WRITER: **JONATHAN HICKMAN**

ARTIST: **ALESSANDRO VITTI**

COLOR ARTIST: **IMAGINARY FRIENDS STUDIO**

LETTERER: **ARTMONKEYS' DAVE LANPHEAR**

COVER ARTIST: **PAUL RENAUD**

ASSISTANT EDITOR: **RACHEL PINNELAS**

EDITOR: **LAUREN SANKOVITCH**

COLLECTION EDITOR: **JENNIFER GRÜNWALD**
EDITORIAL ASSISTANTS: **JAMES EMMETT & JOE HOCHSTEIN**
ASSISTANT EDITORS: **ALEX STARBUCK & NELSON RIBEIRO**
EDITOR, SPECIAL PROJECTS: **MARK D. BEAZLEY**
SENIOR EDITOR, SPECIAL PROJECTS: **JEFF YOUNGQUIST**
SENIOR VICE PRESIDENT OF SALES: **DAVID GABRIEL**
SVP OF BRAND PLANNING & COMMUNICATIONS: **MICHAEL PASCIULLO**

EDITOR IN CHIEF: **AXEL ALONSO**
CHIEF CREATIVE OFFICER: **JOE QUESADA**
PUBLISHER: **DAN BUCKLEY**
EXECUTIVE PRODUCER: **ALAN FINE**

SEC

RET WARRIORS

CREATED BY: **BRIAN MICHAEL BENDIS & ALEX MALEEV**

SECRET WARRIORS VOL. 6: WHEELS WITHIN WHEELS. Contains material originally published in magazine form as SECRET WARRIORS #25-28. First printing 2011. Hardcover ISBN# 978-0-7851-5814-1. Softcover ISBN# 978-0-7851-5815-8. Published by MARVEL WORLDWIDE, INC., a subsidiary of MARVEL ENTERTAINMENT, LLC. OFFICE OF PUBLICATION: 135 West 50th Street, New York, NY 10020. Copyright © 2011 and 2012 Marvel Characters, Inc. All rights reserved. Hardcover: $19.99 per copy in the U.S. and $21.99 in Canada (GST #R127032852). Softcover: $14.99 per copy in the U.S. and $16.99 in Canada (GST #R127032852). Canadian Agreement #40668537. All characters featured in this issue and the distinctive names and likenesses thereof, and all related indicia are trademarks of Marvel Characters, Inc. No similarity between any of the names, characters, persons, and/or institutions in this magazine with those of any living or dead person or institution is intended, and any such similarity which may exist is purely coincidental. **Printed in the U.S.A.** ALAN FINE, EVP - Office of the President, Marvel Worldwide, Inc. and EVP & CMO Marvel Characters B.V.; DAN BUCKLEY, Publisher & President - Print, Animation & Digital Divisions; JOE QUESADA, Chief Creative Officer; JIM SOKOLOWSKI, Chief Operating Officer; DAVID BOGART, SVP of Business Affairs & Talent Management; TOM BREVOORT, SVP of Publishing; C.B. CEBULSKI, SVP of Creator & Content Development; DAVID GABRIEL, SVP of Publishing Sales & Circulation; MICHAEL PASCIULLO, SVP of Brand Planning & Communications; JIM O'KEEFE, VP of Operations & Logistics; DAN CARR, Executive Director of Publishing Technology; SUSAN CRESPI, Editorial Operations Manager; ALEX MORALES, Publishing Operations Manager; STAN LEE, Chairman Emeritus. For information regarding advertising in Marvel Comics or on Marvel.com, please contact John Dokes, SVP Integrated Sales and Marketing, at jdokes@marvel.com. For Marvel subscription inquiries, please call 800-217-9158. **Manufactured between 8/1/2011 and 8/29/2011 (hardcover), and 8/1/2011 and 2/20/2012 (softcover), by R.R. DONNELLEY, INC., SALEM, VA, USA.**

10 9 8 7 6 5 4 3 2 1

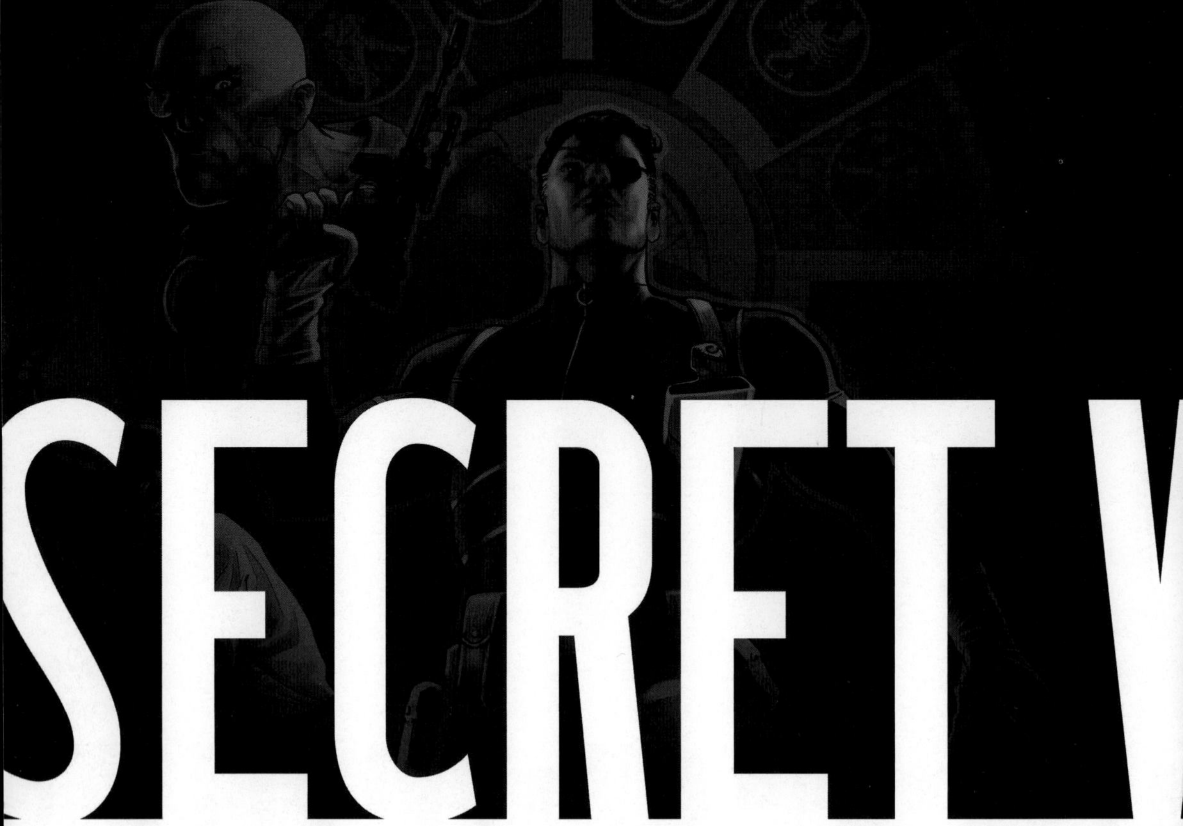
SECRET

WARRIORS

VOL **SIX** WHEELS WITHIN WHEELS

I GET WHAT I WANT... AND YOU GET TI

IE WORLD

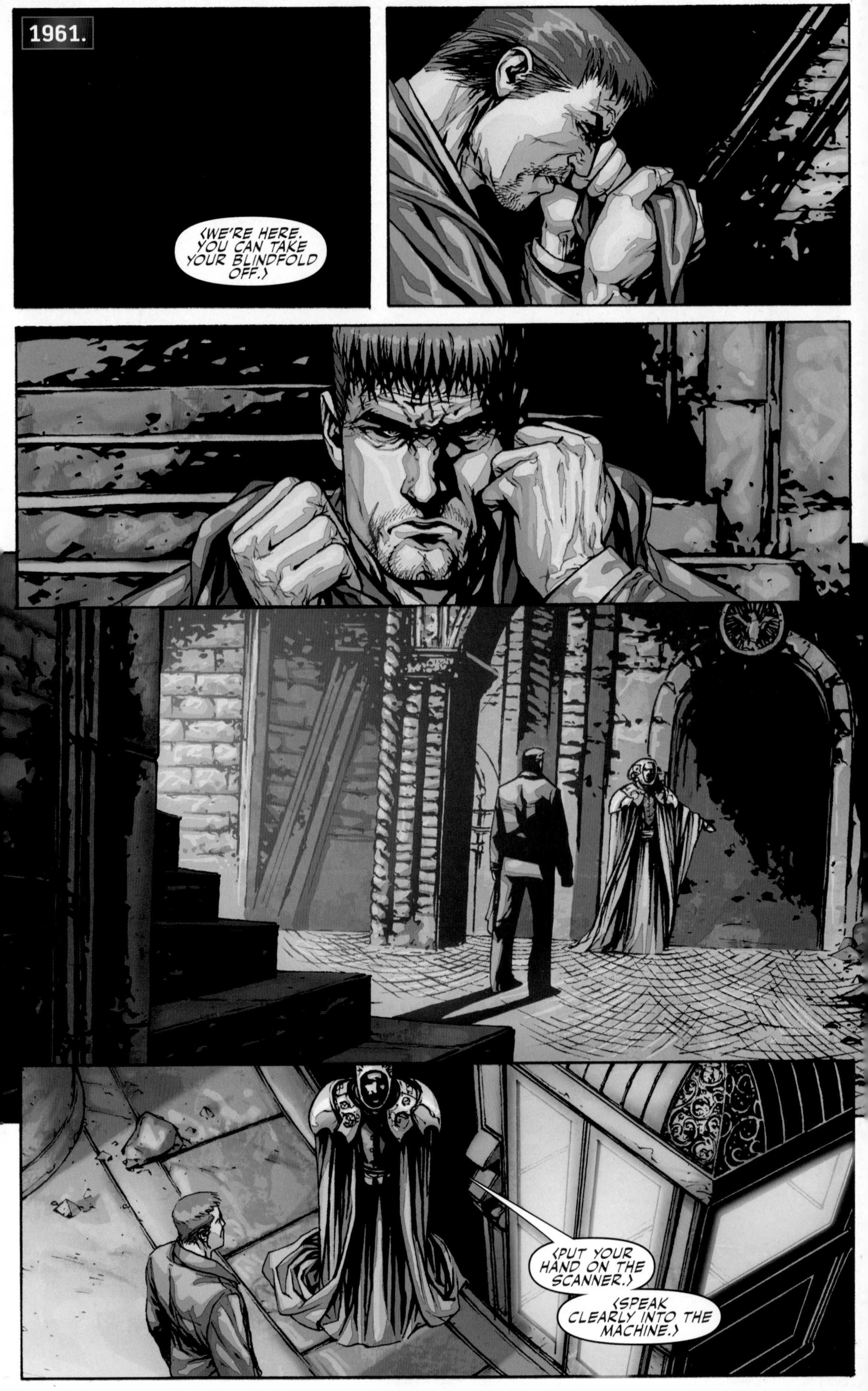
1961.
‹WE'RE HERE. YOU CAN TAKE YOUR BLINDFOLD OFF.›
‹PUT YOUR HAND ON THE SCANNER.›
‹SPEAK CLEARLY INTO THE MACHINE.›

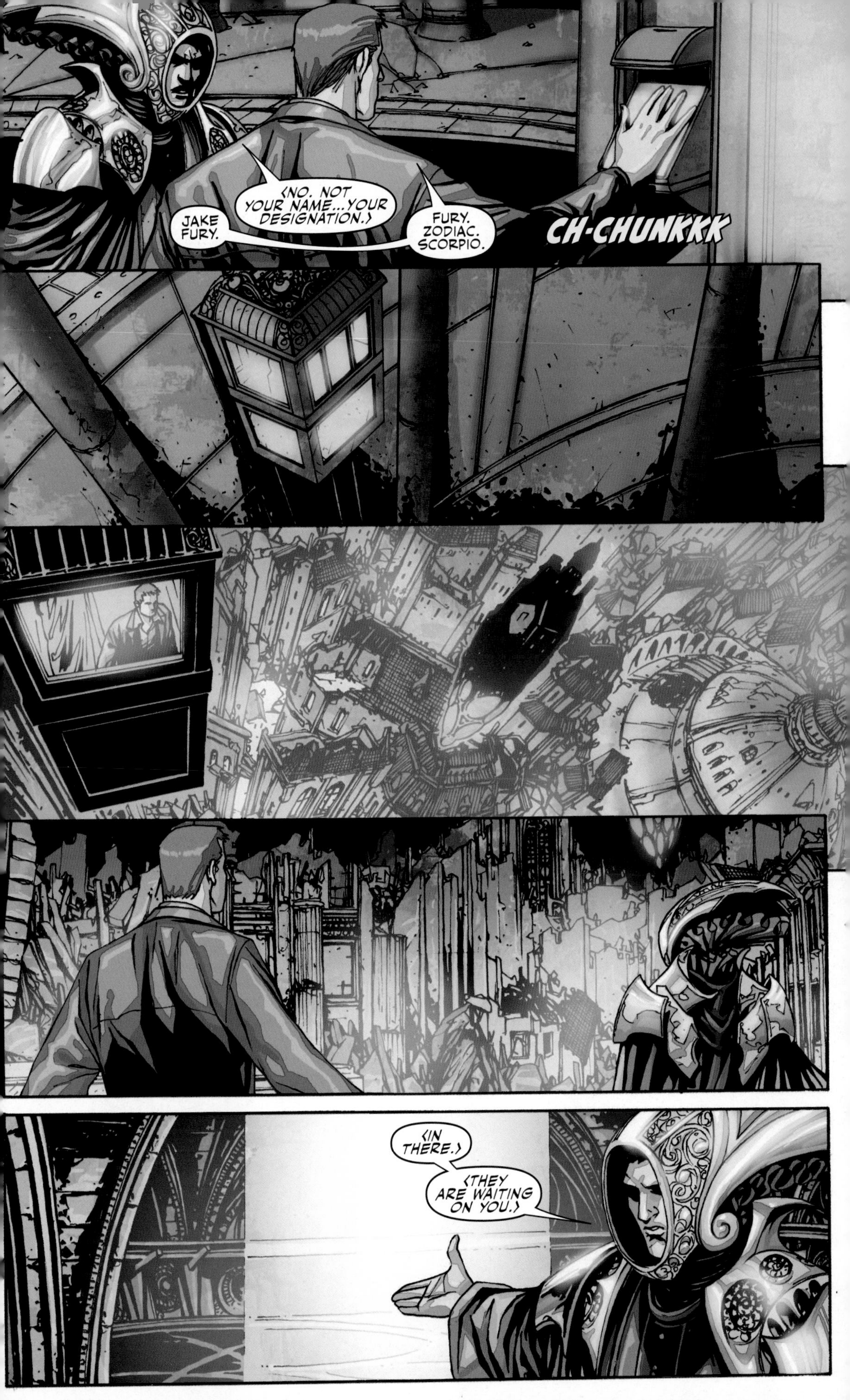
JAKE FURY.
<NO. NOT YOUR NAME...YOUR DESIGNATION.>
FURY. ZODIAC. SCORPIO.
CH-CHUNKKK
<IN THERE.>
<THEY ARE WAITING ON YOU.>

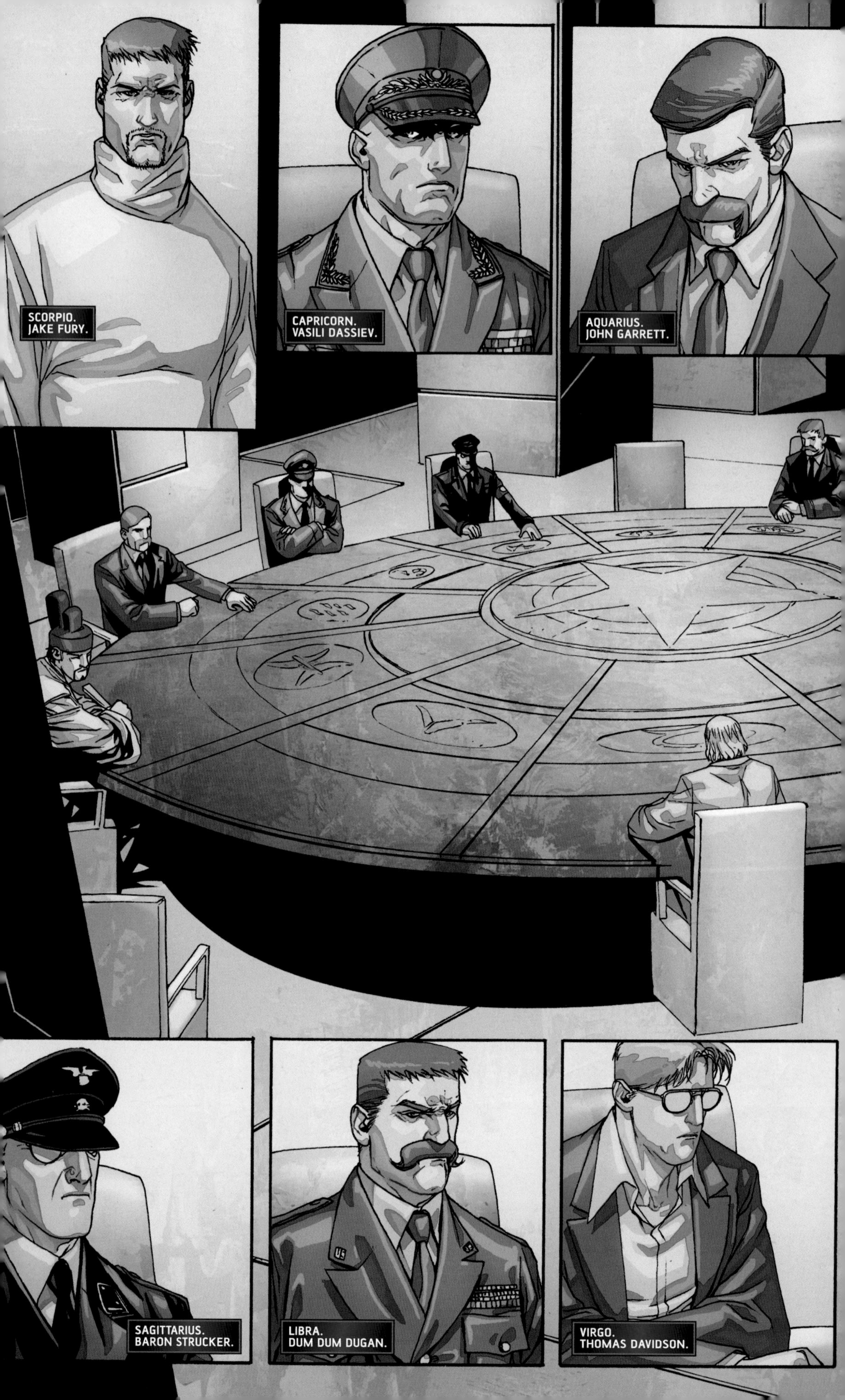
SCORPIO. JAKE FURY.
CAPRICORN. VASILI DASSIEV.
AQUARIUS. JOHN GARRETT.
SAGITTARIUS. BARON STRUCKER.
LIBRA. DUM DUM DUGAN.
VIRGO. THOMAS DAVIDSON.

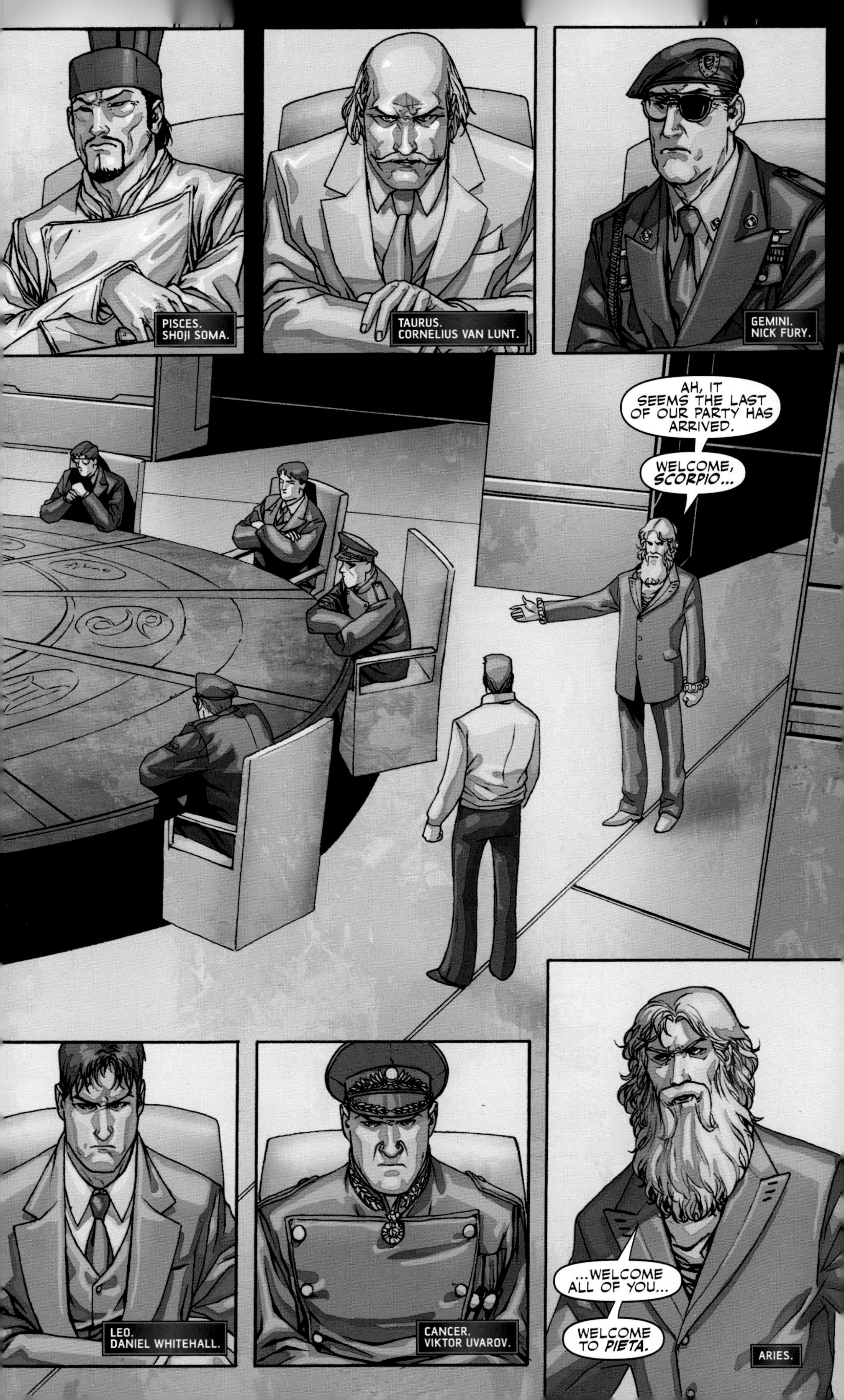
PISCES.
SHOJI SOMA.
TAURUS.
CORNELIUS VAN LUNT.
GEMINI.
NICK FURY.
AH, IT SEEMS THE LAST OF OUR PARTY HAS ARRIVED.
WELCOME, *SCORPIO*...
LEO.
DANIEL WHITEHALL.
CANCER.
VIKTOR UVAROV.
...WELCOME ALL OF YOU...
WELCOME TO *PIETA*.
ARIES.

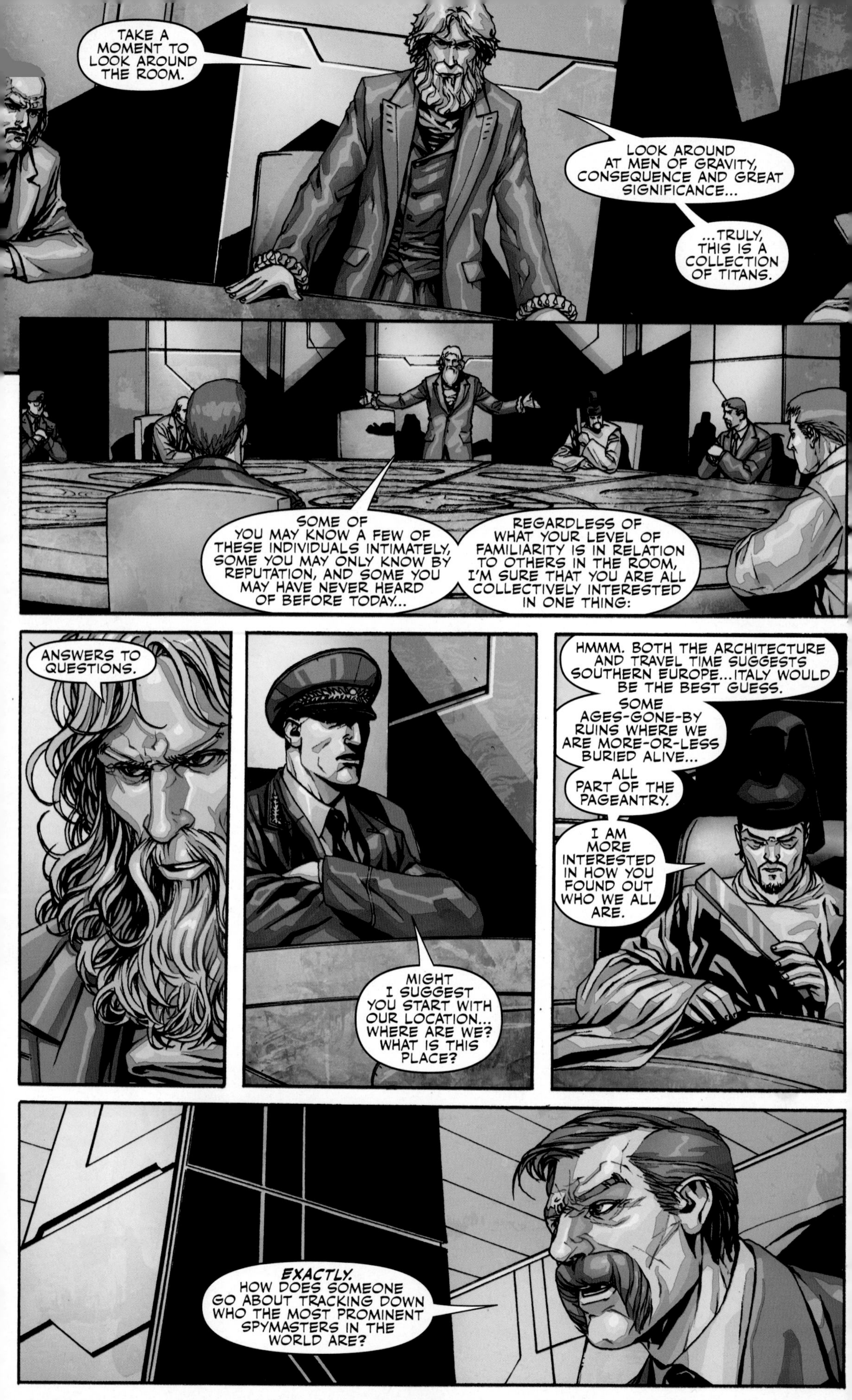
TAKE A MOMENT TO LOOK AROUND THE ROOM.
LOOK AROUND AT MEN OF GRAVITY, CONSEQUENCE AND GREAT SIGNIFICANCE...
...TRULY, THIS IS A COLLECTION OF TITANS.
SOME OF YOU MAY KNOW A FEW OF THESE INDIVIDUALS INTIMATELY, SOME YOU MAY ONLY KNOW BY REPUTATION, AND SOME YOU MAY HAVE NEVER HEARD OF BEFORE TODAY...
REGARDLESS OF WHAT YOUR LEVEL OF FAMILIARITY IS IN RELATION TO OTHERS IN THE ROOM, I'M SURE THAT YOU ARE ALL COLLECTIVELY INTERESTED IN ONE THING:
ANSWERS TO QUESTIONS.
MIGHT I SUGGEST YOU START WITH OUR LOCATION... WHERE ARE WE? WHAT IS THIS PLACE?
HMMM. BOTH THE ARCHITECTURE AND TRAVEL TIME SUGGESTS SOUTHERN EUROPE...ITALY WOULD BE THE BEST GUESS.
SOME AGES-GONE-BY RUINS WHERE WE ARE MORE-OR-LESS BURIED ALIVE...
ALL PART OF THE PAGEANTRY.
I AM MORE INTERESTED IN HOW YOU FOUND OUT WHO WE ALL ARE.
EXACTLY. HOW DOES SOMEONE GO ABOUT TRACKING DOWN WHO THE MOST PROMINENT SPYMASTERS IN THE WORLD ARE?

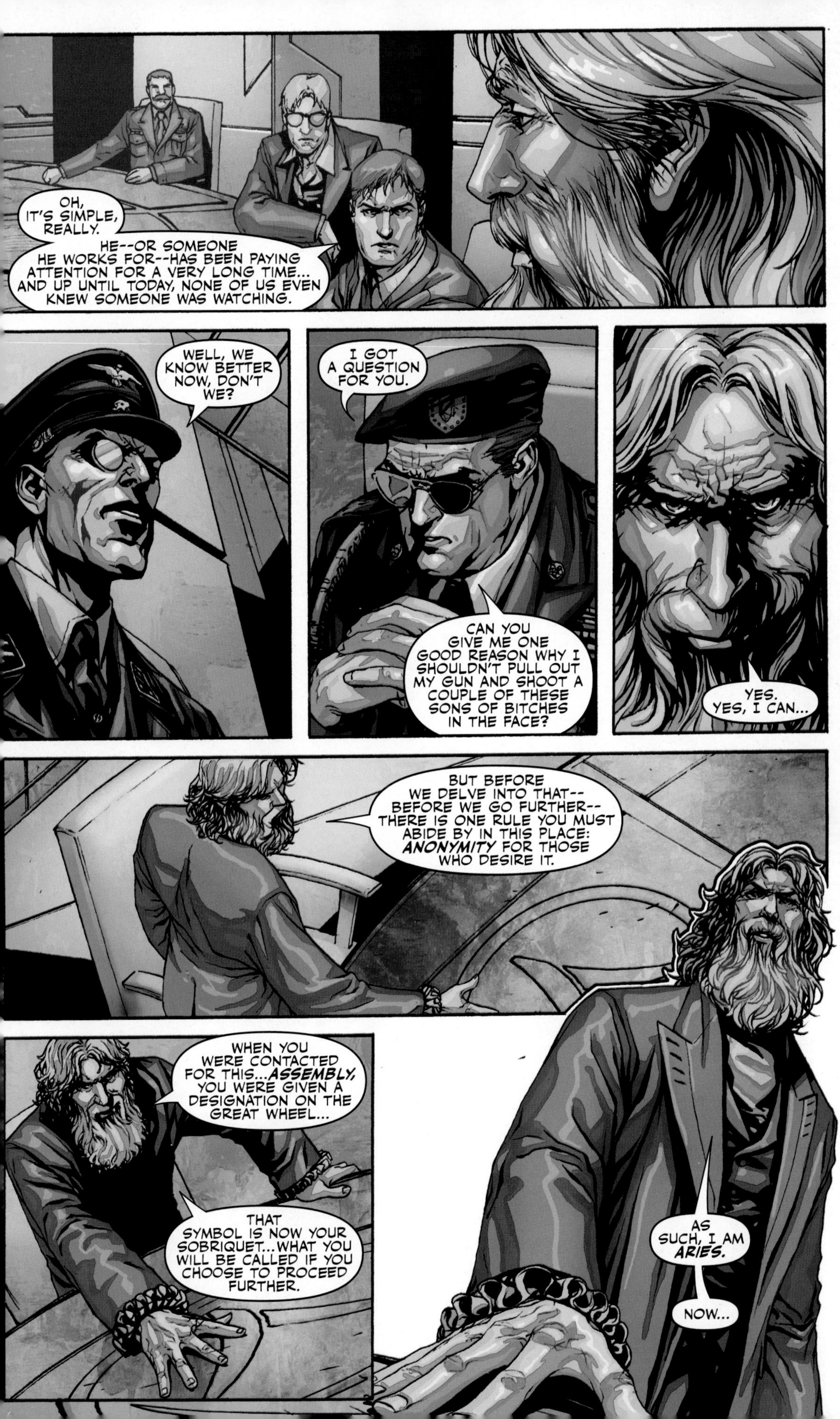
OH, IT'S SIMPLE, REALLY.
HE--OR SOMEONE HE WORKS FOR--HAS BEEN PAYING ATTENTION FOR A VERY LONG TIME... AND UP UNTIL TODAY, NONE OF US EVEN KNEW SOMEONE WAS WATCHING.
WELL, WE KNOW BETTER NOW, DON'T WE?
I GOT A QUESTION FOR YOU.
CAN YOU GIVE ME ONE GOOD REASON WHY I SHOULDN'T PULL OUT MY GUN AND SHOOT A COUPLE OF THESE SONS OF BITCHES IN THE FACE?
YES. YES, I CAN...
BUT BEFORE WE DELVE INTO THAT-- BEFORE WE GO FURTHER-- THERE IS ONE RULE YOU MUST ABIDE BY IN THIS PLACE: ANONYMITY FOR THOSE WHO DESIRE IT.
WHEN YOU WERE CONTACTED FOR THIS...ASSEMBLY, YOU WERE GIVEN A DESIGNATION ON THE GREAT WHEEL...
THAT SYMBOL IS NOW YOUR SOBRIQUET...WHAT YOU WILL BE CALLED IF YOU CHOOSE TO PROCEED FURTHER.
AS SUCH, I AM ARIES.
NOW...

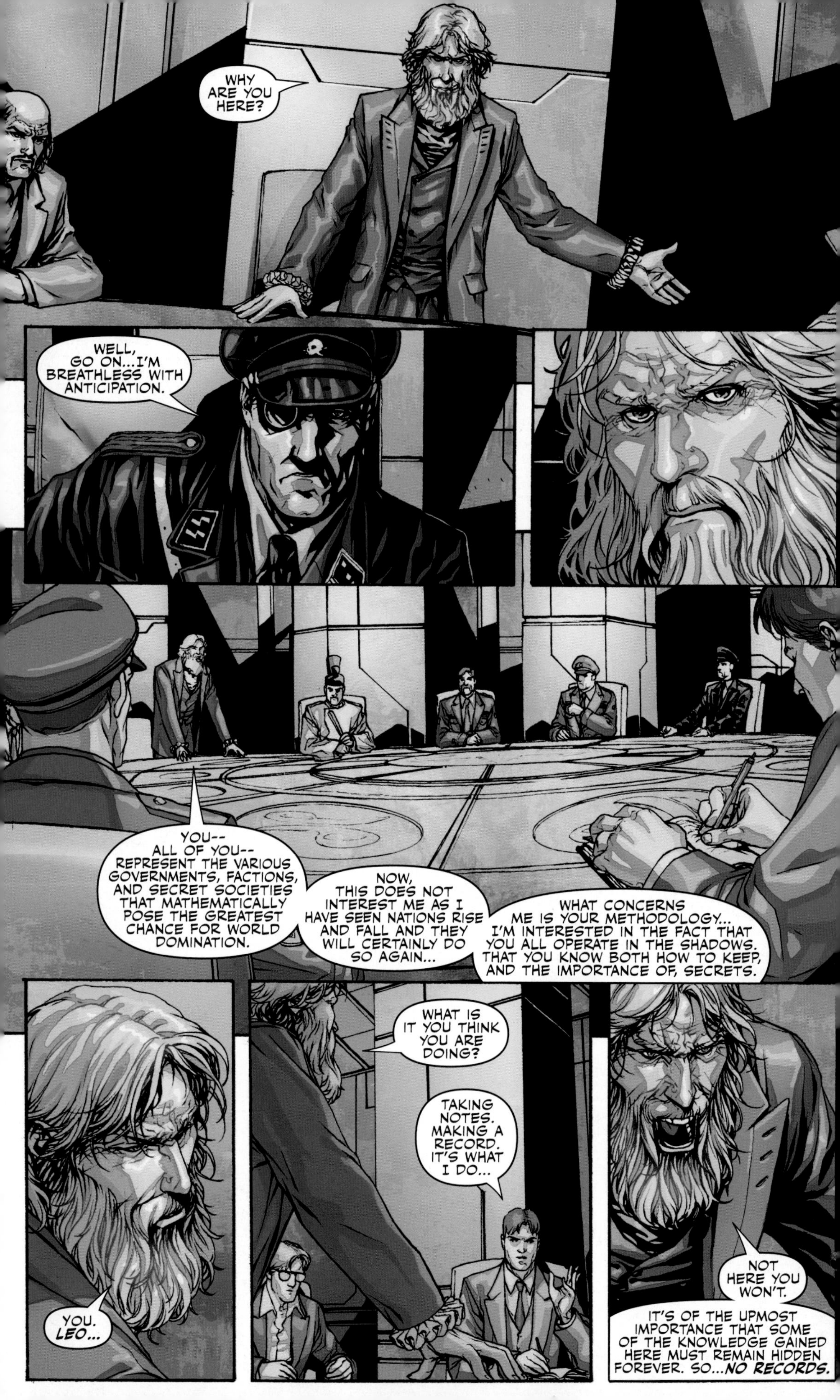
WHY ARE YOU HERE?
WELL, GO ON...I'M BREATHLESS WITH ANTICIPATION.
YOU-- ALL OF YOU-- REPRESENT THE VARIOUS GOVERNMENTS, FACTIONS, AND SECRET SOCIETIES THAT MATHEMATICALLY POSE THE GREATEST CHANCE FOR WORLD DOMINATION.
NOW, THIS DOES NOT INTEREST ME AS I HAVE SEEN NATIONS RISE AND FALL AND THEY WILL CERTAINLY DO SO AGAIN...
WHAT CONCERNS ME IS YOUR METHODOLOGY... I'M INTERESTED IN THE FACT THAT YOU ALL OPERATE IN THE SHADOWS. THAT YOU KNOW BOTH HOW TO KEEP, AND THE IMPORTANCE OF, SECRETS.
YOU. LEO...
WHAT IS IT YOU THINK YOU ARE DOING?
TAKING NOTES. MAKING A RECORD. IT'S WHAT I DO...
NOT HERE YOU WON'T.
IT'S OF THE UPMOST IMPORTANCE THAT SOME OF THE KNOWLEDGE GAINED HERE MUST REMAIN HIDDEN FOREVER. SO...NO RECORDS.

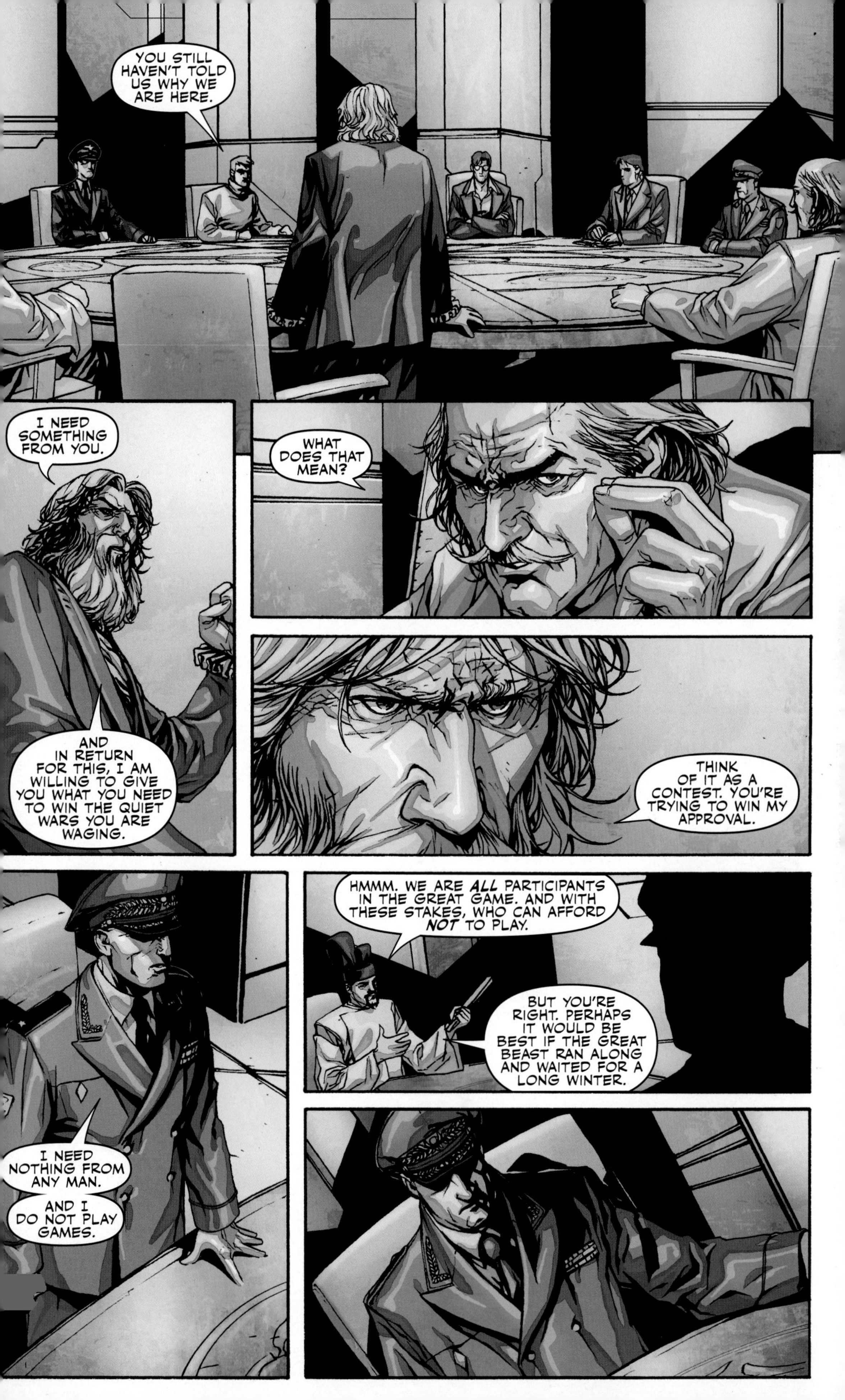
YOU STILL HAVEN'T TOLD US WHY WE ARE HERE.
I NEED SOMETHING FROM YOU.
WHAT DOES THAT MEAN?
AND IN RETURN FOR THIS, I AM WILLING TO GIVE YOU WHAT YOU NEED TO WIN THE QUIET WARS YOU ARE WAGING.
THINK OF IT AS A CONTEST. YOU'RE TRYING TO WIN MY APPROVAL.
I NEED NOTHING FROM ANY MAN.
AND I DO NOT PLAY GAMES.
HMMM. WE ARE ALL PARTICIPANTS IN THE GREAT GAME. AND WITH THESE STAKES, WHO CAN AFFORD NOT TO PLAY.
BUT YOU'RE RIGHT. PERHAPS IT WOULD BE BEST IF THE GREAT BEAST RAN ALONG AND WAITED FOR A LONG WINTER.

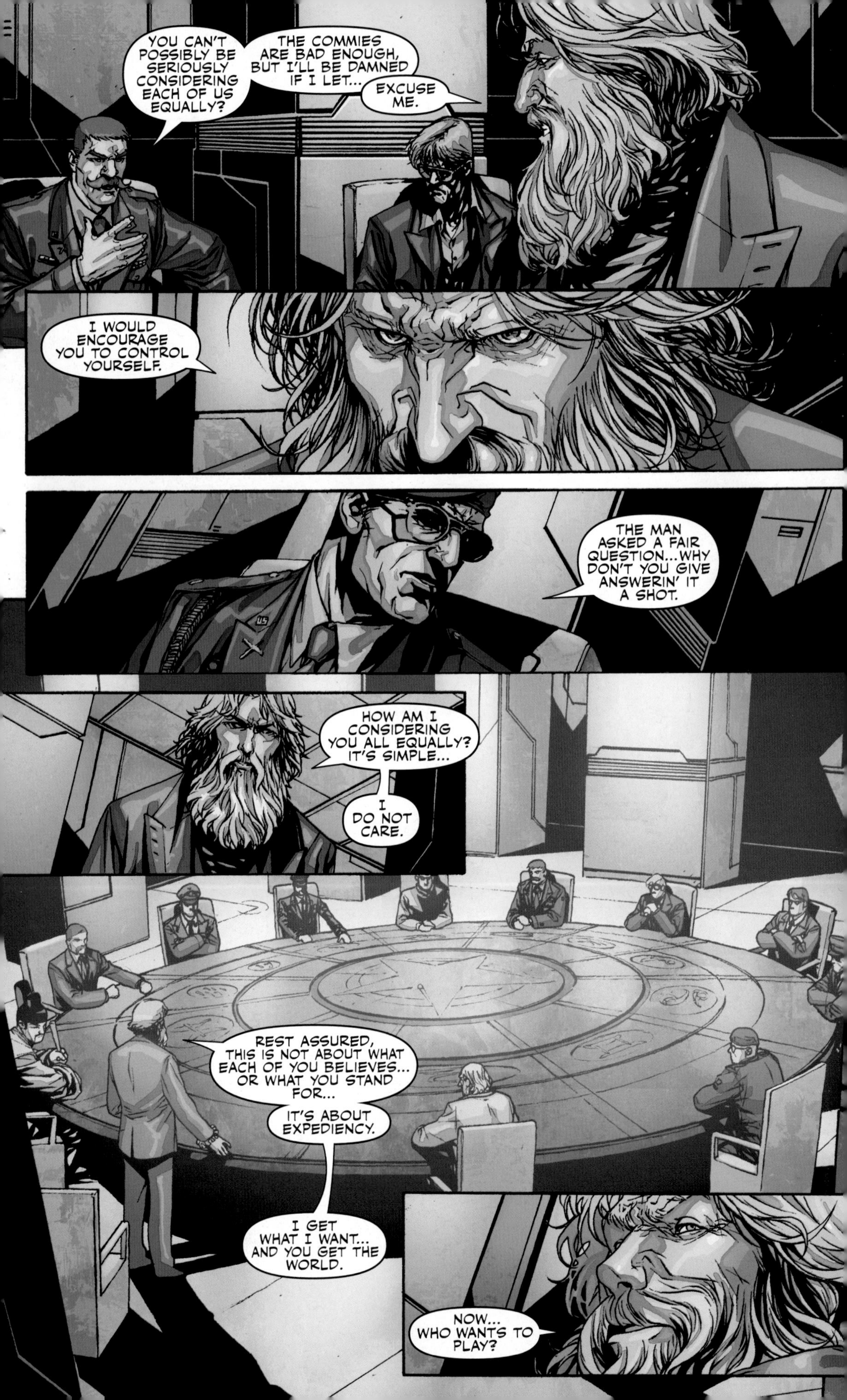
YOU CAN'T POSSIBLY BE SERIOUSLY CONSIDERING EACH OF US EQUALLY?
THE COMMIES ARE BAD ENOUGH, BUT I'LL BE DAMNED IF I LET...
EXCUSE ME.
I WOULD ENCOURAGE YOU TO CONTROL YOURSELF.
THE MAN ASKED A FAIR QUESTION...WHY DON'T YOU GIVE ANSWERIN' IT A SHOT.
HOW AM I CONSIDERING YOU ALL EQUALLY? IT'S SIMPLE...
I DO NOT CARE.
REST ASSURED, THIS IS NOT ABOUT WHAT EACH OF YOU BELIEVES... OR WHAT YOU STAND FOR...
IT'S ABOUT EXPEDIENCY.
I GET WHAT I WANT... AND YOU GET THE WORLD.
NOW... WHO WANTS TO PLAY?

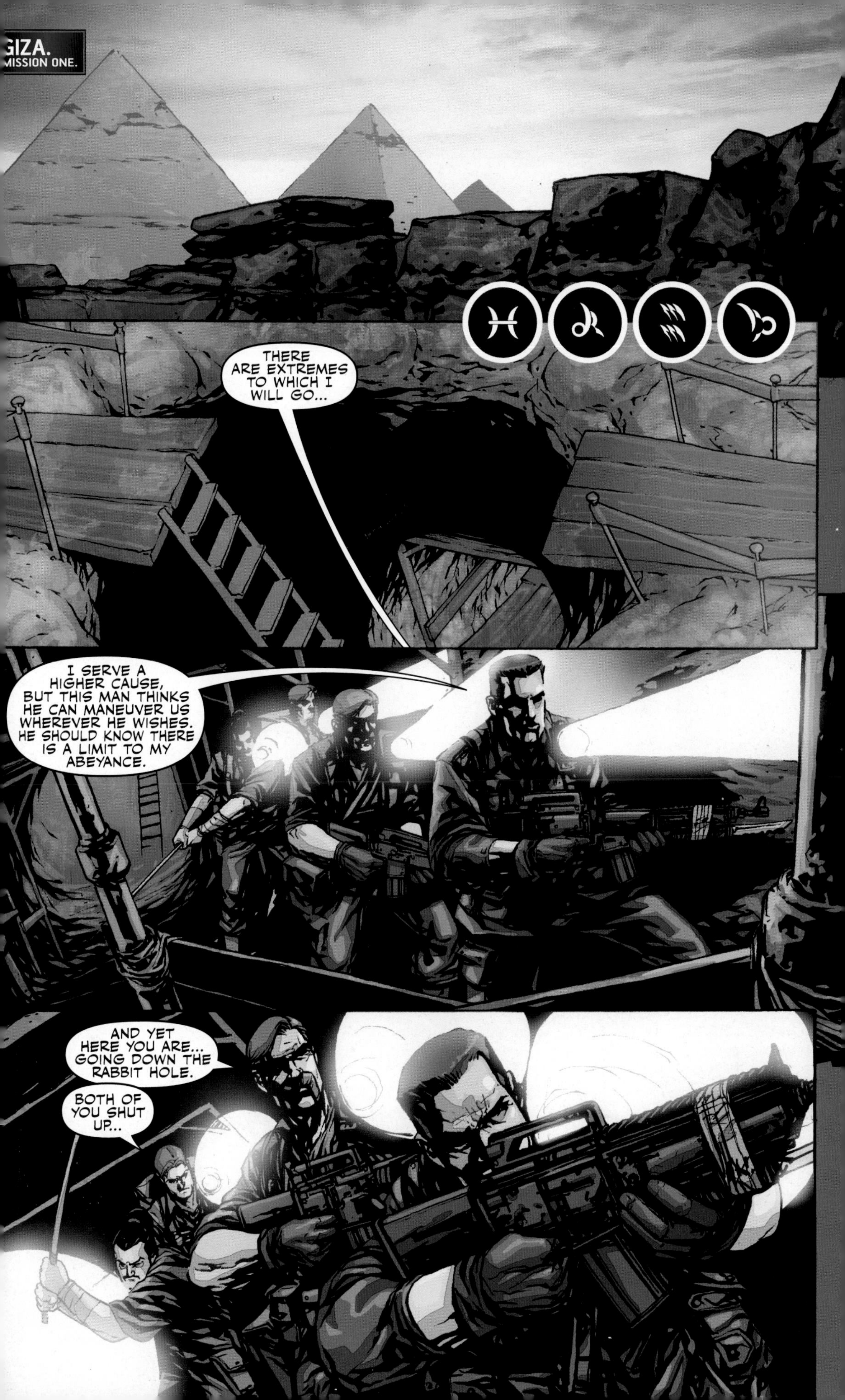
GIZA.
MISSION ONE.
THERE ARE EXTREMES TO WHICH I WILL GO...
I SERVE A HIGHER CAUSE, BUT THIS MAN THINKS HE CAN MANEUVER US WHEREVER HE WISHES. HE SHOULD KNOW THERE IS A LIMIT TO MY ABEYANCE.
AND YET HERE YOU ARE... GOING DOWN THE RABBIT HOLE.
BOTH OF YOU SHUT UP...

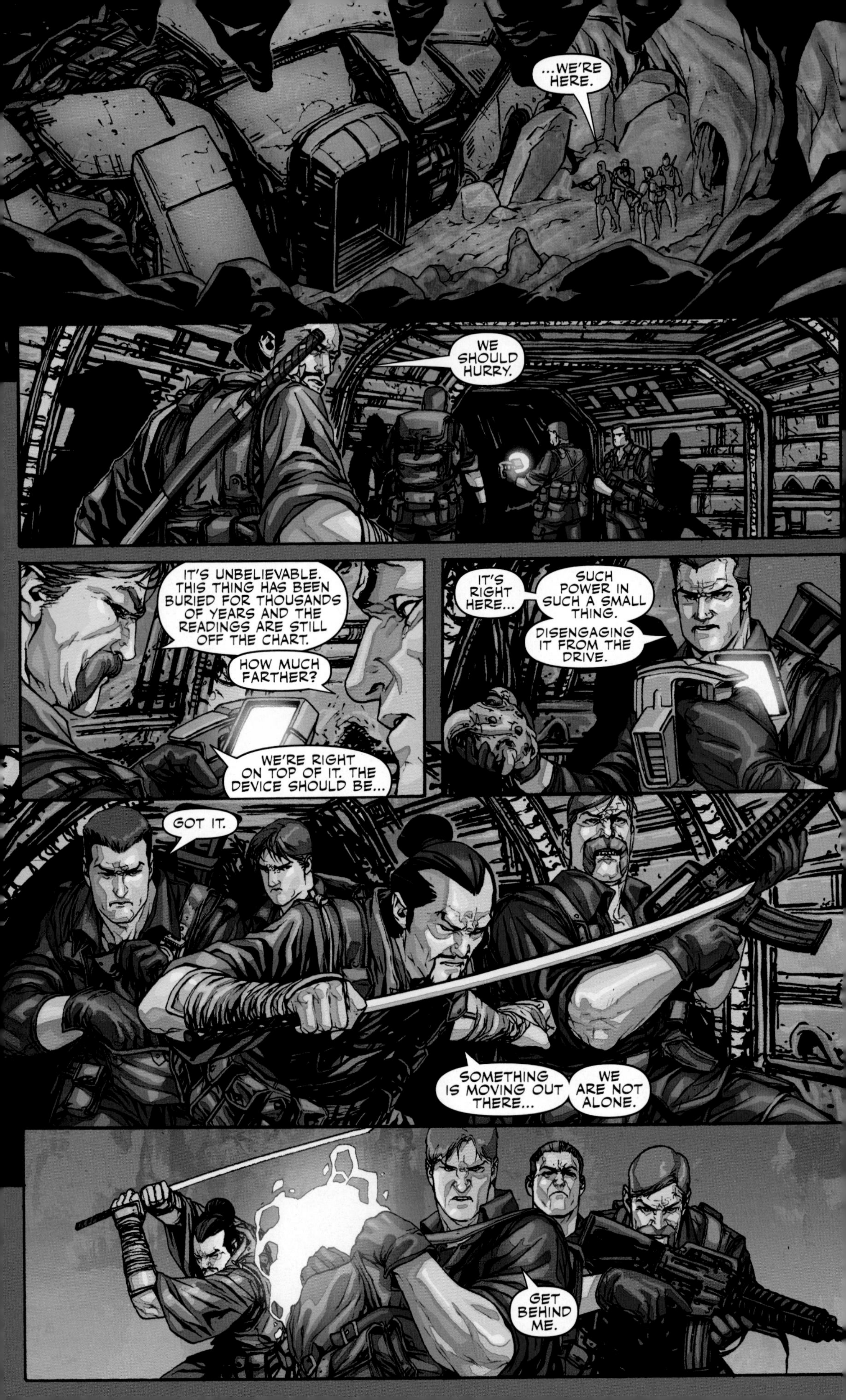
...WE'RE HERE.
WE SHOULD HURRY.
IT'S UNBELIEVABLE. THIS THING HAS BEEN BURIED FOR THOUSANDS OF YEARS AND THE READINGS ARE STILL OFF THE CHART.
HOW MUCH FARTHER?
WE'RE RIGHT ON TOP OF IT. THE DEVICE SHOULD BE...
IT'S RIGHT HERE...
SUCH POWER IN SUCH A SMALL THING.
DISENGAGING IT FROM THE DRIVE.
GOT IT.
SOMETHING IS MOVING OUT THERE...
WE ARE NOT ALONE.
GET BEHIND ME.

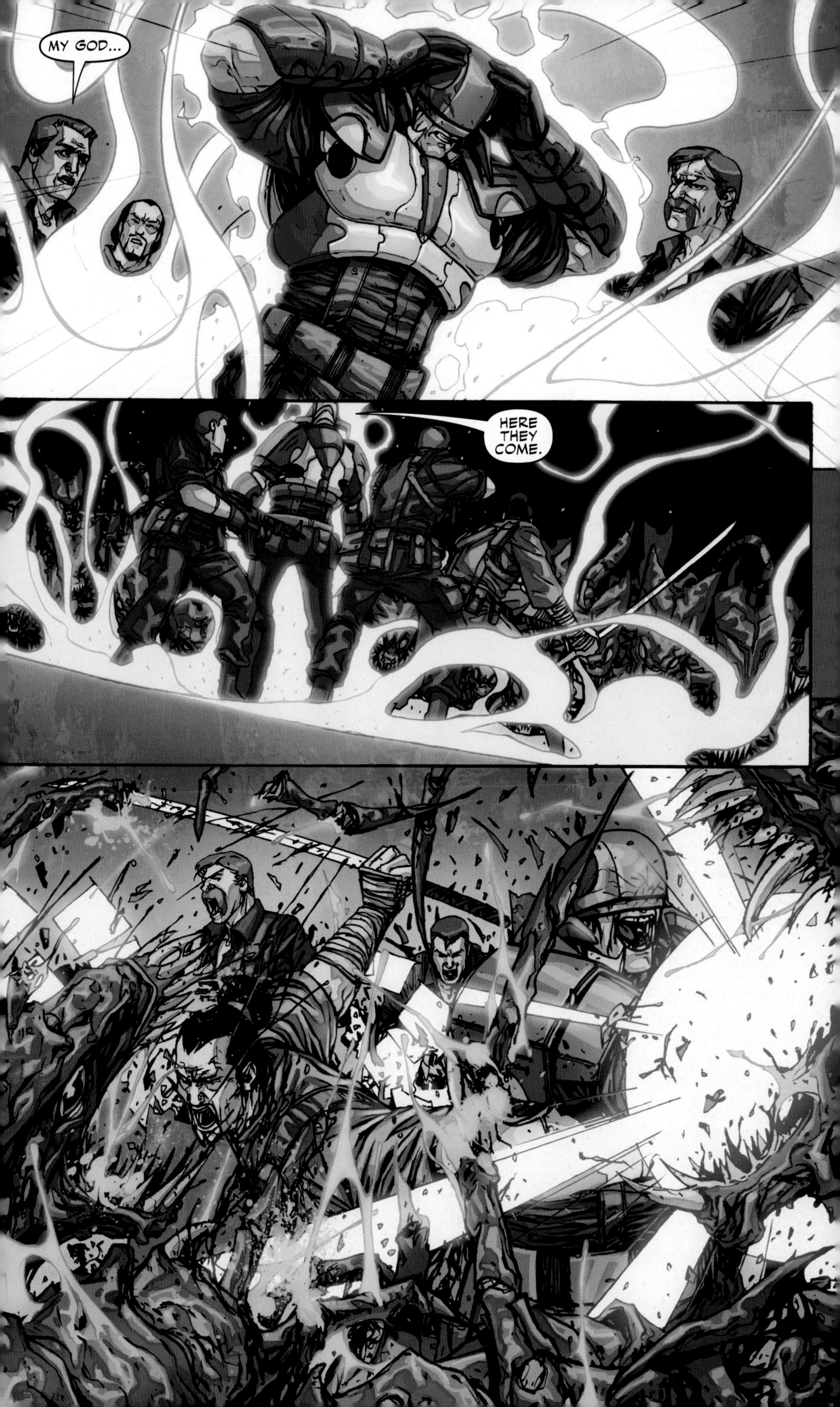
MY GOD...
HERE THEY COME.

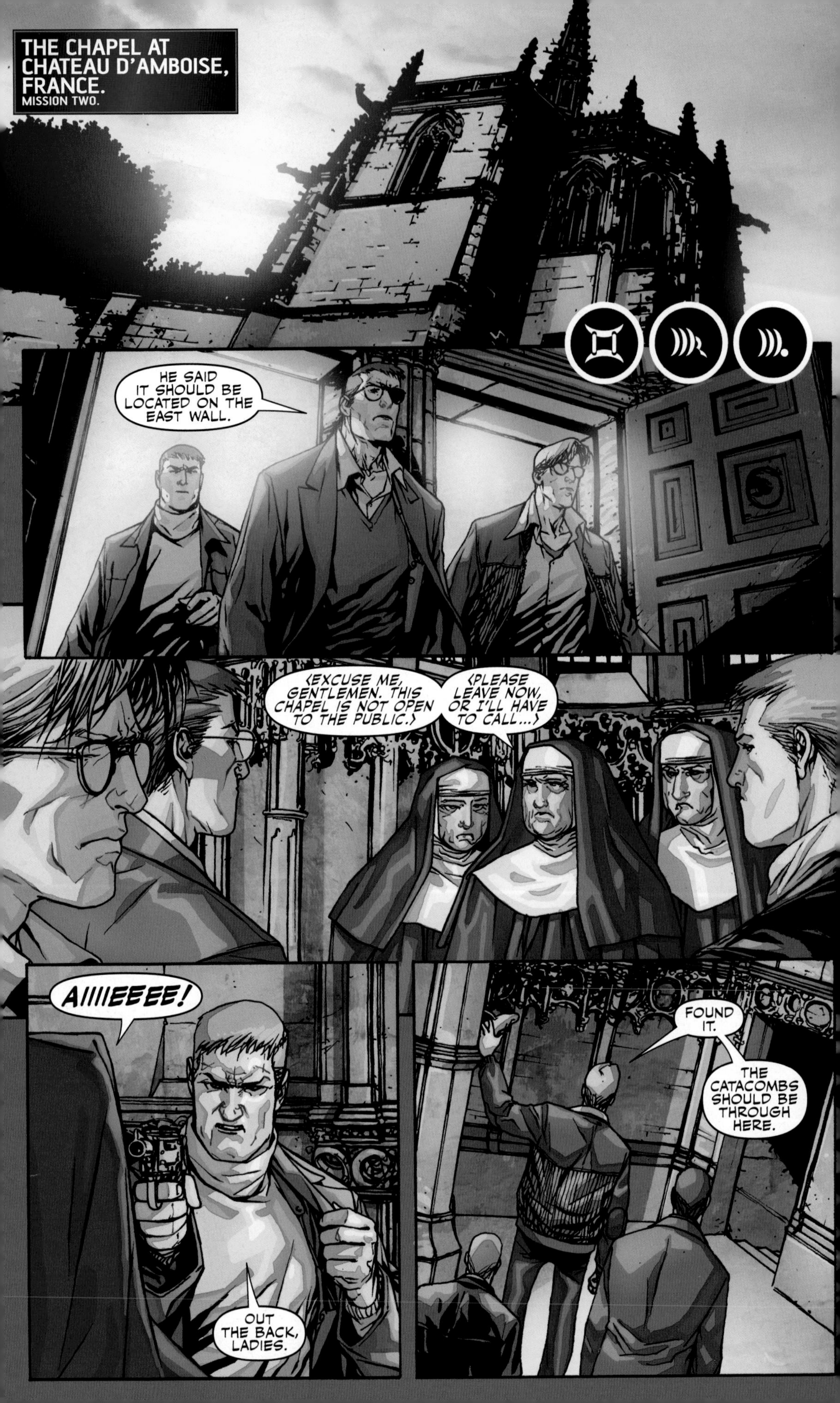
THE CHAPEL AT CHATEAU D'AMBOISE, FRANCE.
MISSION TWO.
HE SAID IT SHOULD BE LOCATED ON THE EAST WALL.
‹EXCUSE ME, GENTLEMEN. THIS CHAPEL IS NOT OPEN TO THE PUBLIC.›
‹PLEASE LEAVE NOW, OR I'LL HAVE TO CALL...›
AIIIIEEEE!
OUT THE BACK, LADIES.
FOUND IT.
THE CATACOMBS SHOULD BE THROUGH HERE.

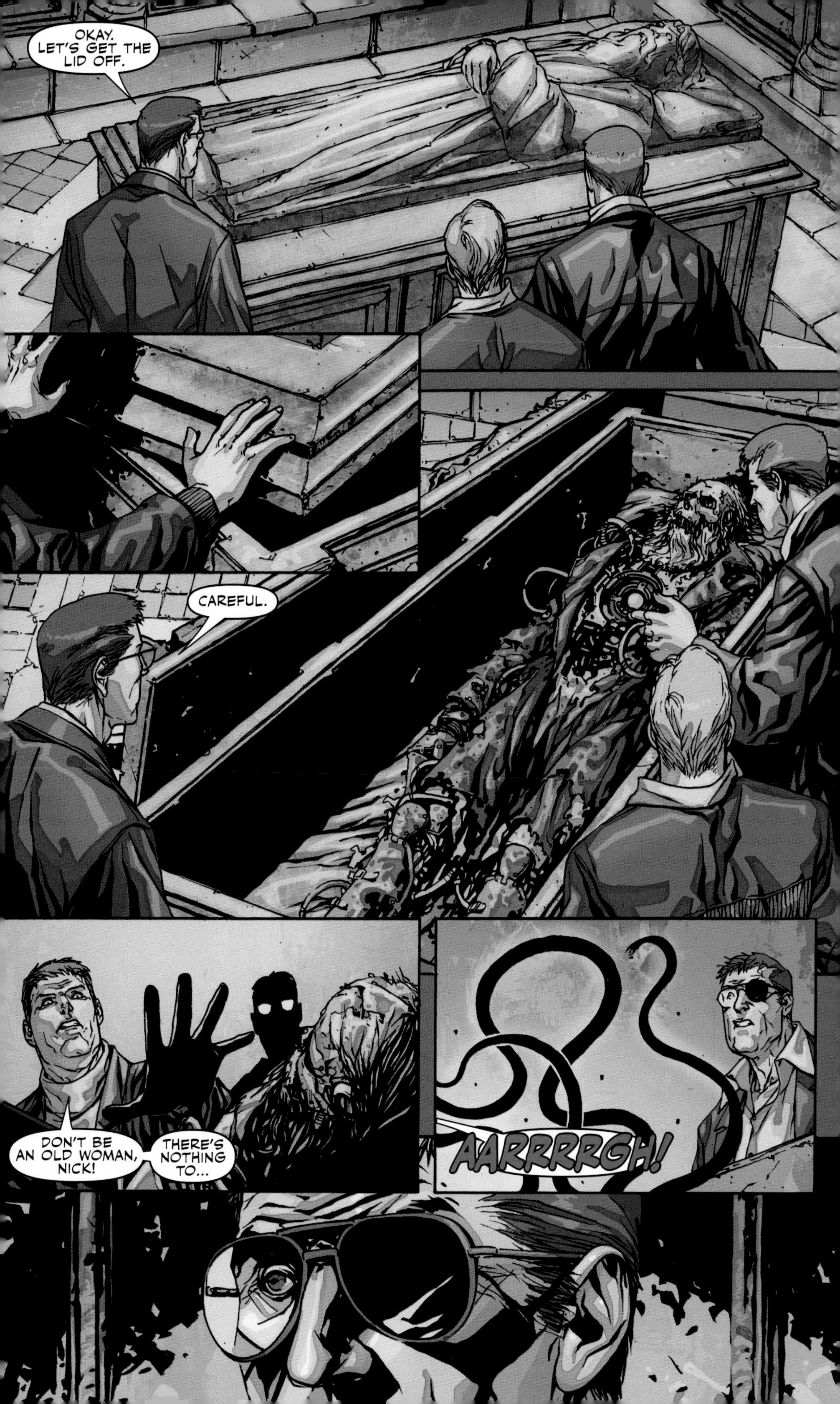
OKAY. LET'S GET THE LID OFF.
CAREFUL.
DON'T BE AN OLD WOMAN, NICK!
THERE'S NOTHING TO...
AARRRRGH!

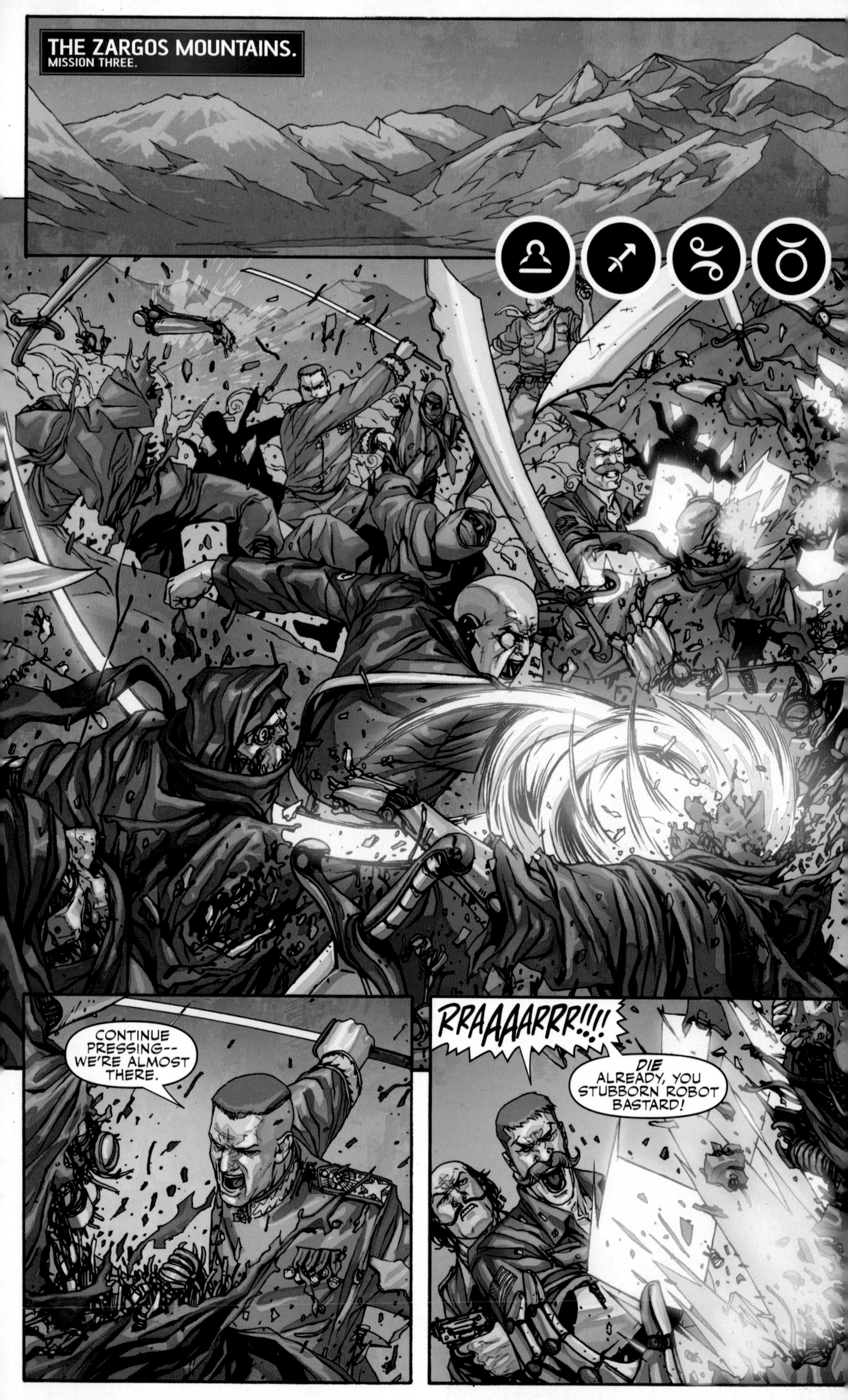
THE ZARGOS MOUNTAINS.
MISSION THREE.
CONTINUE PRESSING--WE'RE ALMOST THERE.
RRAAAARRR!!!!
DIE ALREADY, YOU STUBBORN ROBOT BASTARD!

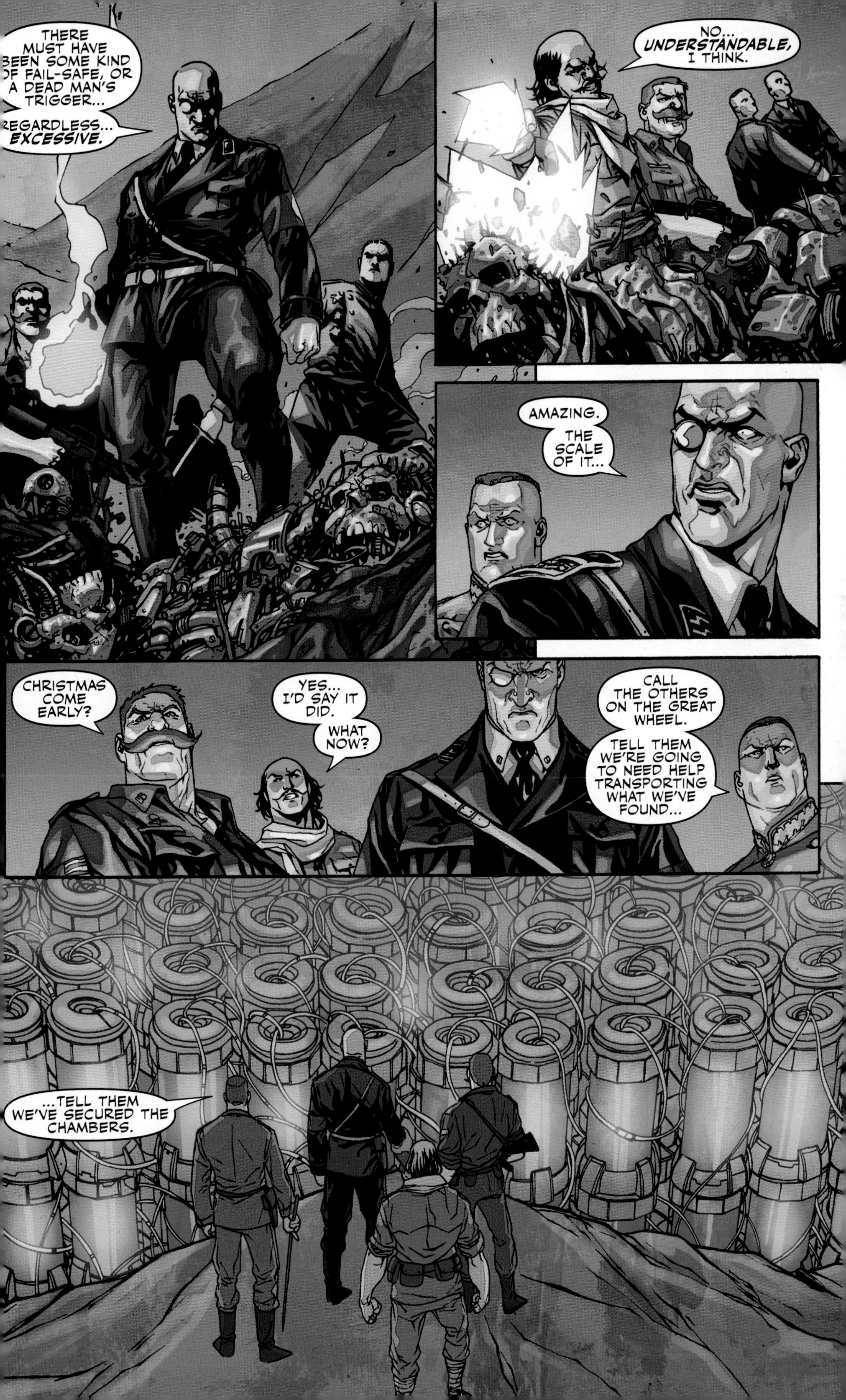
THERE MUST HAVE BEEN SOME KIND OF FAIL-SAFE, OR A DEAD MAN'S TRIGGER...
REGARDLESS... *EXCESSIVE.*
NO... *UNDERSTANDABLE,* I THINK.
AMAZING. THE SCALE OF IT...
CHRISTMAS COME EARLY?
YES... I'D SAY IT DID.
WHAT NOW?
CALL THE OTHERS ON THE GREAT WHEEL.
TELL THEM WE'RE GOING TO NEED HELP TRANSPORTING WHAT WE'VE FOUND...
...TELL THEM WE'VE SECURED THE CHAMBERS.

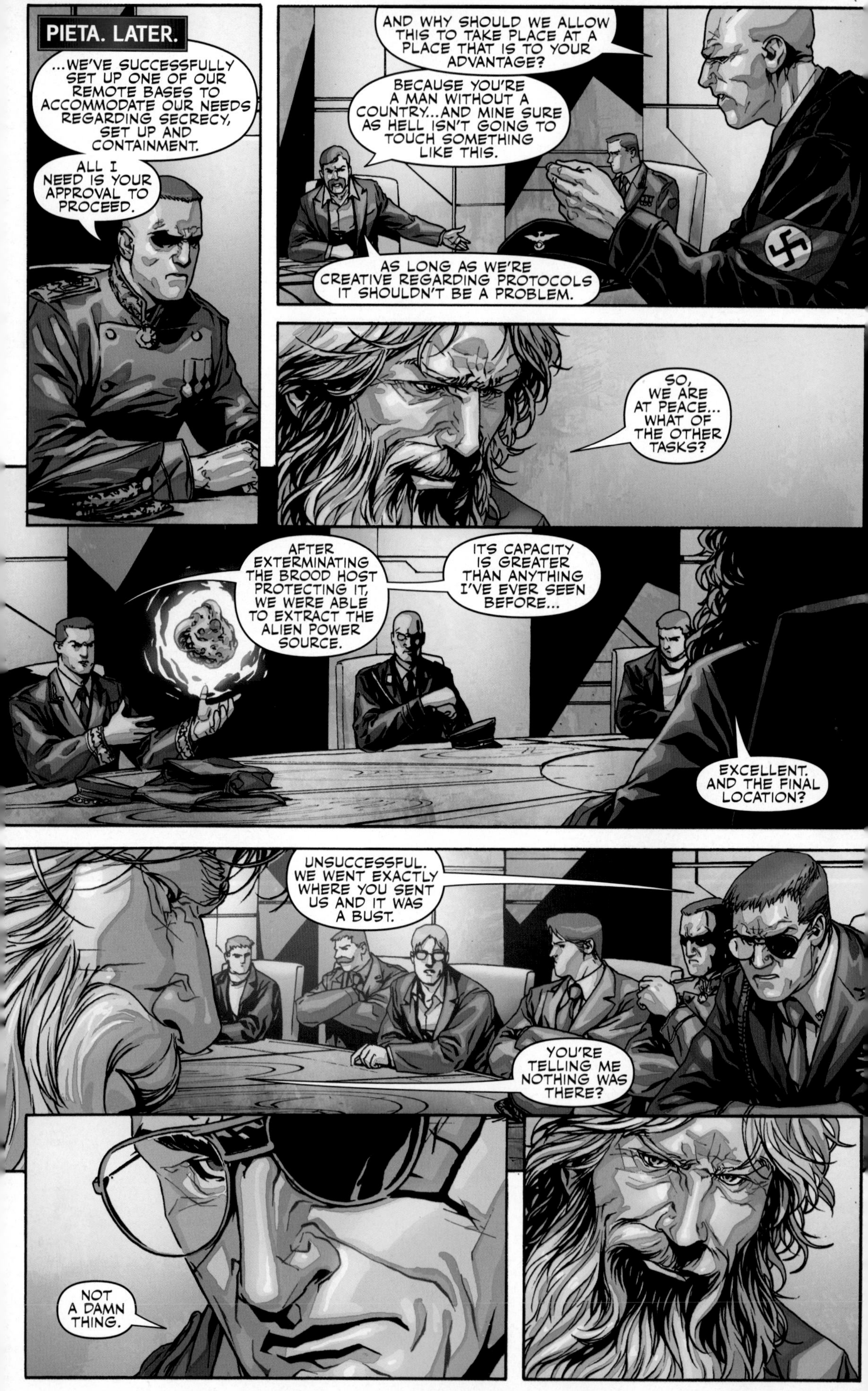
PIETA. LATER.
...WE'VE SUCCESSFULLY SET UP ONE OF OUR REMOTE BASES TO ACCOMMODATE OUR NEEDS REGARDING SECRECY, SET UP AND CONTAINMENT.
ALL I NEED IS YOUR APPROVAL TO PROCEED.
AND WHY SHOULD WE ALLOW THIS TO TAKE PLACE AT A PLACE THAT IS TO YOUR ADVANTAGE?
BECAUSE YOU'RE A MAN WITHOUT A COUNTRY...AND MINE SURE AS HELL ISN'T GOING TO TOUCH SOMETHING LIKE THIS.
AS LONG AS WE'RE CREATIVE REGARDING PROTOCOLS IT SHOULDN'T BE A PROBLEM.
SO, WE ARE AT PEACE... WHAT OF THE OTHER TASKS?
AFTER EXTERMINATING THE BROOD HOST PROTECTING IT, WE WERE ABLE TO EXTRACT THE ALIEN POWER SOURCE.
ITS CAPACITY IS GREATER THAN ANYTHING I'VE EVER SEEN BEFORE...
EXCELLENT. AND THE FINAL LOCATION?
UNSUCCESSFUL. WE WENT EXACTLY WHERE YOU SENT US AND IT WAS A BUST.
YOU'RE TELLING ME NOTHING WAS THERE?
NOT A DAMN THING.

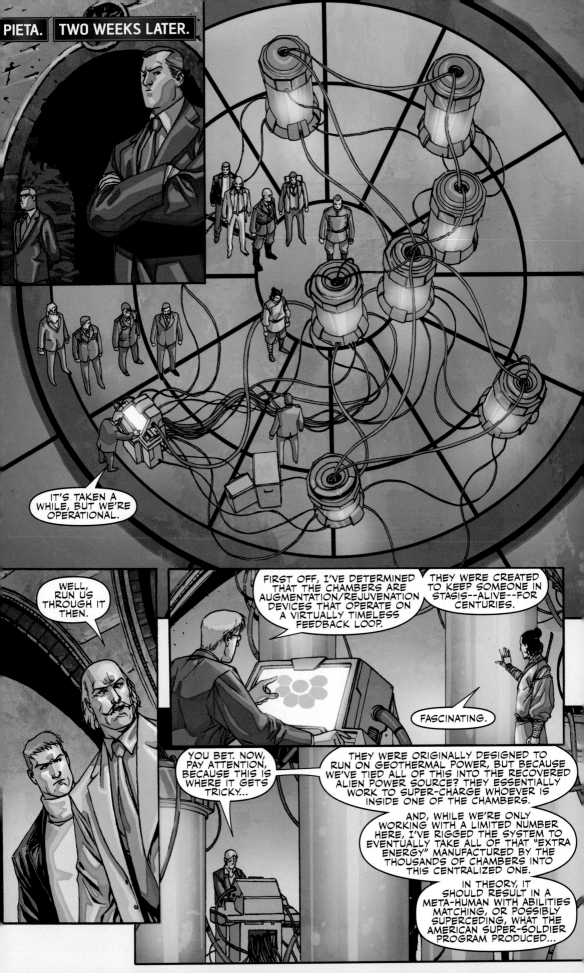

IT'S TAKEN A WHILE, BUT WE'RE OPERATIONAL.

WELL, RUN US THROUGH IT THEN.

FIRST OFF, I'VE DETERMINED THAT THE CHAMBERS ARE AUGMENTATION/REJUVENATION DEVICES THAT OPERATE ON A VIRTUALLY TIMELESS FEEDBACK LOOP.

THEY WERE CREATED TO KEEP SOMEONE IN STASIS--ALIVE--FOR CENTURIES.

FASCINATING.

YOU BET. NOW, PAY ATTENTION, BECAUSE THIS IS WHERE IT GETS TRICKY...

THEY WERE ORIGINALLY DESIGNED TO RUN ON GEOTHERMAL POWER, BUT BECAUSE WE'VE TIED ALL OF THIS INTO THE RECOVERED ALIEN POWER SOURCE? THEY ESSENTIALLY WORK TO SUPER-CHARGE WHOEVER IS INSIDE ONE OF THE CHAMBERS.

AND, WHILE WE'RE ONLY WORKING WITH A LIMITED NUMBER HERE, I'VE RIGGED THE SYSTEM TO EVENTUALLY TAKE ALL OF THAT "EXTRA ENERGY" MANUFACTURED BY THE THOUSANDS OF CHAMBERS INTO THIS CENTRALIZED ONE.

IN THEORY, IT SHOULD RESULT IN A META-HUMAN WITH ABILITIES MATCHING, OR POSSIBLY SUPERCEDING, WHAT THE AMERICAN SUPER-SOLDIER PROGRAM PRODUCED...

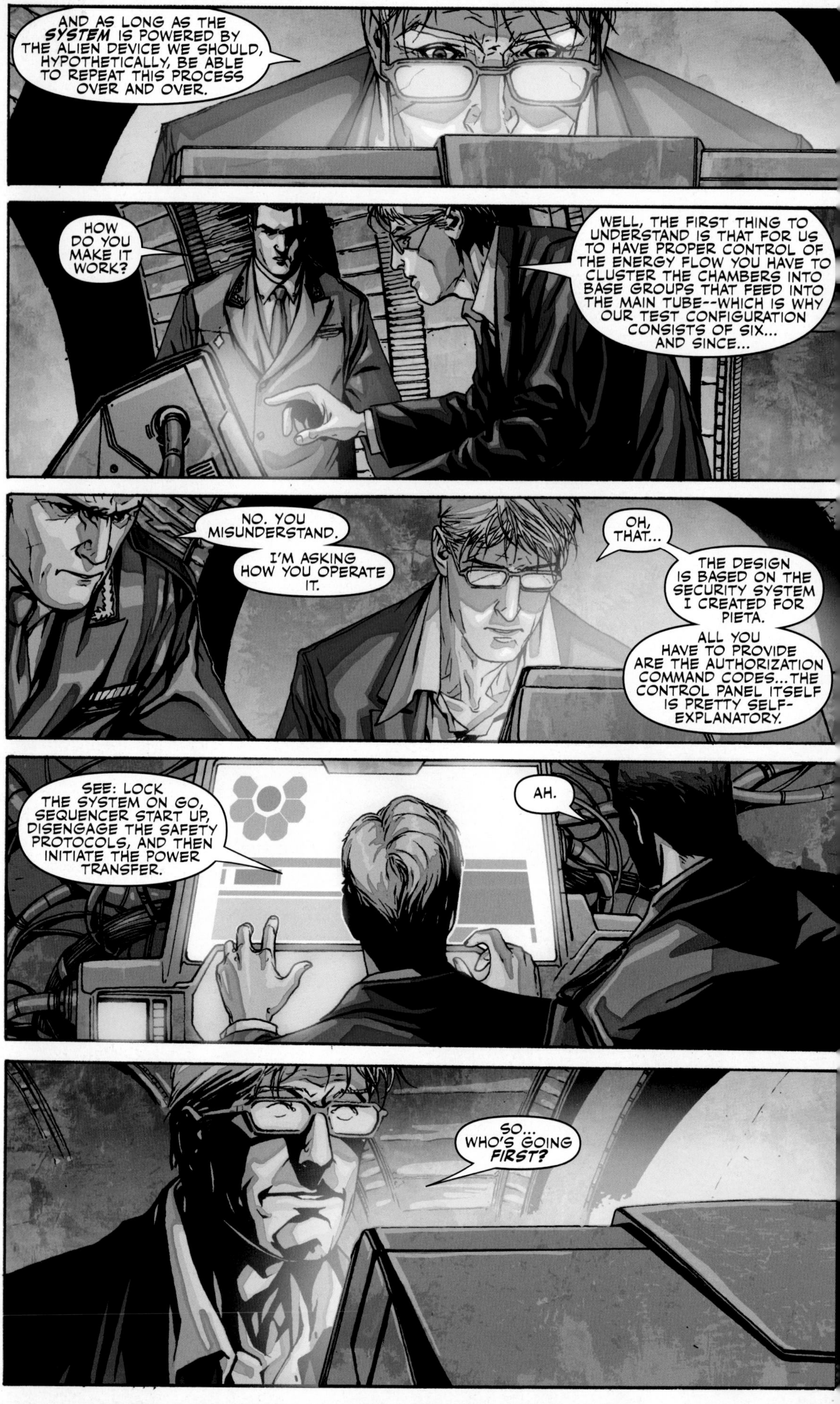
AND AS LONG AS THE SYSTEM IS POWERED BY THE ALIEN DEVICE WE SHOULD, HYPOTHETICALLY, BE ABLE TO REPEAT THIS PROCESS OVER AND OVER.
HOW DO YOU MAKE IT WORK?
WELL, THE FIRST THING TO UNDERSTAND IS THAT FOR US TO HAVE PROPER CONTROL OF THE ENERGY FLOW YOU HAVE TO CLUSTER THE CHAMBERS INTO BASE GROUPS THAT FEED INTO THE MAIN TUBE--WHICH IS WHY OUR TEST CONFIGURATION CONSISTS OF SIX... AND SINCE...
NO. YOU MISUNDERSTAND.
I'M ASKING HOW YOU OPERATE IT.
OH, THAT...
THE DESIGN IS BASED ON THE SECURITY SYSTEM I CREATED FOR PIETA.
ALL YOU HAVE TO PROVIDE ARE THE AUTHORIZATION COMMAND CODES...THE CONTROL PANEL ITSELF IS PRETTY SELF-EXPLANATORY.
SEE: LOCK THE SYSTEM ON GO, SEQUENCER START UP, DISENGAGE THE SAFETY PROTOCOLS, AND THEN INITIATE THE POWER TRANSFER.
AH.
SO... WHO'S GOING FIRST?

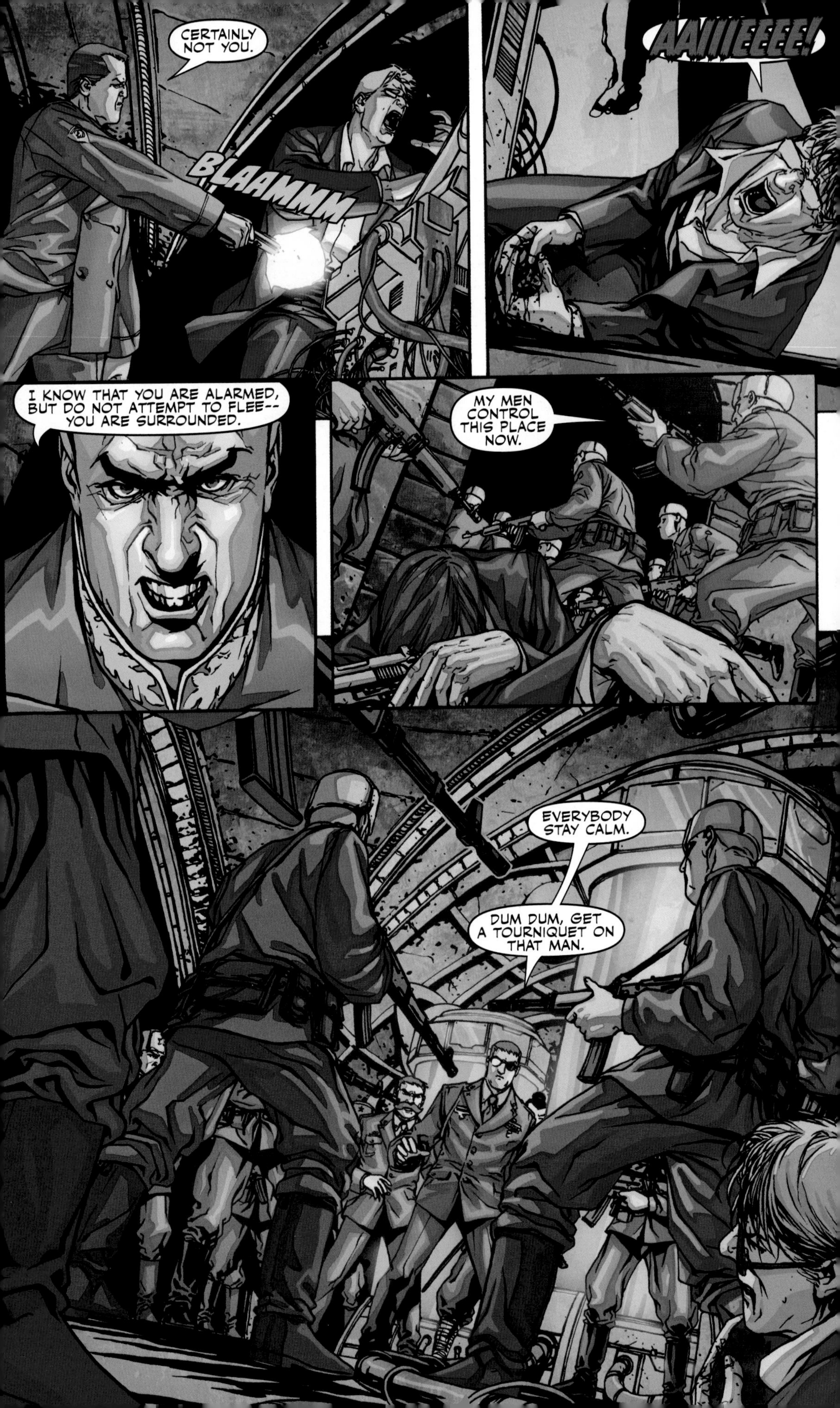
CERTAINLY NOT YOU.
BLAAMMM
AAIIIEEEE!
I KNOW THAT YOU ARE ALARMED, BUT DO NOT ATTEMPT TO FLEE-- YOU ARE SURROUNDED.
MY MEN CONTROL THIS PLACE NOW.
EVERYBODY STAY CALM.
DUM DUM, GET A TOURNIQUET ON THAT MAN.

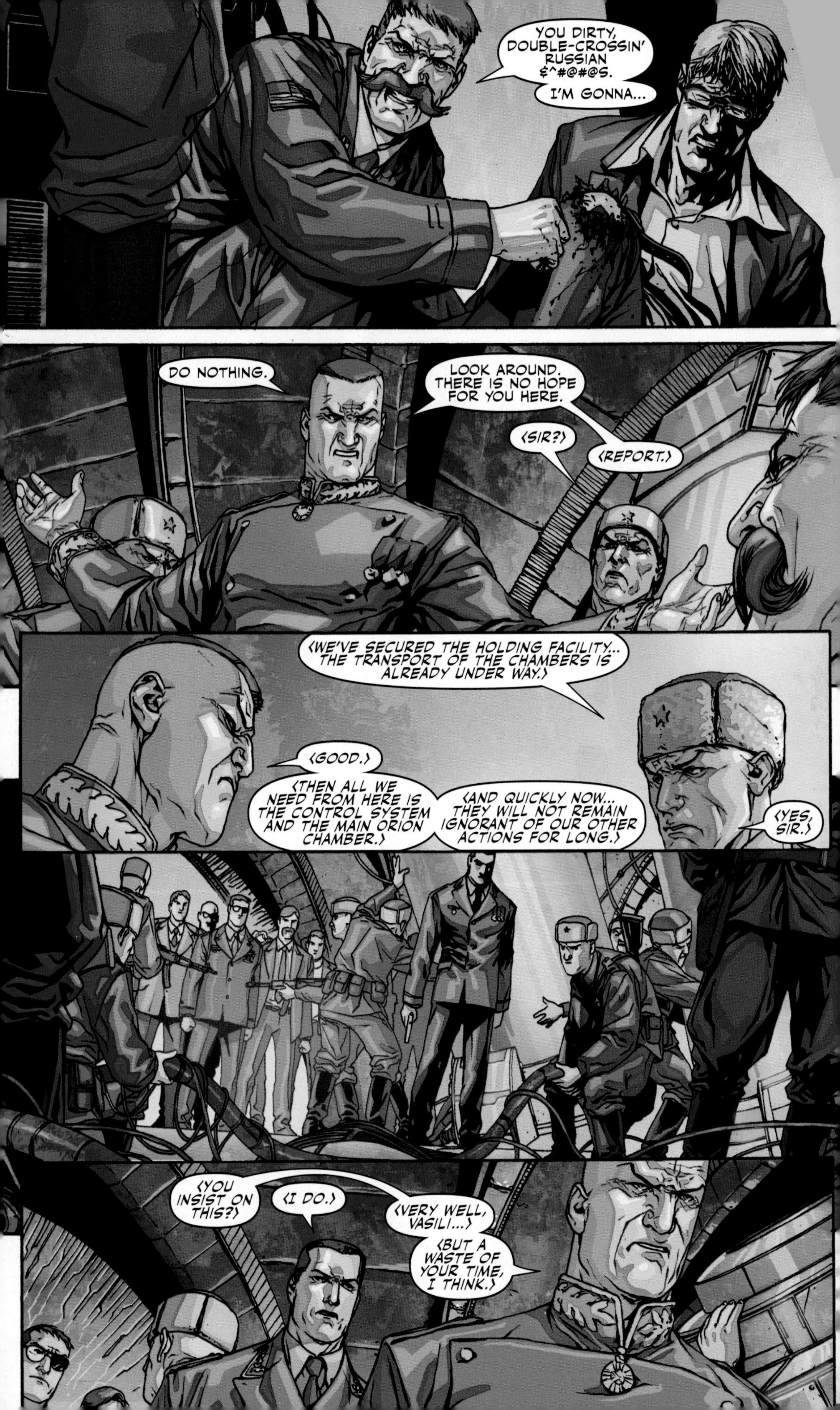
YOU DIRTY, DOUBLE-CROSSIN' RUSSIAN &^#@#@S.
I'M GONNA...
DO NOTHING.
LOOK AROUND. THERE IS NO HOPE FOR YOU HERE.
‹SIR?›
‹REPORT.›
‹WE'VE SECURED THE HOLDING FACILITY... THE TRANSPORT OF THE CHAMBERS IS ALREADY UNDER WAY.›
‹GOOD.›
‹THEN ALL WE NEED FROM HERE IS THE CONTROL SYSTEM AND THE MAIN ORION CHAMBER.›
‹AND QUICKLY NOW... THEY WILL NOT REMAIN IGNORANT OF OUR OTHER ACTIONS FOR LONG.›
‹YES, SIR.›
‹YOU INSIST ON THIS?›
‹I DO.›
‹VERY WELL, VASILI...›
‹BUT A WASTE OF YOUR TIME, I THINK.›

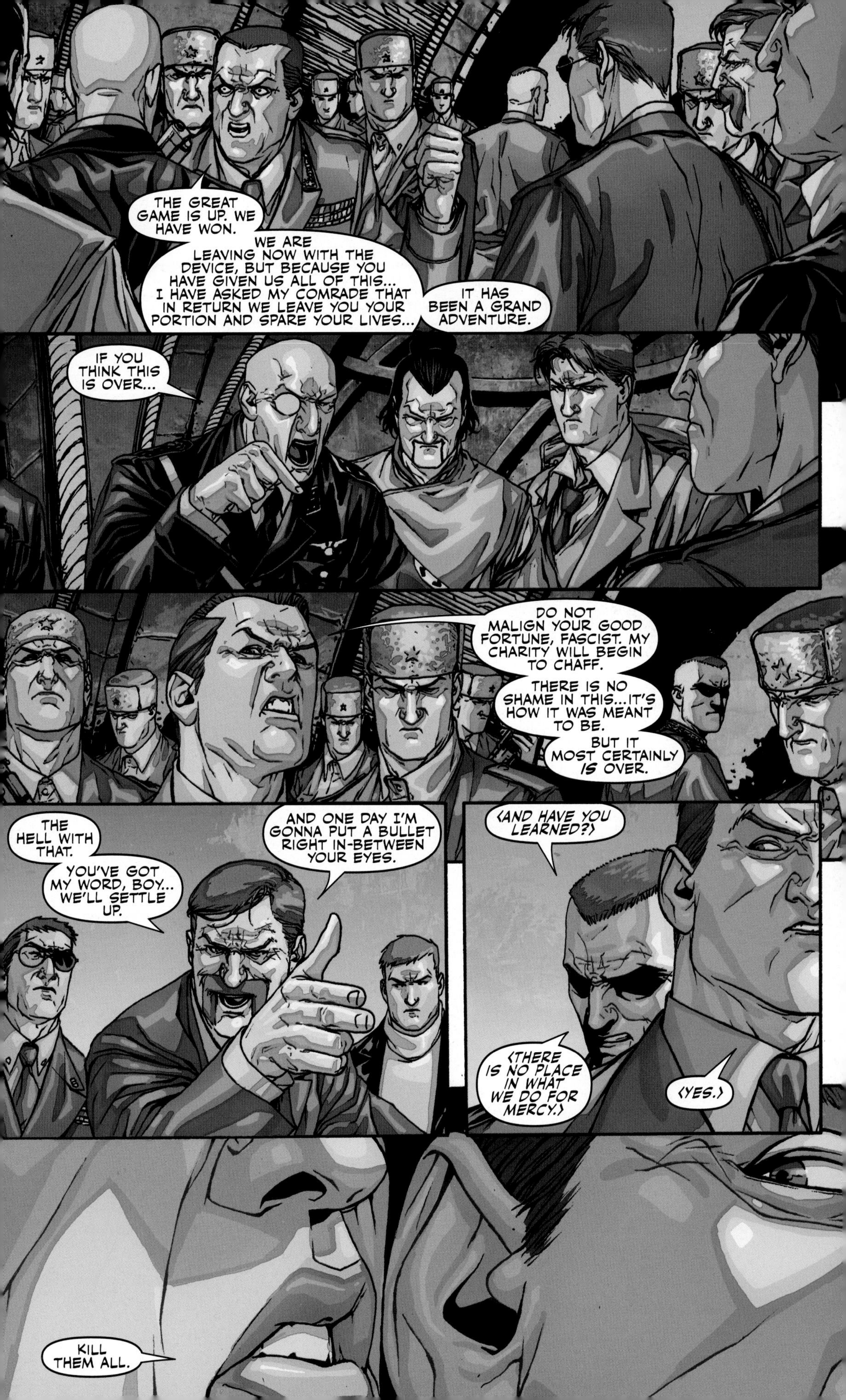
THE GREAT GAME IS UP. WE HAVE WON.
WE ARE LEAVING NOW WITH THE DEVICE, BUT BECAUSE YOU HAVE GIVEN US ALL OF THIS... I HAVE ASKED MY COMRADE THAT IN RETURN WE LEAVE YOU YOUR PORTION AND SPARE YOUR LIVES...
IT HAS BEEN A GRAND ADVENTURE.
IF YOU THINK THIS IS OVER...
DO NOT MALIGN YOUR GOOD FORTUNE, FASCIST. MY CHARITY WILL BEGIN TO CHAFF.
THERE IS NO SHAME IN THIS...IT'S HOW IT WAS MEANT TO BE.
BUT IT MOST CERTAINLY *IS* OVER.
THE HELL WITH THAT.
YOU'VE GOT MY WORD, BOY... WE'LL SETTLE UP.
AND ONE DAY I'M GONNA PUT A BULLET RIGHT IN-BETWEEN YOUR EYES.
‹AND HAVE YOU LEARNED?›
‹THERE IS NO PLACE IN WHAT WE DO FOR MERCY.›
‹YES.›
KILL THEM ALL.

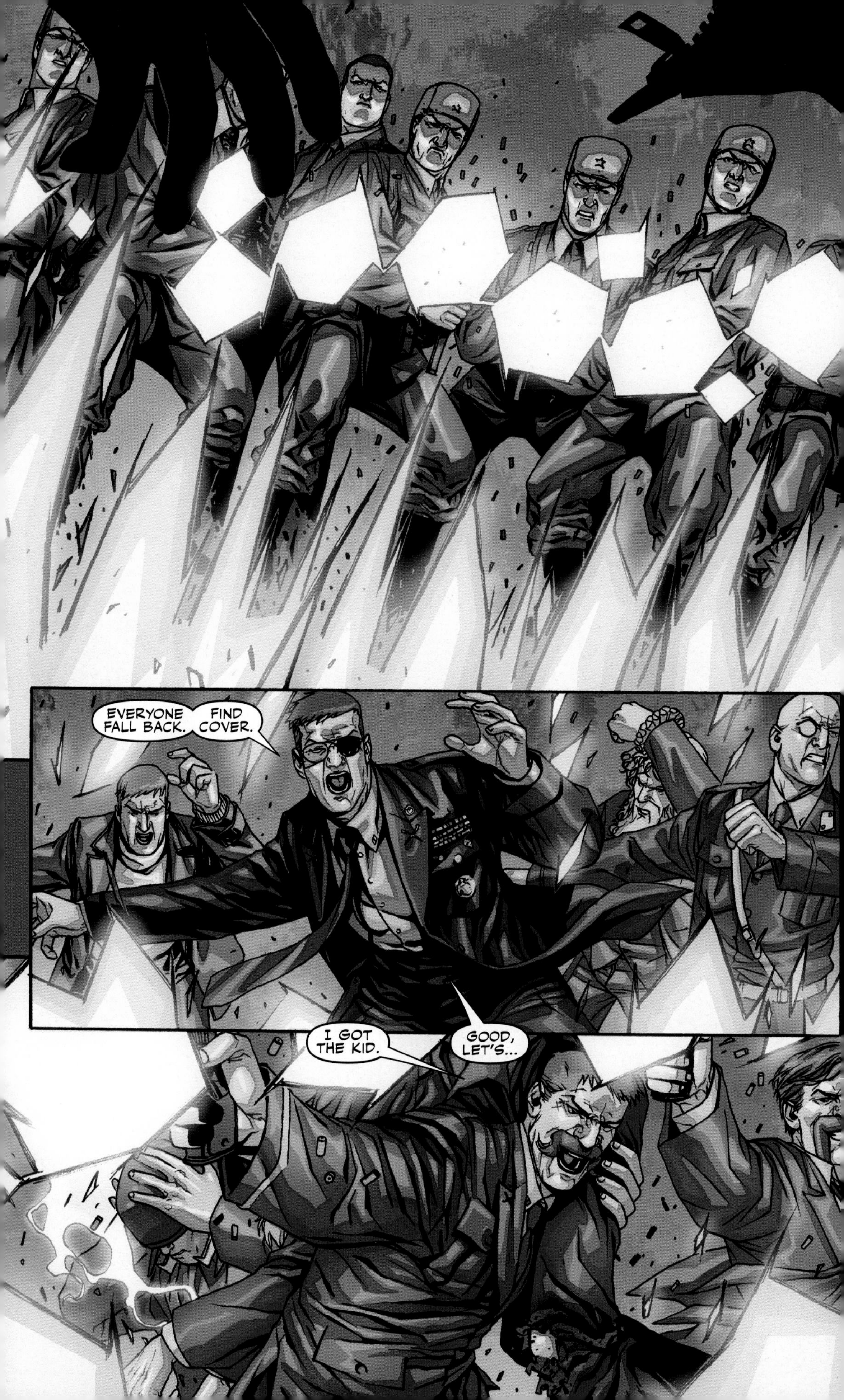
EVERYONE FALL BACK.
FIND COVER.
I GOT THE KID.
GOOD, LET'S...

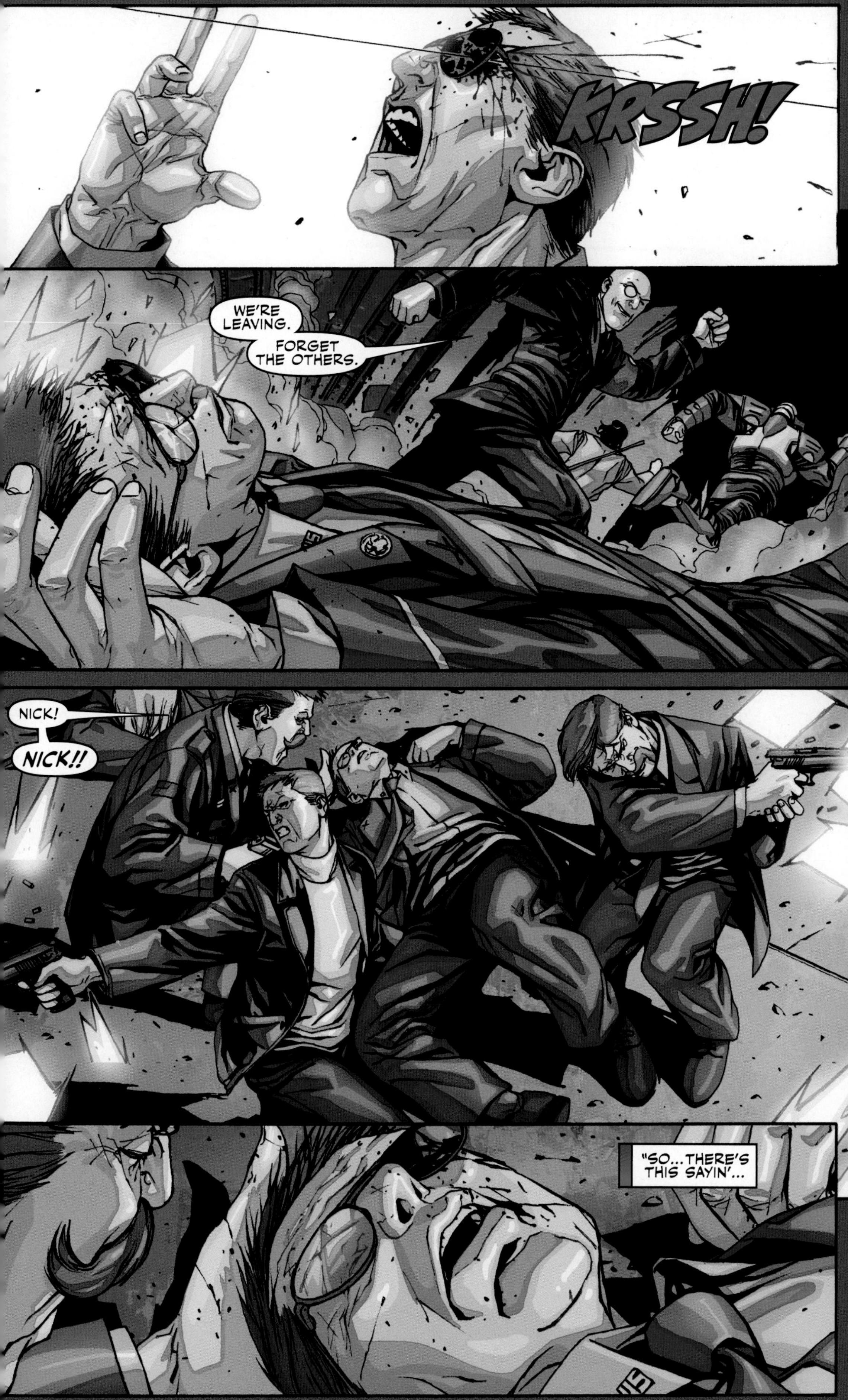
KRSSH!
WE'RE LEAVING.
FORGET THE OTHERS.
NICK!
NICK!!
"SO...THERE'S THIS SAYIN'...

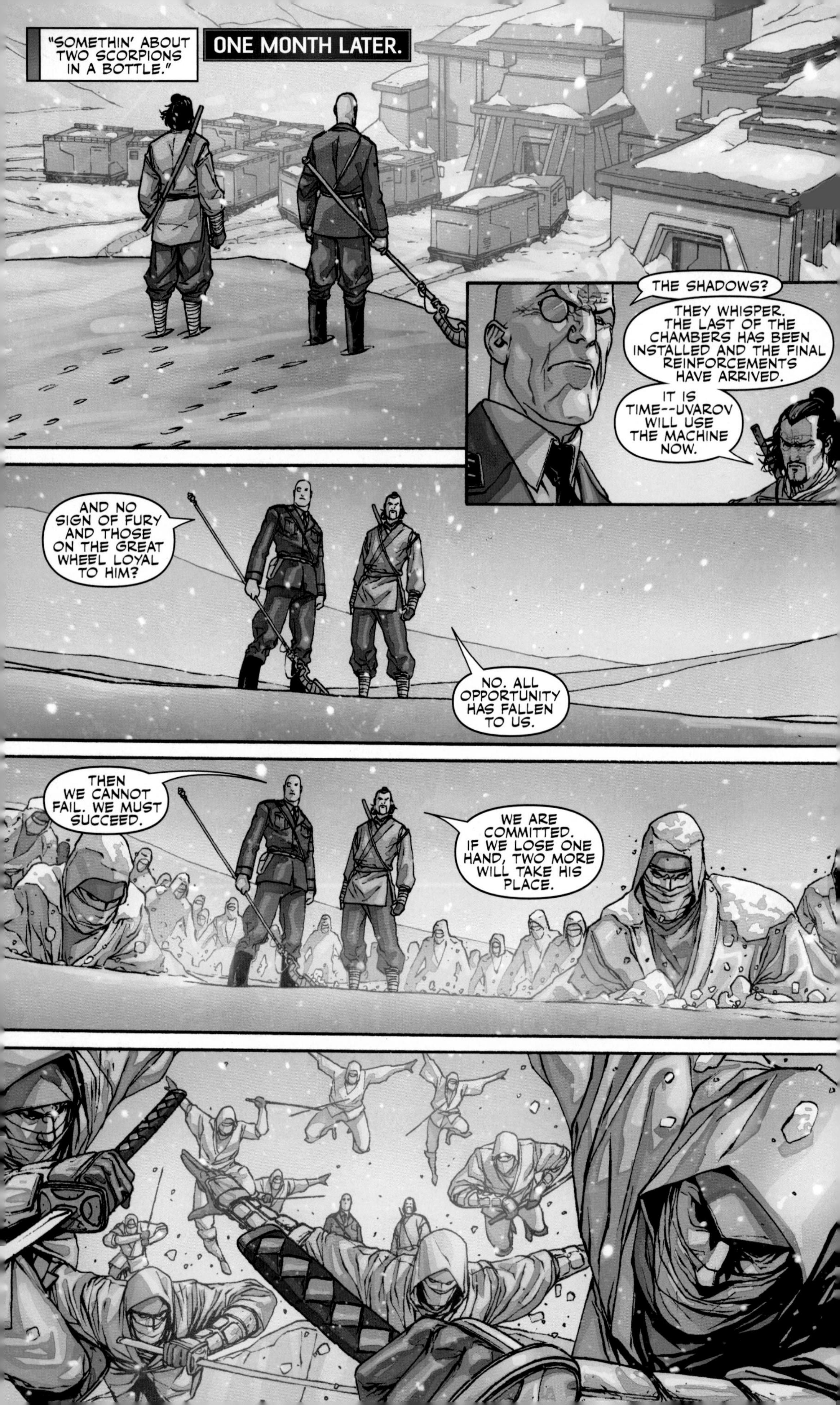

"SOMETHIN' ABOUT TWO SCORPIONS IN A BOTTLE."
ONE MONTH LATER.
THE SHADOWS?
THEY WHISPER. THE LAST OF THE CHAMBERS HAS BEEN INSTALLED AND THE FINAL REINFORCEMENTS HAVE ARRIVED.
IT IS TIME--UVAROV WILL USE THE MACHINE NOW.
AND NO SIGN OF FURY AND THOSE ON THE GREAT WHEEL LOYAL TO HIM?
NO. ALL OPPORTUNITY HAS FALLEN TO US.
THEN WE CANNOT FAIL. WE MUST SUCCEED.
WE ARE COMMITTED. IF WE LOSE ONE HAND, TWO MORE WILL TAKE HIS PLACE.

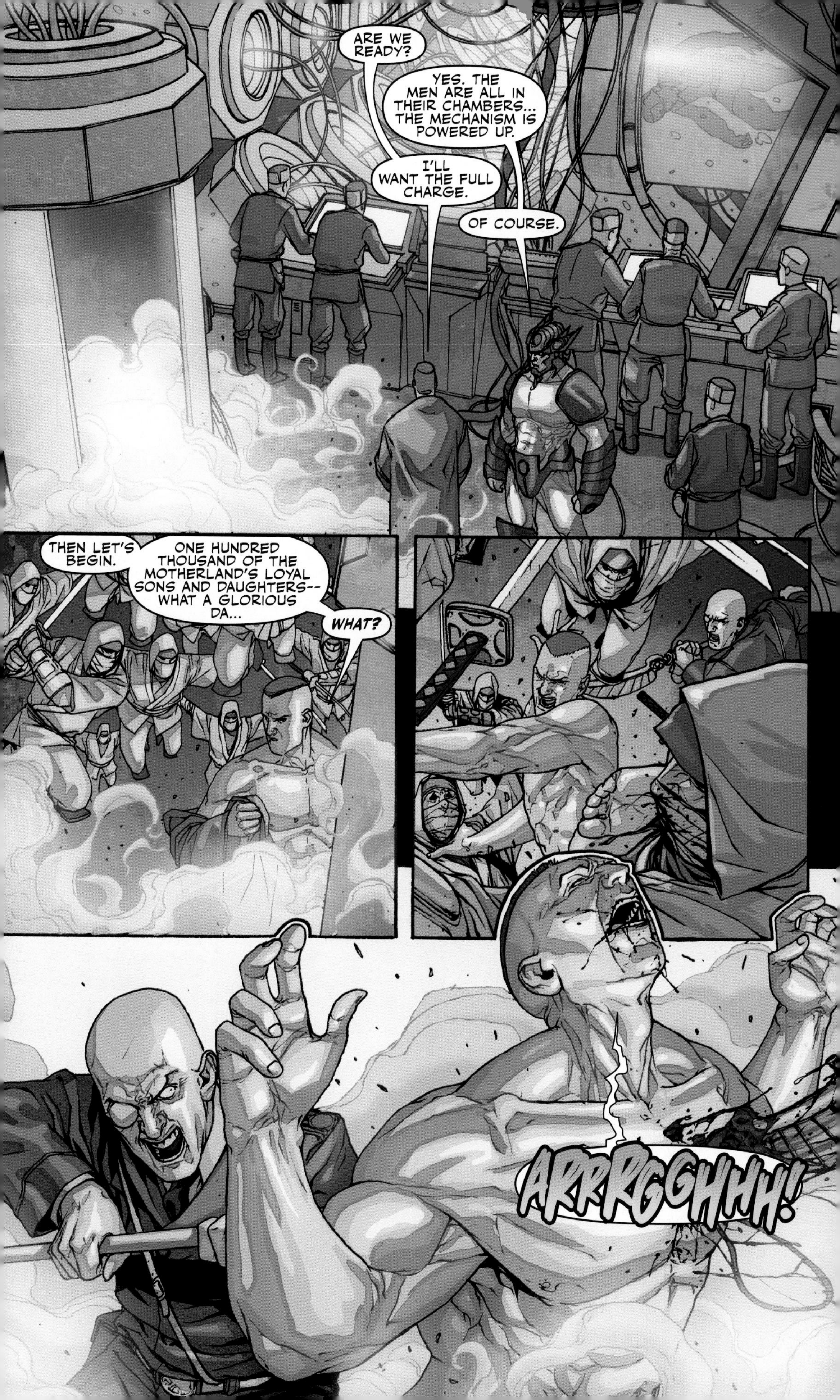
ARE WE READY?
YES. THE MEN ARE ALL IN THEIR CHAMBERS... THE MECHANISM IS POWERED UP.
I'LL WANT THE FULL CHARGE.
OF COURSE.
THEN LET'S BEGIN.
ONE HUNDRED THOUSAND OF THE MOTHERLAND'S LOYAL SONS AND DAUGHTERS-- WHAT A GLORIOUS DA...
WHAT?
ARRRGGHHH!

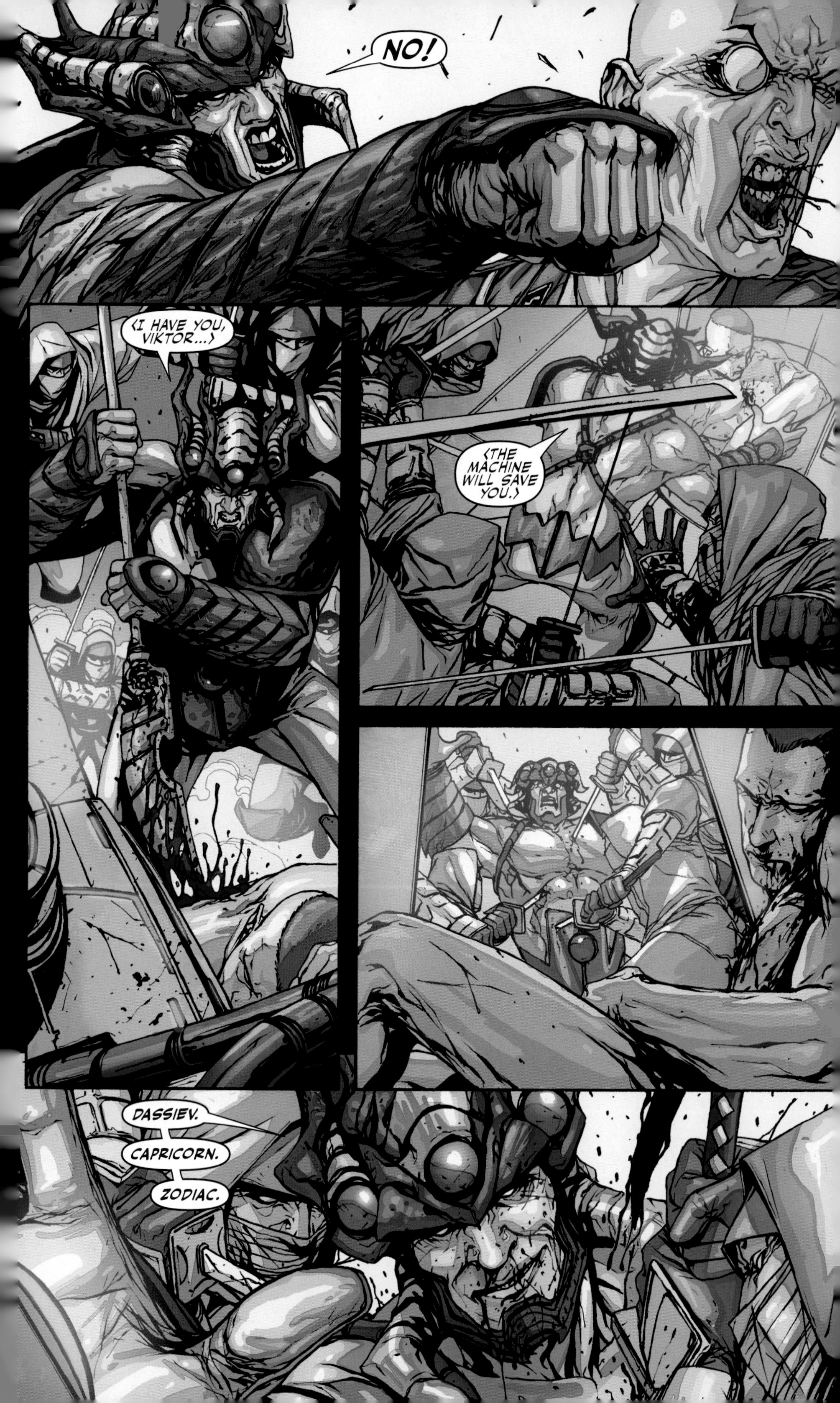
NO!
‹I HAVE YOU, VIKTOR...›
‹THE MACHINE WILL SAVE YOU.›
DASSIEV.
CAPRICORN.
ZODIAC.

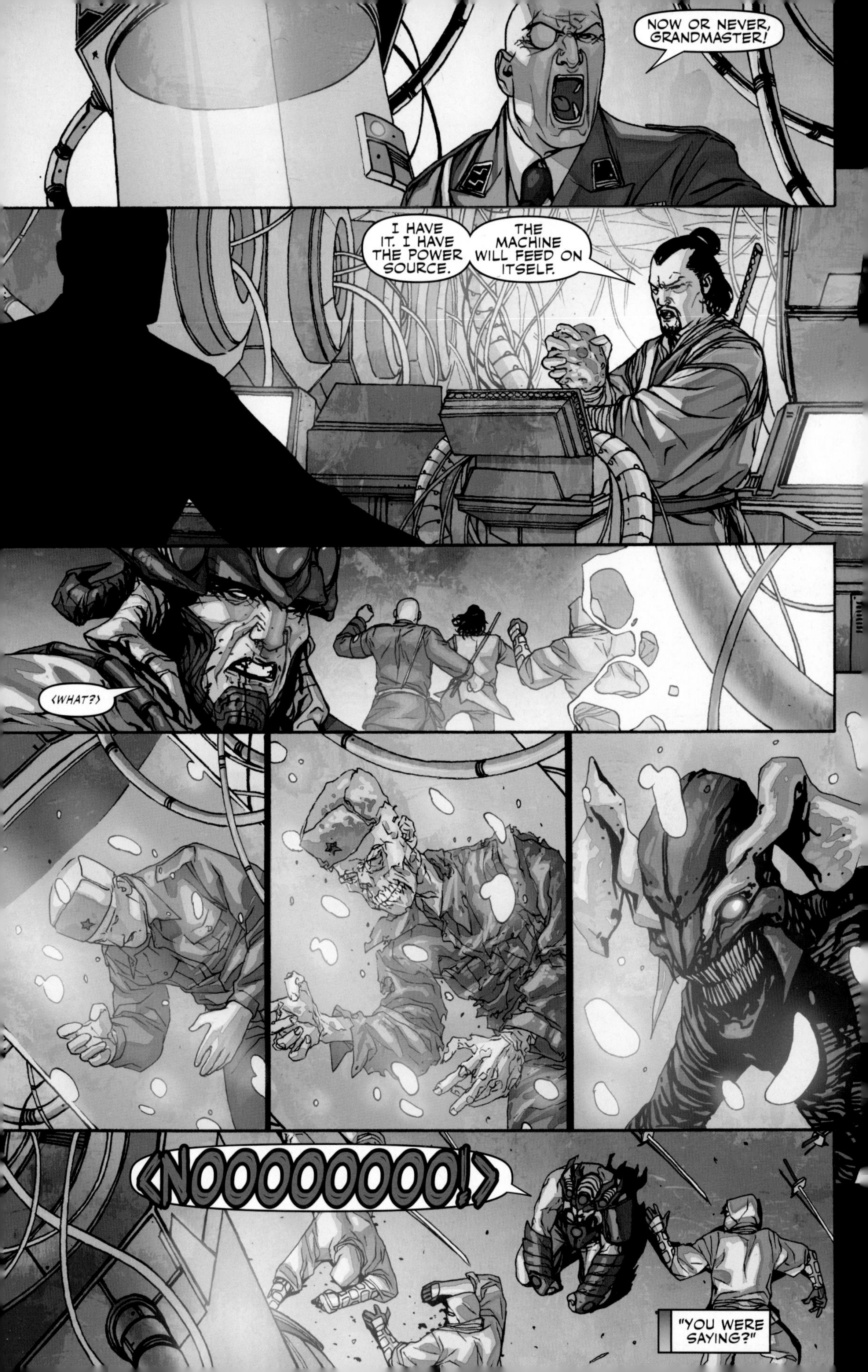
NOW OR NEVER, GRANDMASTER!
I HAVE IT. I HAVE THE POWER SOURCE.
THE MACHINE WILL FEED ON ITSELF.
<WHAT?>
<NOOOOOOOO!>
"YOU WERE SAYING?"

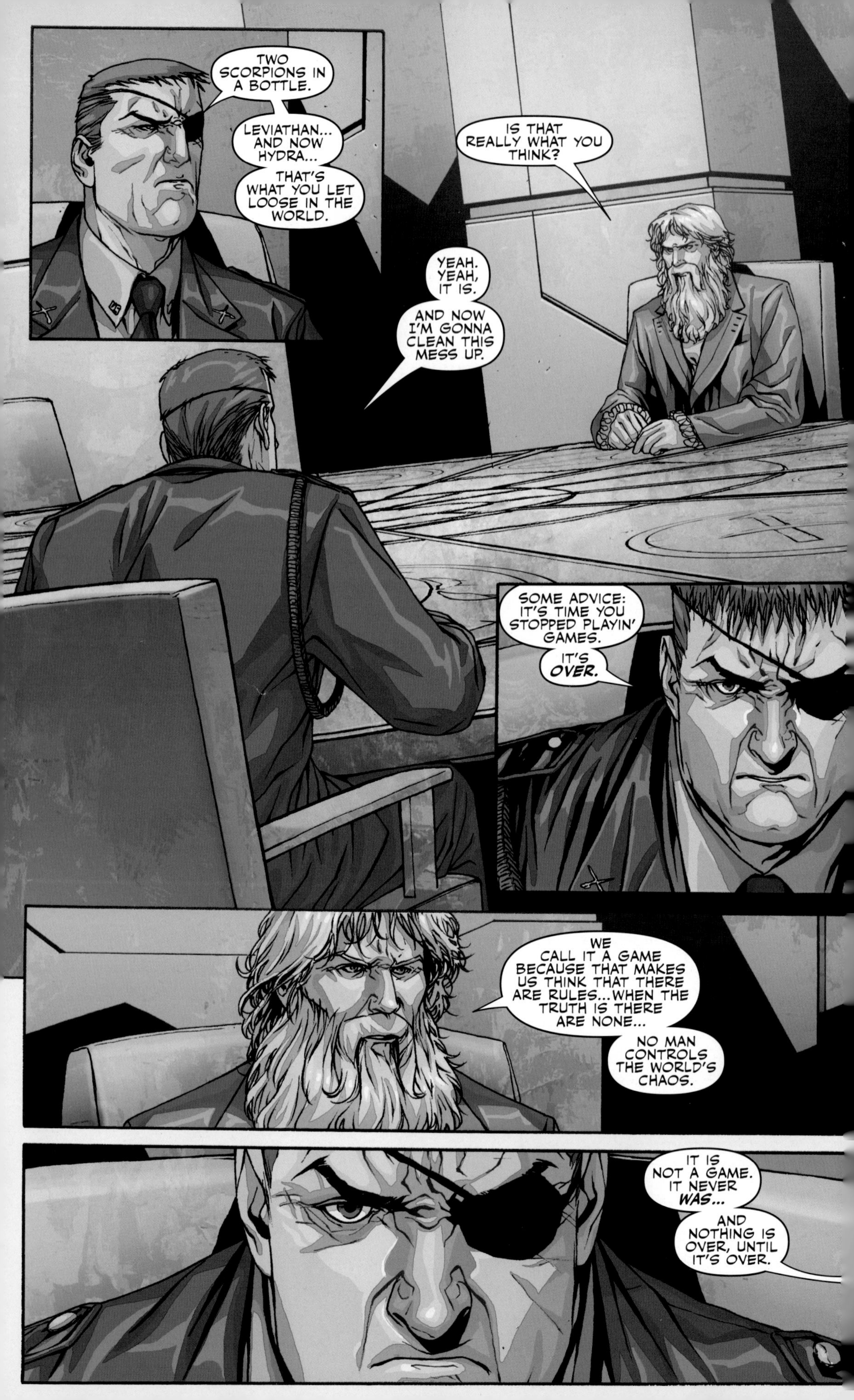
TWO SCORPIONS IN A BOTTLE.
LEVIATHAN... AND NOW HYDRA...
THAT'S WHAT YOU LET LOOSE IN THE WORLD.
IS THAT REALLY WHAT YOU THINK?
YEAH. YEAH, IT IS.
AND NOW I'M GONNA CLEAN THIS MESS UP.
SOME ADVICE: IT'S TIME YOU STOPPED PLAYIN' GAMES.
IT'S *OVER.*
WE CALL IT A GAME BECAUSE THAT MAKES US THINK THAT THERE ARE RULES...WHEN THE TRUTH IS THERE ARE NONE...
NO MAN CONTROLS THE WORLD'S CHAOS.
IT IS NOT A GAME. IT NEVER *WAS...*
AND NOTHING IS OVER, UNTIL IT'S OVER.

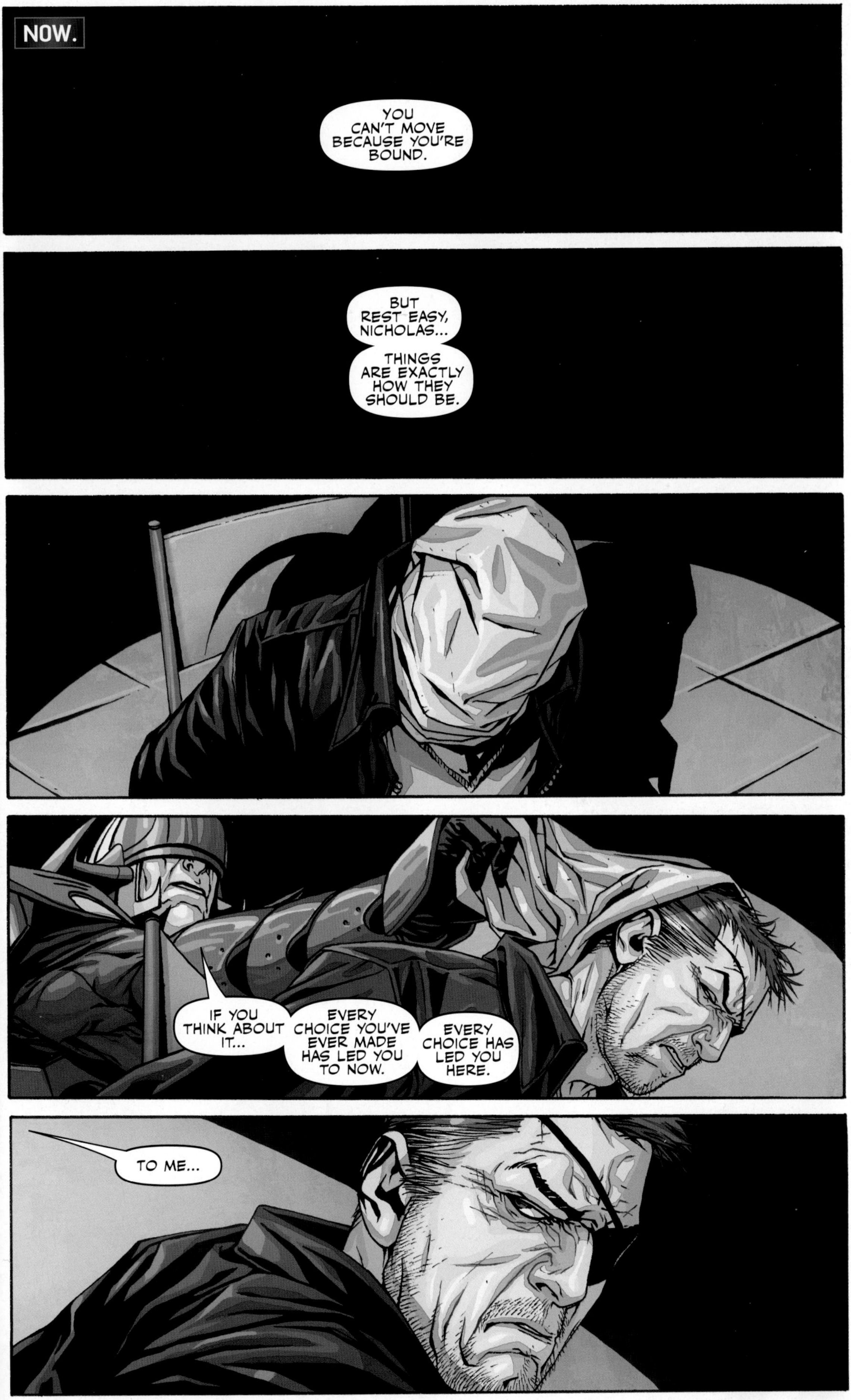
NOW.
YOU CAN'T MOVE BECAUSE YOU'RE BOUND.
BUT REST EASY, NICHOLAS...
THINGS ARE EXACTLY HOW THEY SHOULD BE.
IF YOU THINK ABOUT IT...
EVERY CHOICE YOU'VE EVER MADE HAS LED YOU TO NOW.
EVERY CHOICE HAS LED YOU HERE.
TO ME...

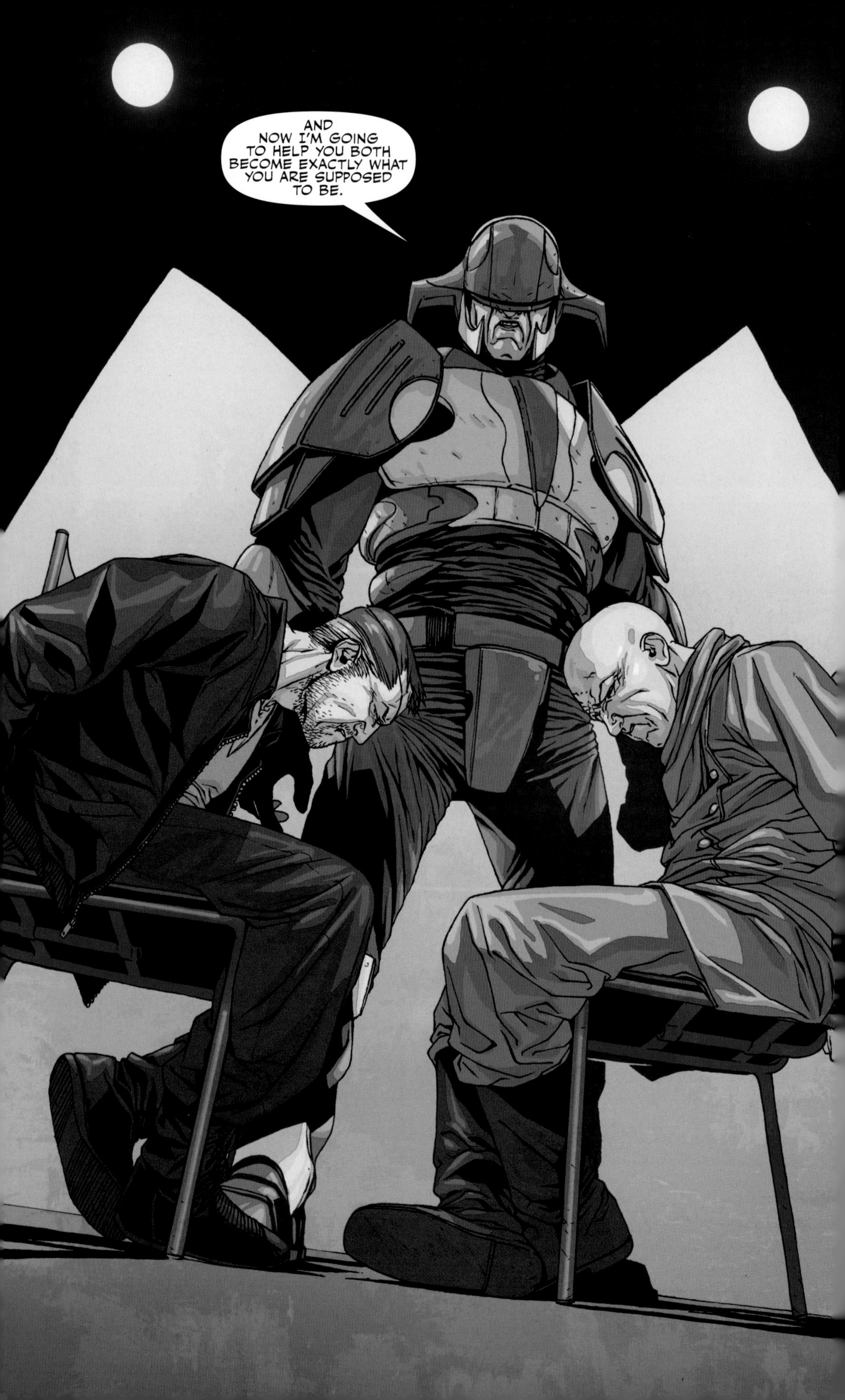
AND NOW I'M GOING TO HELP YOU BOTH BECOME EXACTLY WHAT YOU ARE SUPPOSED TO BE.

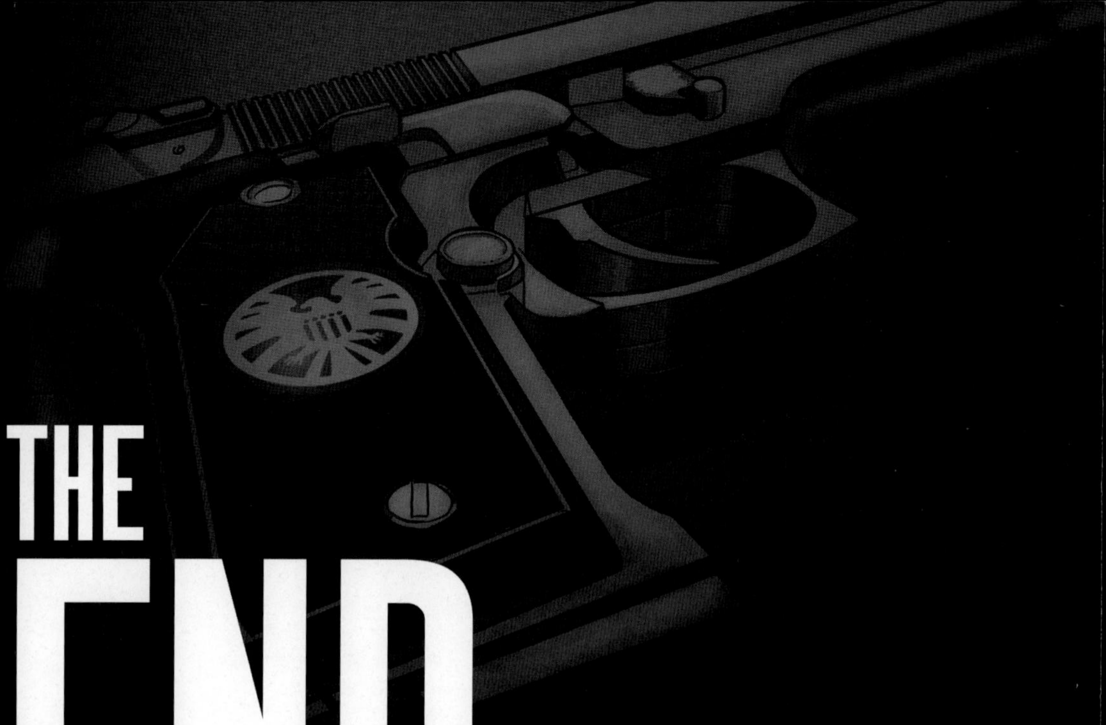

THE END IS NIGH

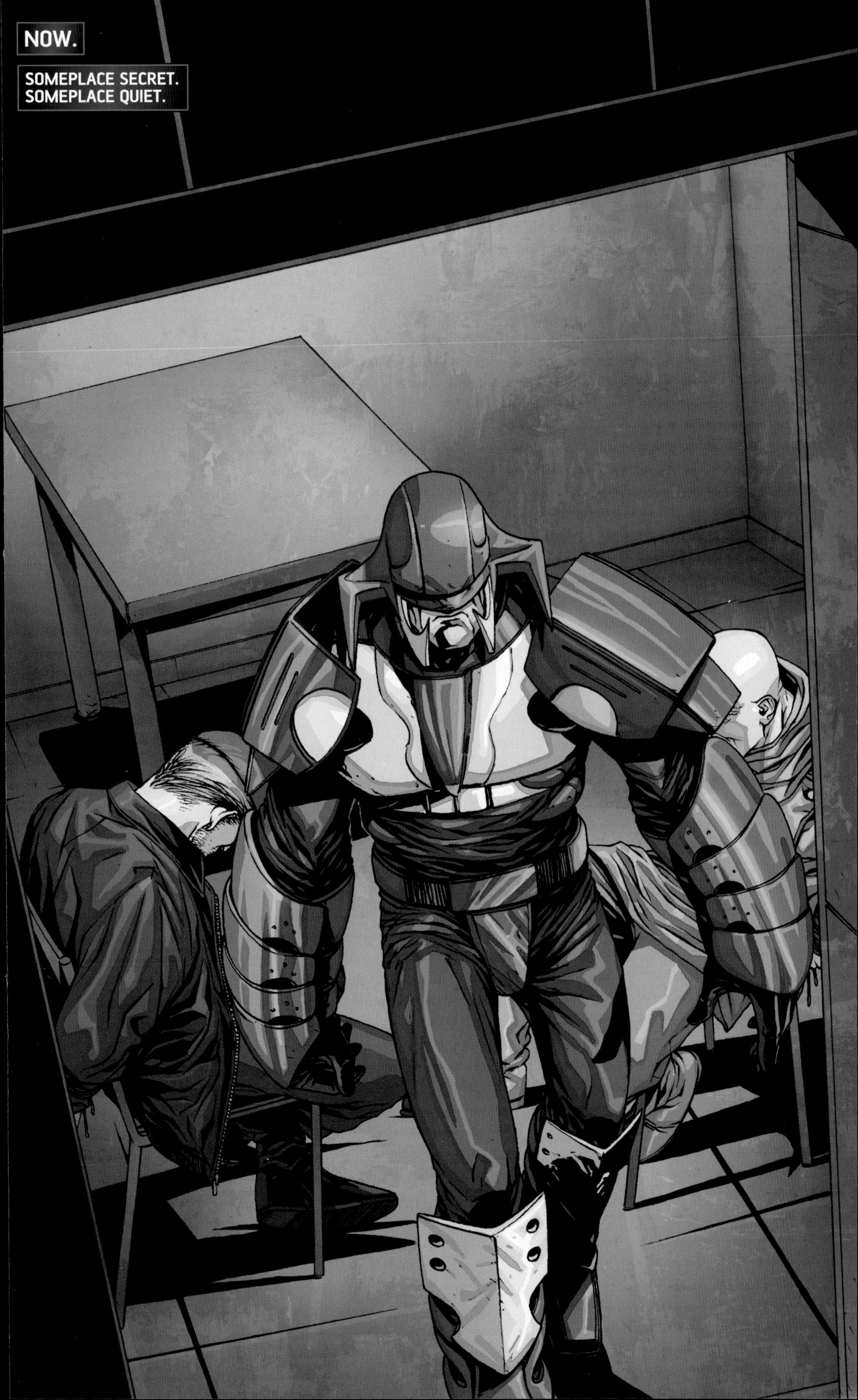
NOW.
SOMEPLACE SECRET. SOMEPLACE QUIET.

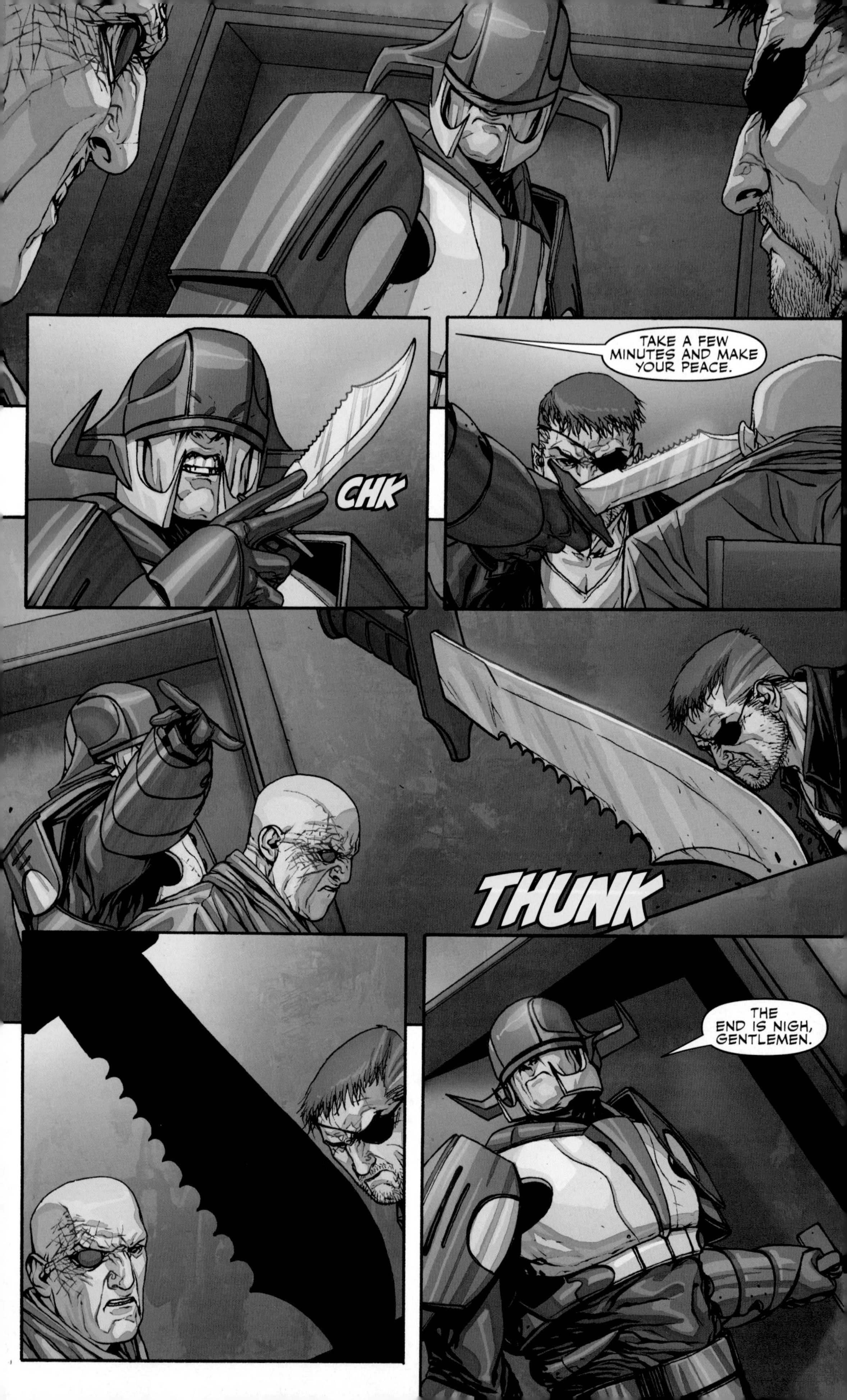
CHK
TAKE A FEW MINUTES AND MAKE YOUR PEACE.
THUNK
THE END IS NIGH, GENTLEMEN.

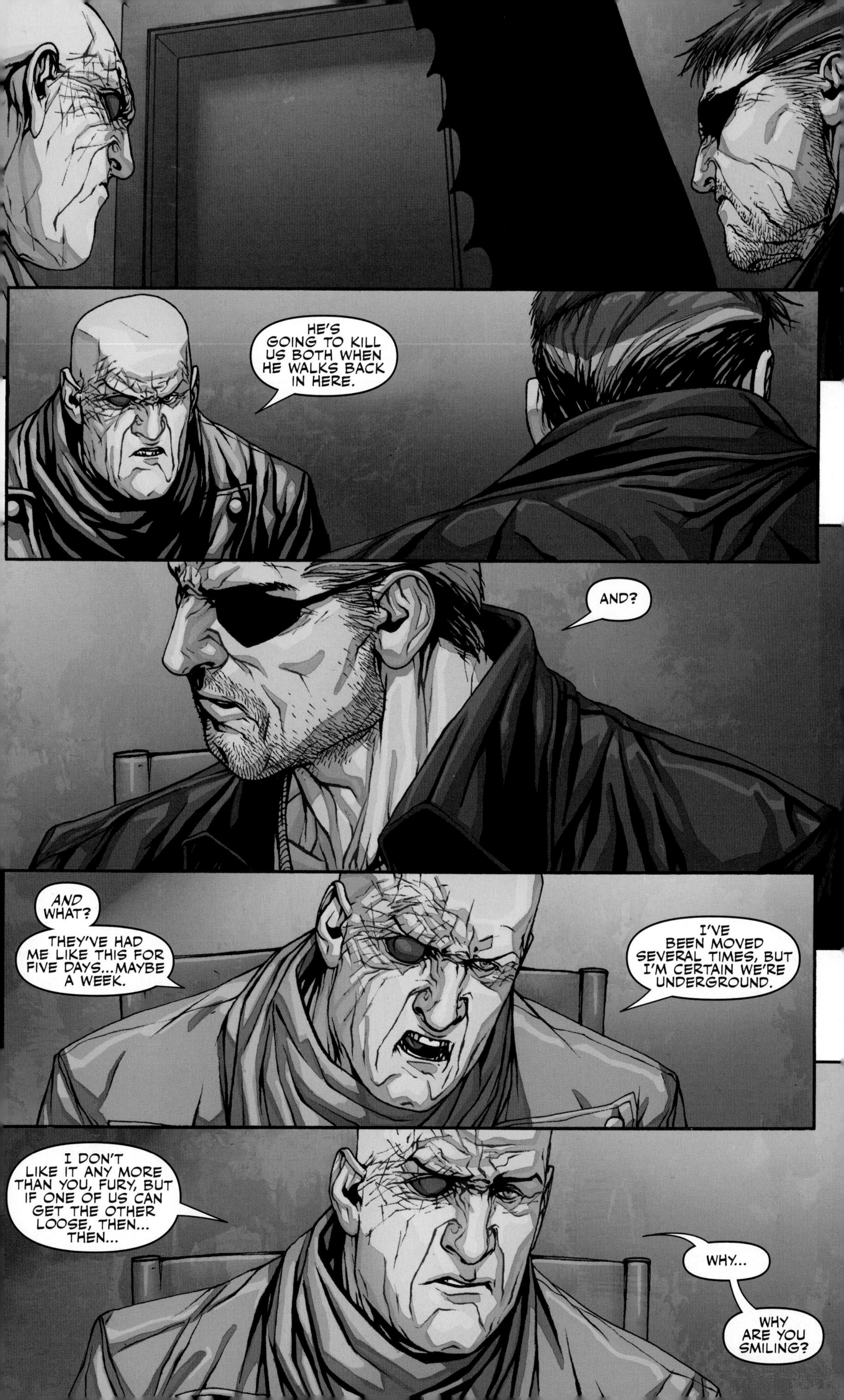
HE'S GOING TO KILL US BOTH WHEN HE WALKS BACK IN HERE.
AND?
AND WHAT?
THEY'VE HAD ME LIKE THIS FOR FIVE DAYS...MAYBE A WEEK.
I'VE BEEN MOVED SEVERAL TIMES, BUT I'M CERTAIN WE'RE UNDERGROUND.
I DON'T LIKE IT ANY MORE THAN YOU, FURY, BUT IF ONE OF US CAN GET THE OTHER LOOSE, THEN... THEN...
WHY...
WHY ARE YOU SMILING?

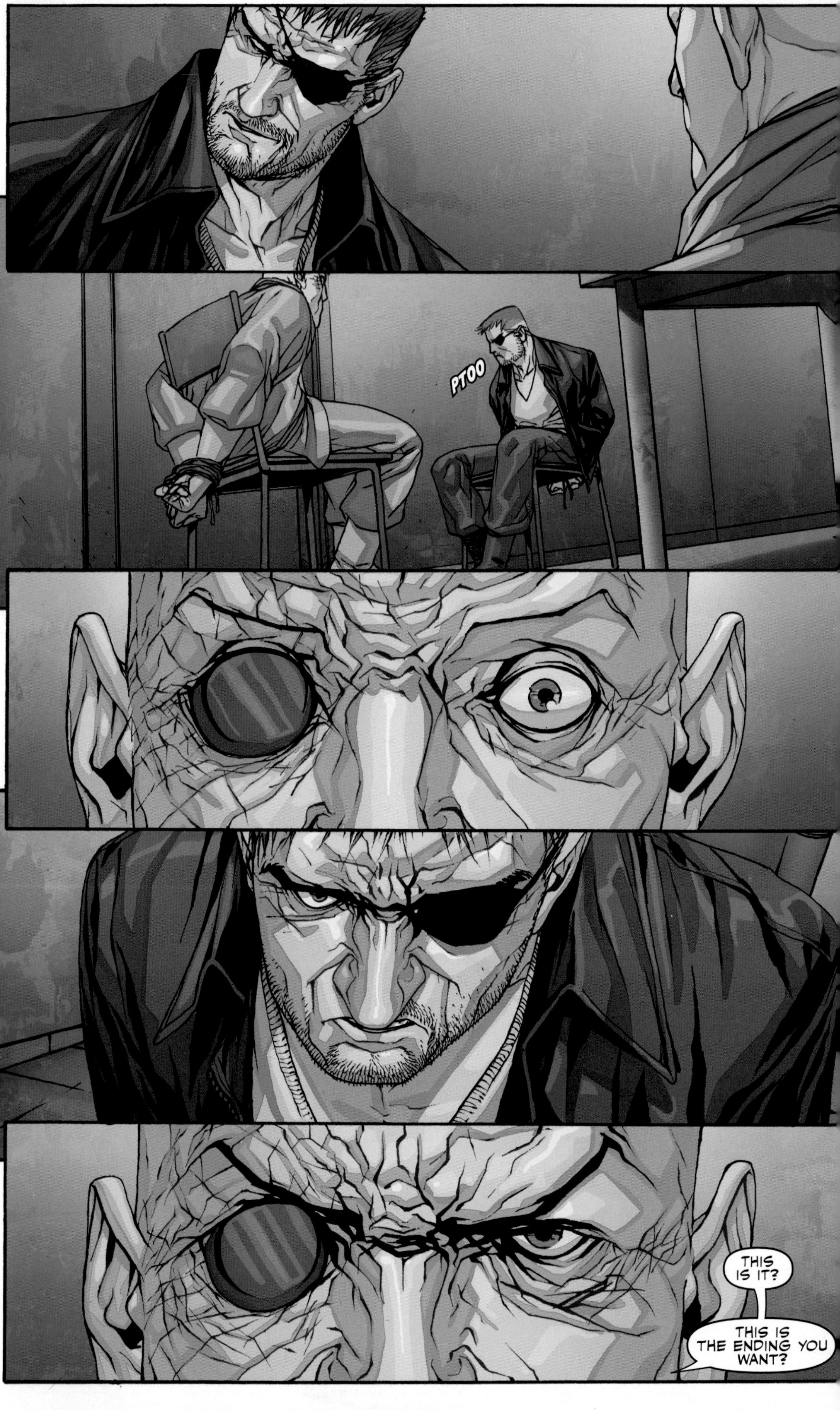
PTOO
THIS IS IT?
THIS IS THE ENDING YOU WANT?

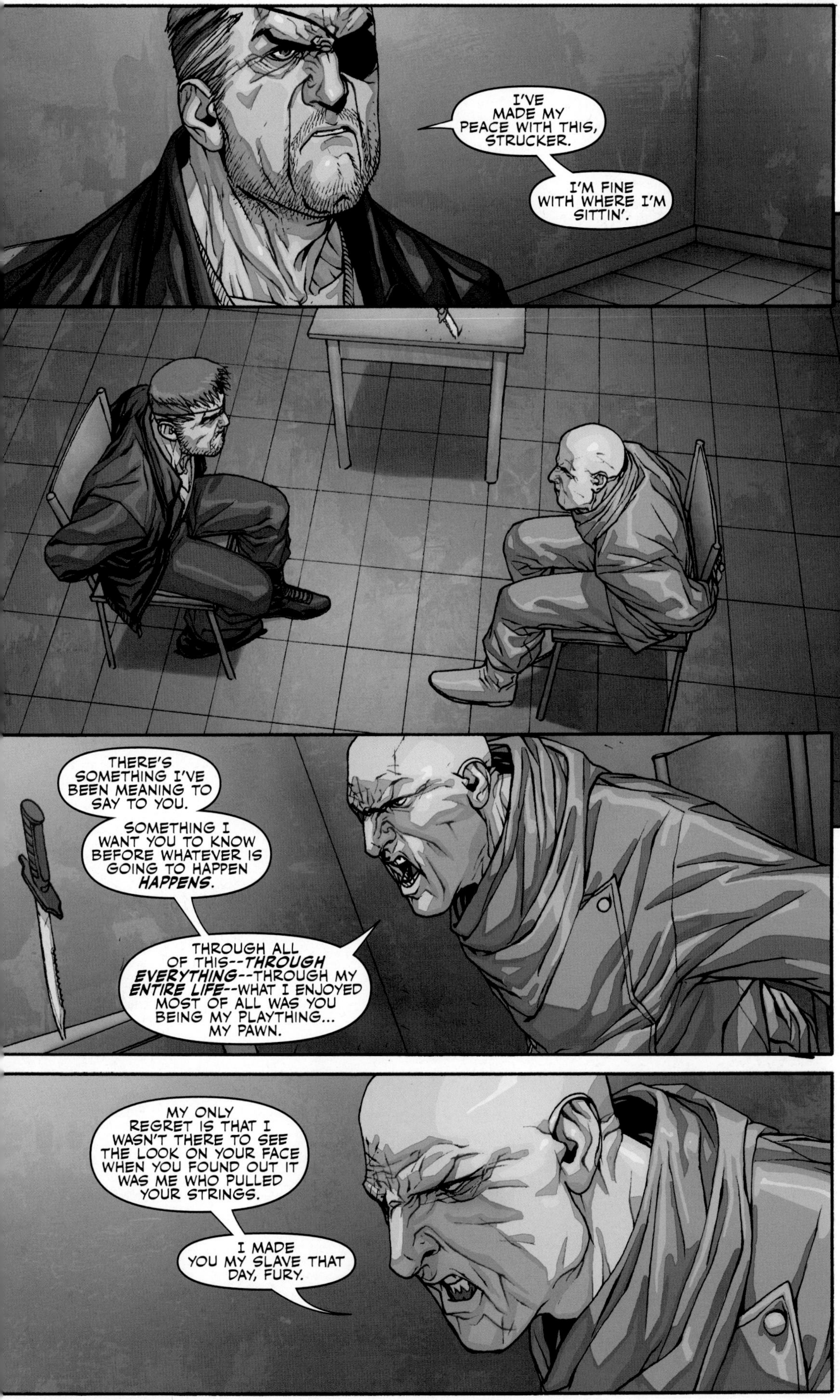
I'VE MADE MY PEACE WITH THIS, STRUCKER.
I'M FINE WITH WHERE I'M SITTIN'.
THERE'S SOMETHING I'VE BEEN MEANING TO SAY TO YOU.
SOMETHING I WANT YOU TO KNOW BEFORE WHATEVER IS GOING TO HAPPEN *HAPPENS*.
THROUGH ALL OF THIS--*THROUGH EVERYTHING*--THROUGH MY *ENTIRE LIFE*--WHAT I ENJOYED MOST OF ALL WAS YOU BEING MY PLAYTHING... MY PAWN.
MY ONLY REGRET IS THAT I WASN'T THERE TO SEE THE LOOK ON YOUR FACE WHEN YOU FOUND OUT IT WAS ME WHO PULLED YOUR STRINGS.
I MADE YOU MY SLAVE THAT DAY, FURY.

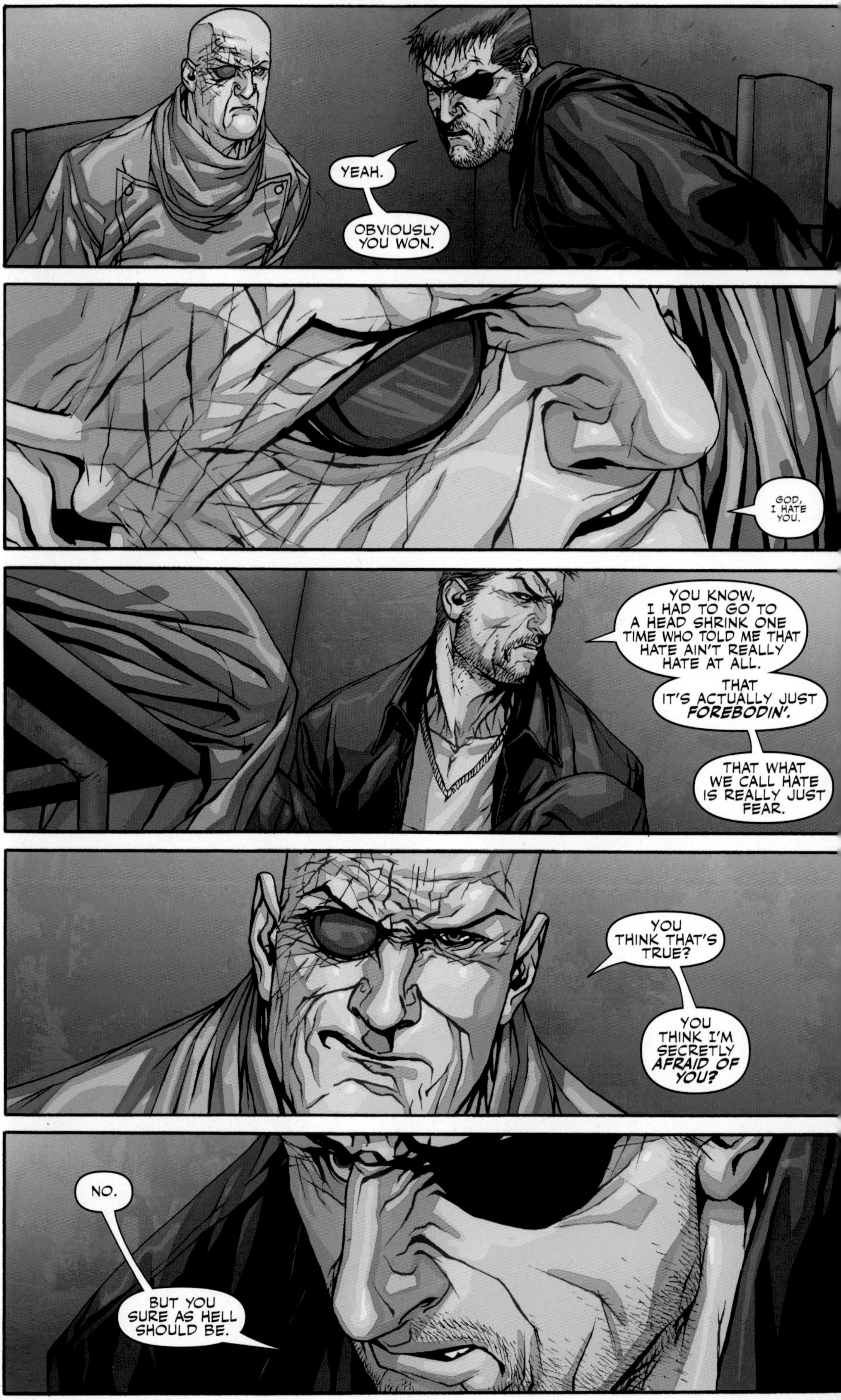
YEAH.
OBVIOUSLY YOU WON.
GOD, I HATE YOU.
YOU KNOW, I HAD TO GO TO A HEAD SHRINK ONE TIME WHO TOLD ME THAT HATE AIN'T REALLY HATE AT ALL.
THAT IT'S ACTUALLY JUST FOREBODIN'.
THAT WHAT WE CALL HATE IS REALLY JUST FEAR.
YOU THINK THAT'S TRUE?
YOU THINK I'M SECRETLY AFRAID OF YOU?
NO.
BUT YOU SURE AS HELL SHOULD BE.

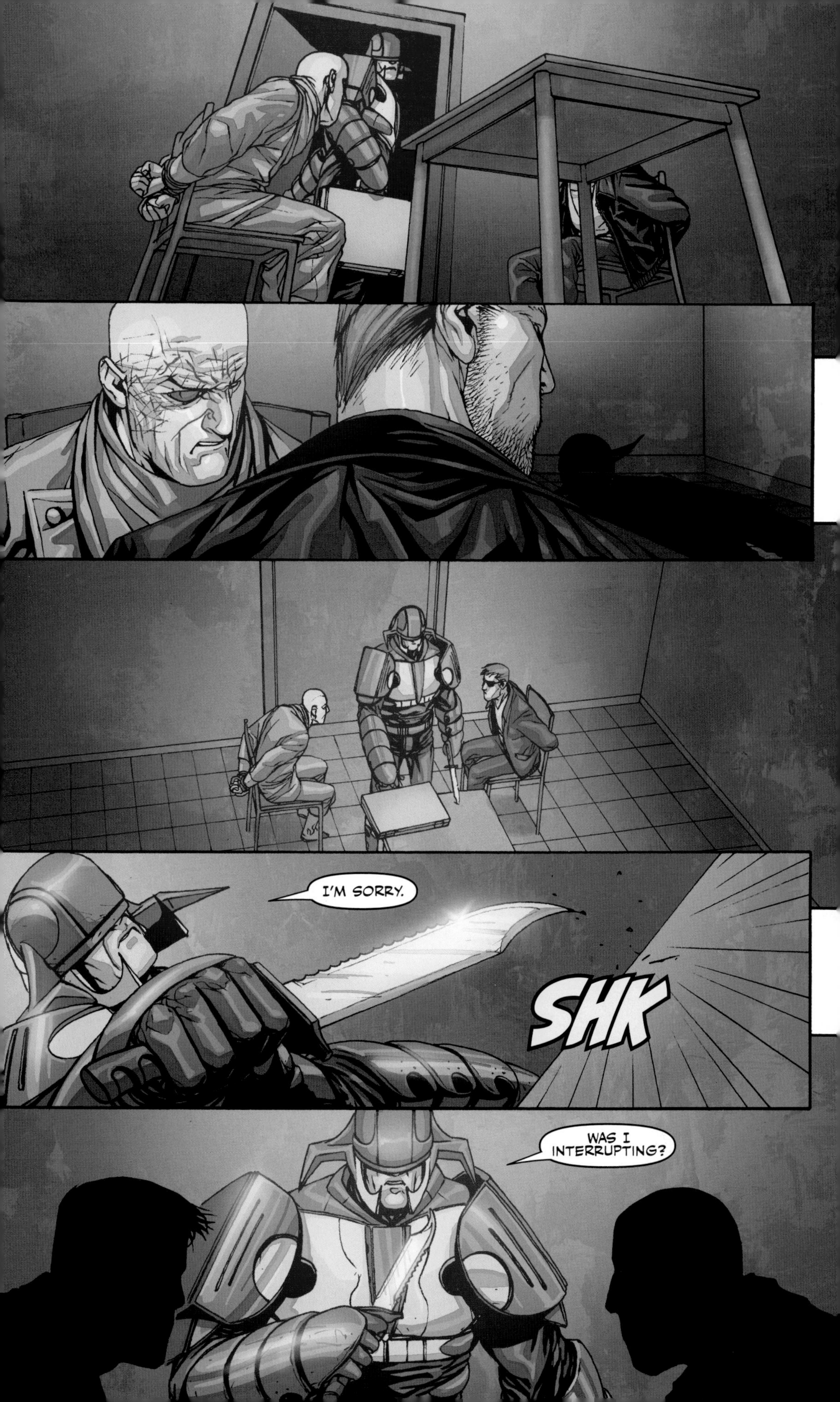
I'M SORRY.
SHK
WAS I INTERRUPTING?

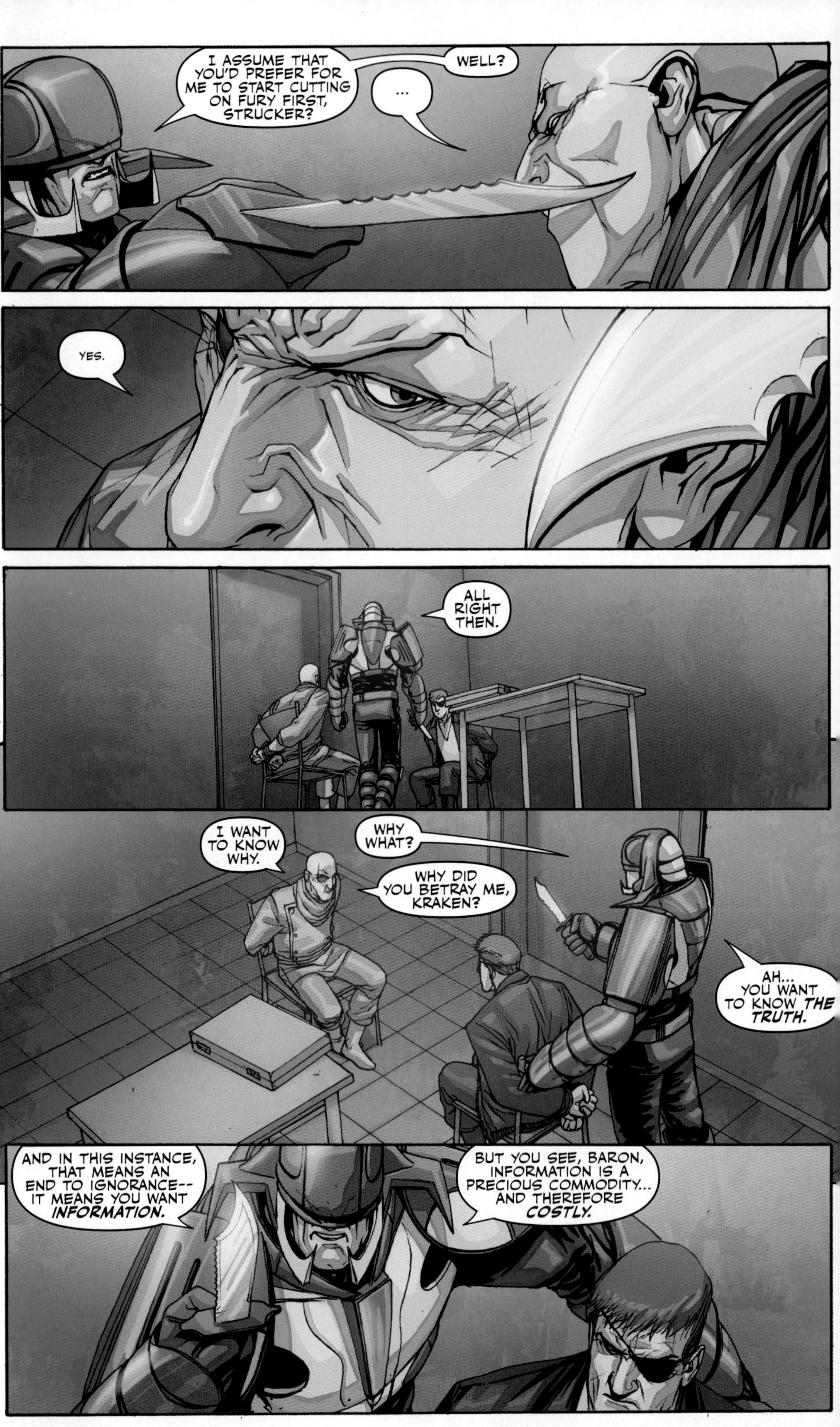
I ASSUME THAT YOU'D PREFER FOR ME TO START CUTTING ON FURY FIRST, STRUCKER?
WELL?
...
YES.
ALL RIGHT THEN.
I WANT TO KNOW WHY.
WHY WHAT?
WHY DID YOU BETRAY ME, KRAKEN?
AH... YOU WANT TO KNOW *THE TRUTH.*
AND IN THIS INSTANCE, THAT MEANS AN END TO IGNORANCE-- IT MEANS YOU WANT *INFORMATION.*
BUT YOU SEE, BARON, INFORMATION IS A PRECIOUS COMMODITY... AND THEREFORE *COSTLY.*

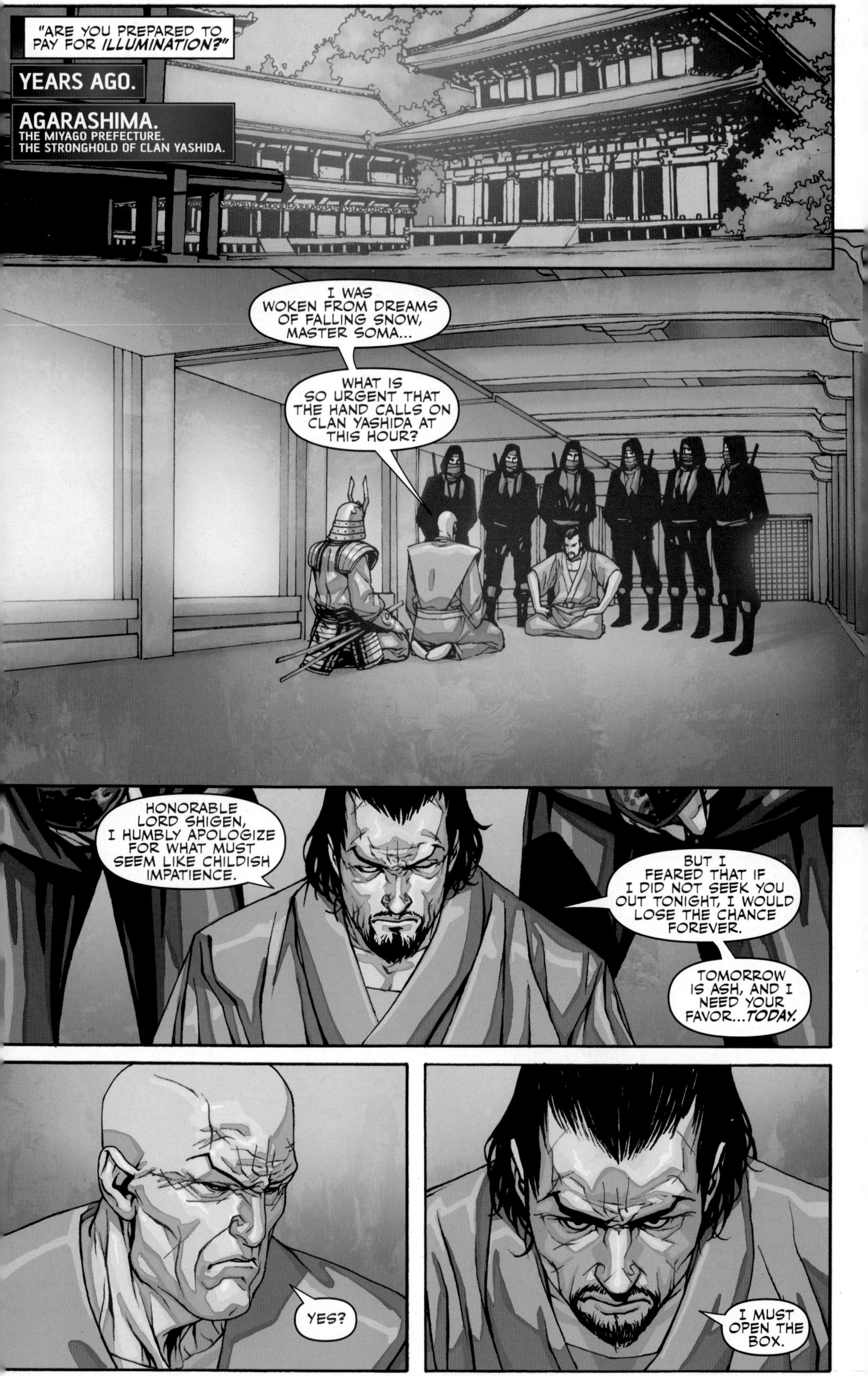
"ARE YOU PREPARED TO PAY FOR *ILLUMINATION?*"
YEARS AGO.
AGARASHIMA.
THE MIYAGO PREFECTURE.
THE STRONGHOLD OF CLAN YASHIDA.
I WAS WOKEN FROM DREAMS OF FALLING SNOW, MASTER SOMA...
WHAT IS SO URGENT THAT THE HAND CALLS ON CLAN YASHIDA AT THIS HOUR?
HONORABLE LORD SHIGEN, I HUMBLY APOLOGIZE FOR WHAT MUST SEEM LIKE CHILDISH IMPATIENCE.
BUT I FEARED THAT IF I DID NOT SEEK YOU OUT TONIGHT, I WOULD LOSE THE CHANCE FOREVER.
TOMORROW IS ASH, AND I NEED YOUR FAVOR...*TODAY.*
YES?
I MUST OPEN THE BOX.

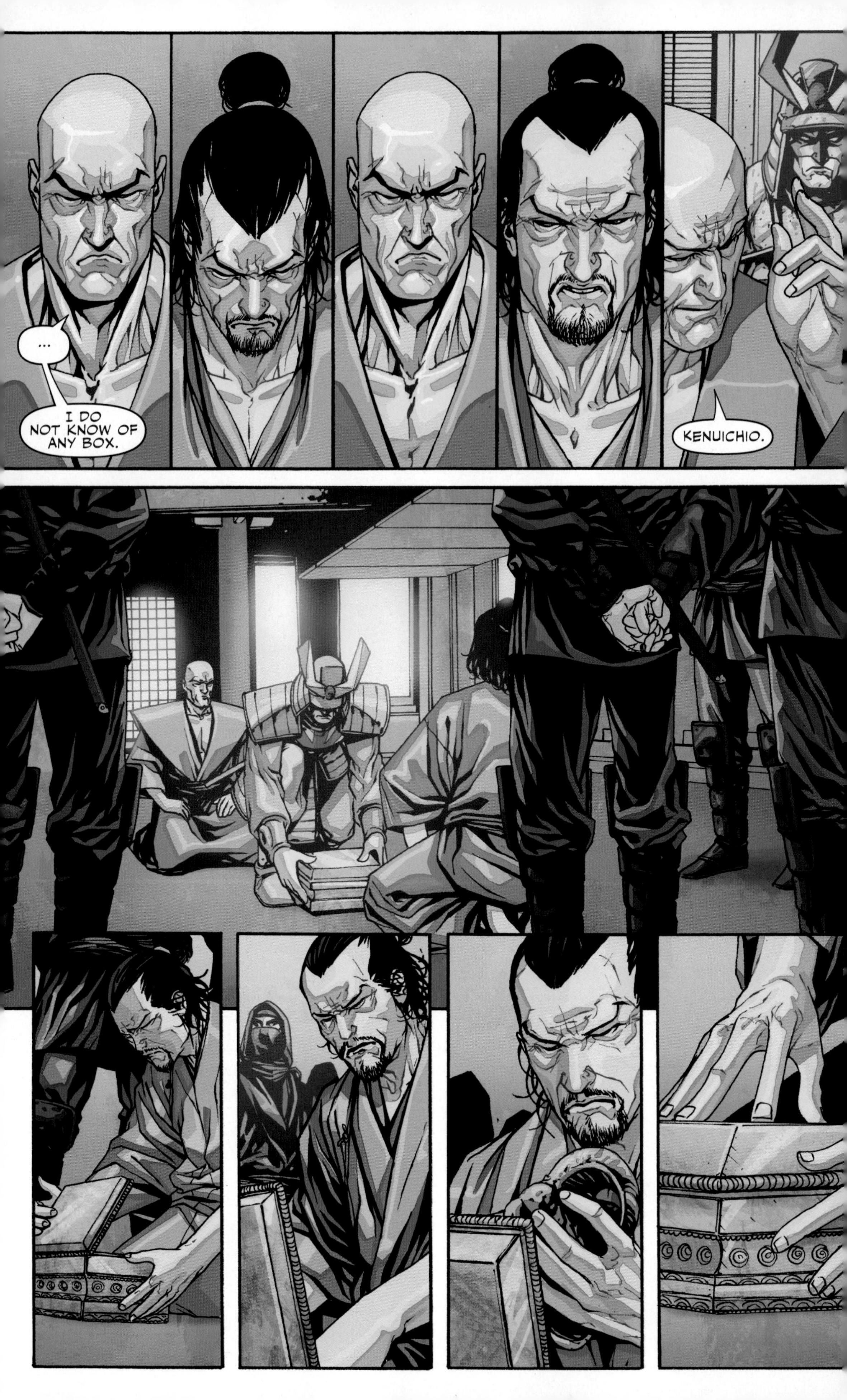
...
I DO NOT KNOW OF ANY BOX.
KENUICHIO.

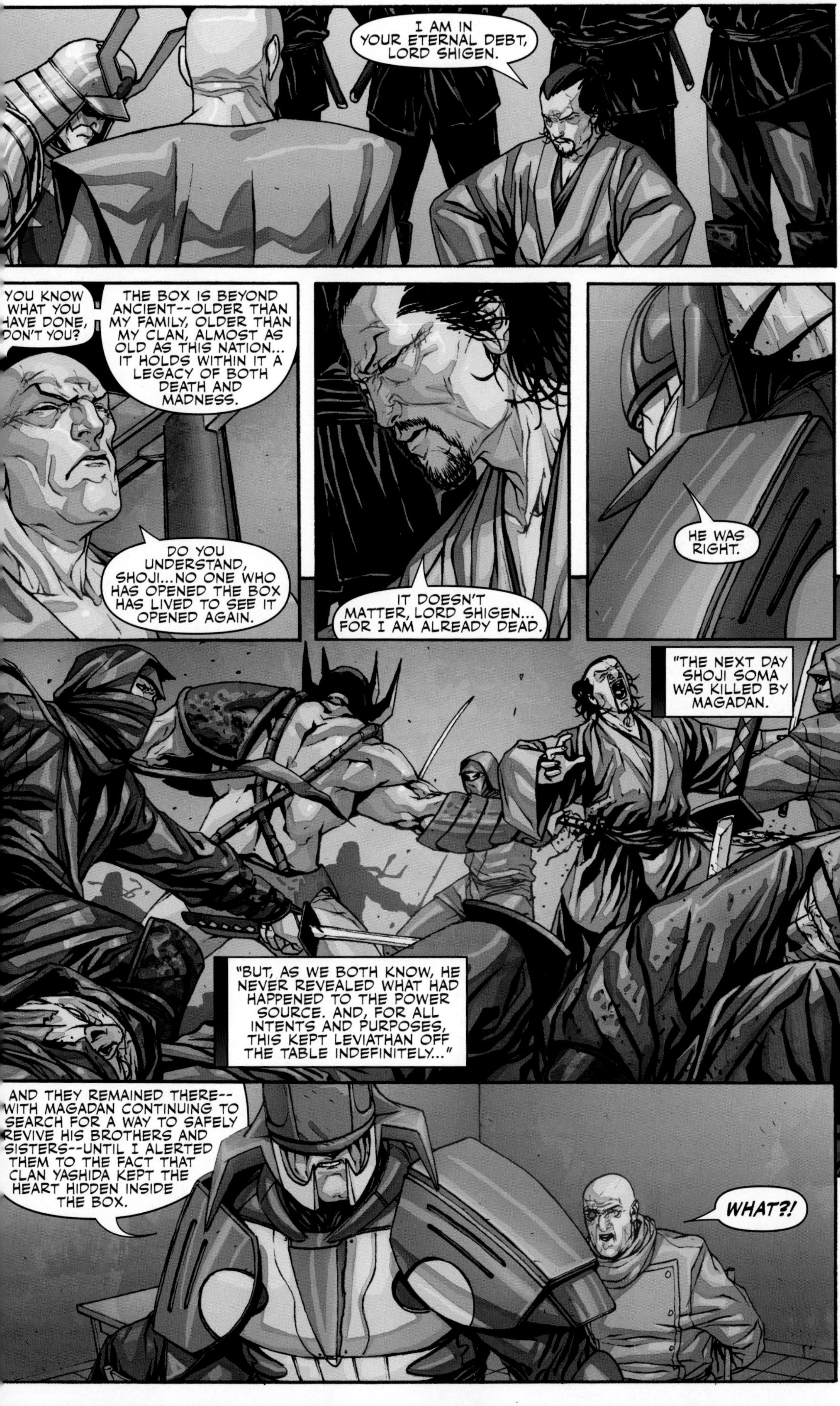
I AM IN YOUR ETERNAL DEBT, LORD SHIGEN.
YOU KNOW WHAT YOU HAVE DONE, DON'T YOU?
THE BOX IS BEYOND ANCIENT--OLDER THAN MY FAMILY, OLDER THAN MY CLAN, ALMOST AS OLD AS THIS NATION... IT HOLDS WITHIN IT A LEGACY OF BOTH DEATH AND MADNESS.
DO YOU UNDERSTAND, SHOJI...NO ONE WHO HAS OPENED THE BOX HAS LIVED TO SEE IT OPENED AGAIN.
IT DOESN'T MATTER, LORD SHIGEN... FOR I AM ALREADY DEAD.
HE WAS RIGHT.
"THE NEXT DAY SHOJI SOMA WAS KILLED BY MAGADAN.
"BUT, AS WE BOTH KNOW, HE NEVER REVEALED WHAT HAD HAPPENED TO THE POWER SOURCE. AND, FOR ALL INTENTS AND PURPOSES, THIS KEPT LEVIATHAN OFF THE TABLE INDEFINITELY..."
AND THEY REMAINED THERE--WITH MAGADAN CONTINUING TO SEARCH FOR A WAY TO SAFELY REVIVE HIS BROTHERS AND SISTERS--UNTIL I ALERTED THEM TO THE FACT THAT CLAN YASHIDA KEPT THE HEART HIDDEN INSIDE THE BOX.
WHAT?!

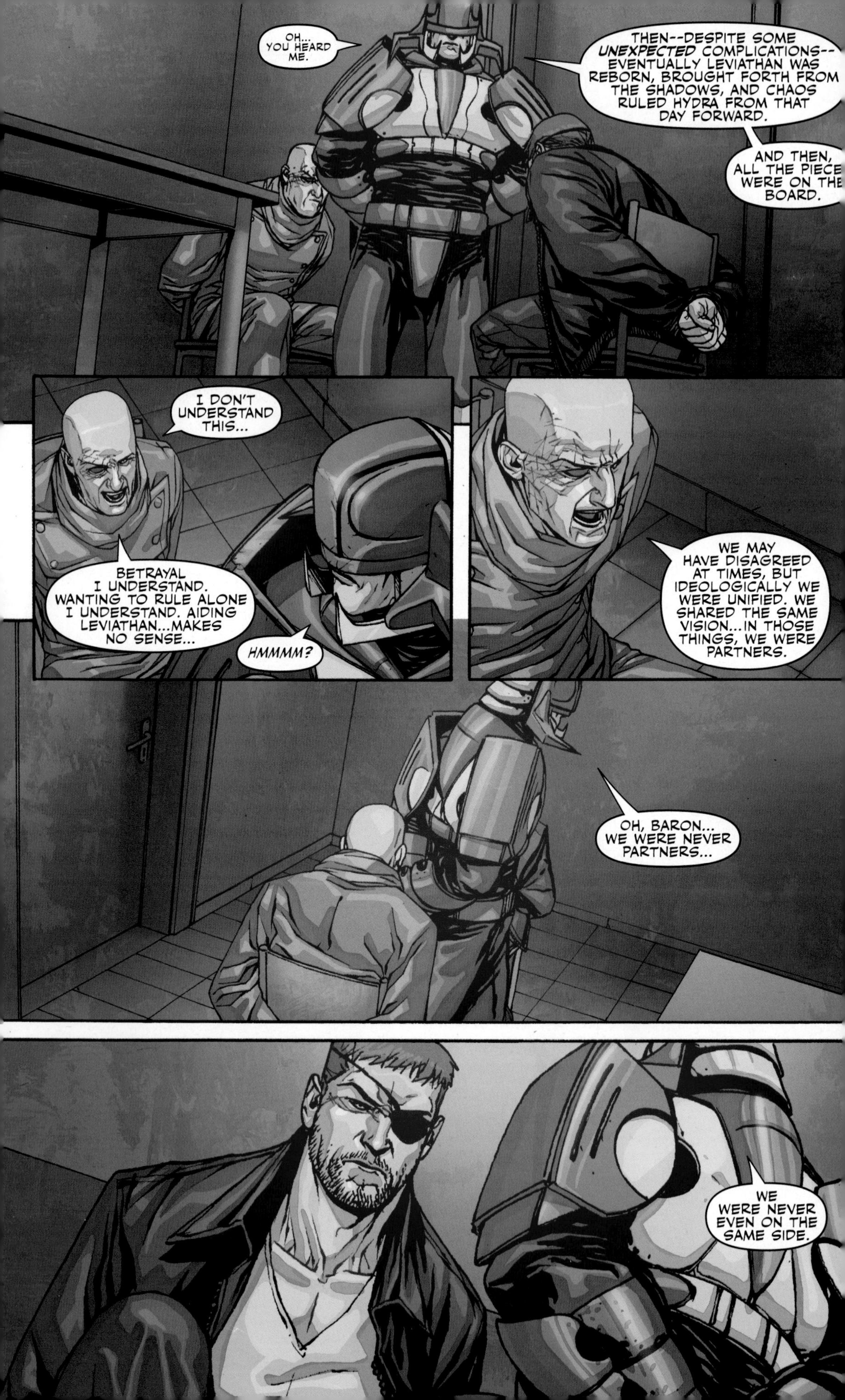
OH... YOU HEARD ME.
THEN--DESPITE SOME UNEXPECTED COMPLICATIONS--EVENTUALLY LEVIATHAN WAS REBORN, BROUGHT FORTH FROM THE SHADOWS, AND CHAOS RULED HYDRA FROM THAT DAY FORWARD.
AND THEN, ALL THE PIECE WERE ON THE BOARD.
I DON'T UNDERSTAND THIS...
BETRAYAL I UNDERSTAND. WANTING TO RULE ALONE I UNDERSTAND. AIDING LEVIATHAN...MAKES NO SENSE...
HMMMM?
WE MAY HAVE DISAGREED AT TIMES, BUT IDEOLOGICALLY WE WERE UNIFIED. WE SHARED THE SAME VISION...IN THOSE THINGS, WE WERE PARTNERS.
OH, BARON... WE WERE NEVER PARTNERS...
WE WERE NEVER EVEN ON THE SAME SIDE.

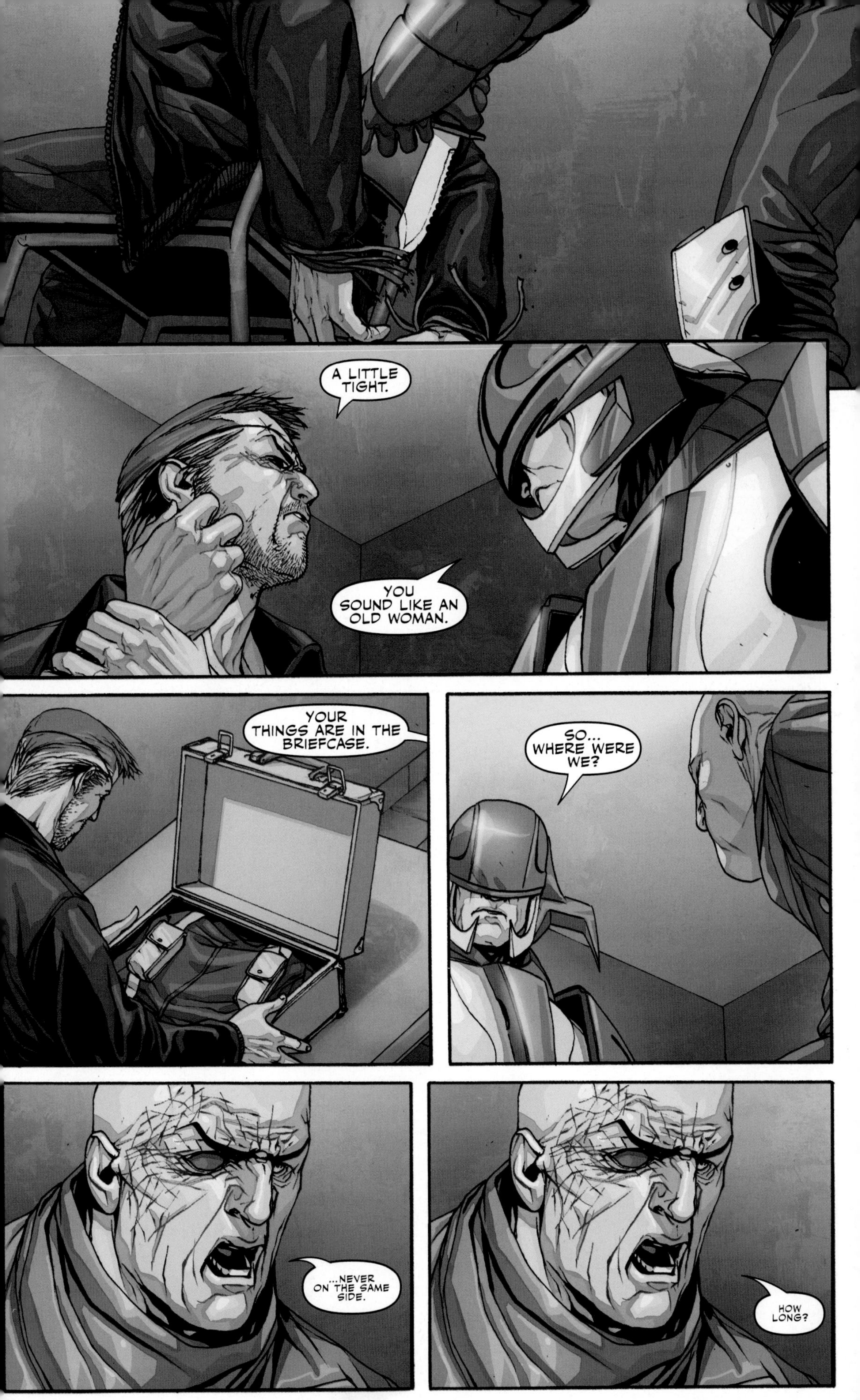
A LITTLE TIGHT.
YOU SOUND LIKE AN OLD WOMAN.
YOUR THINGS ARE IN THE BRIEFCASE.
SO... WHERE WERE WE?
...NEVER ON THE SAME SIDE.
HOW LONG?

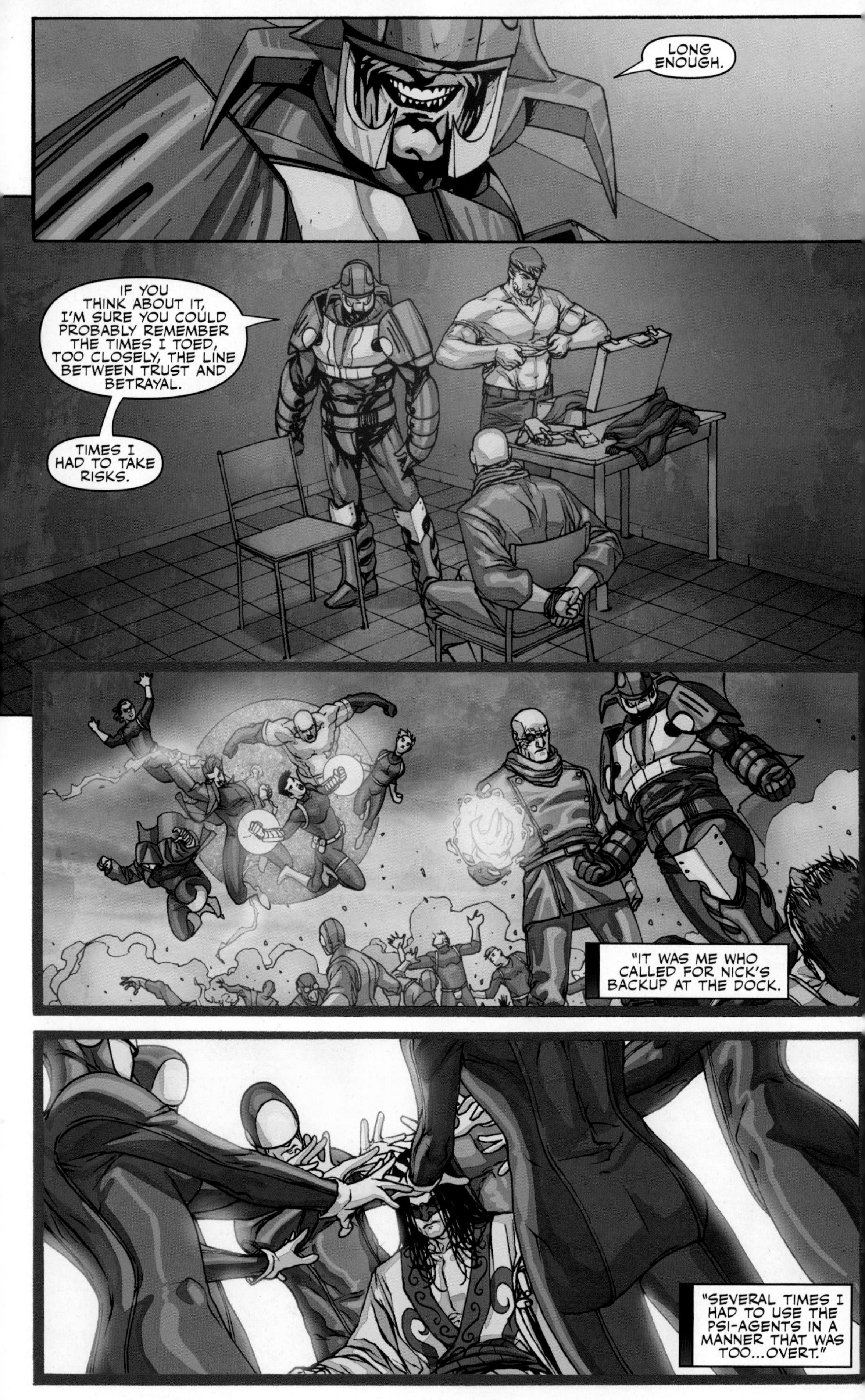
LONG ENOUGH.
IF YOU THINK ABOUT IT, I'M SURE YOU COULD PROBABLY REMEMBER THE TIMES I TOED, TOO CLOSELY, THE LINE BETWEEN TRUST AND BETRAYAL.
TIMES I HAD TO TAKE RISKS.
"IT WAS ME WHO CALLED FOR NICK'S BACKUP AT THE DOCK.
"SEVERAL TIMES I HAD TO USE THE PSI-AGENTS IN A MANNER THAT WAS TOO...OVERT."

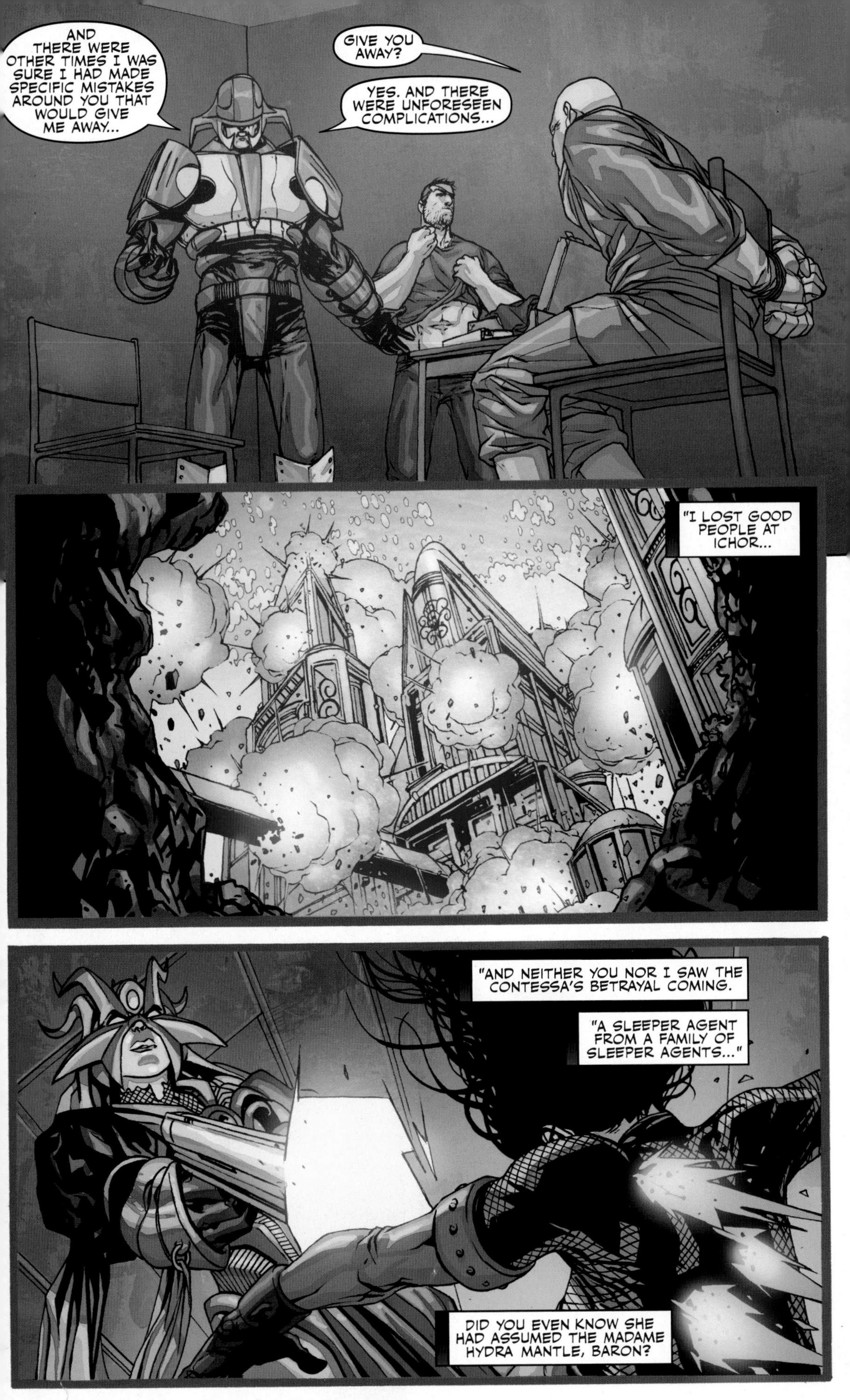
AND THERE WERE OTHER TIMES I WAS SURE I HAD MADE SPECIFIC MISTAKES AROUND YOU THAT WOULD GIVE ME AWAY...
GIVE YOU AWAY?
YES. AND THERE WERE UNFORESEEN COMPLICATIONS...
"I LOST GOOD PEOPLE AT ICHOR...
"AND NEITHER YOU NOR I SAW THE CONTESSA'S BETRAYAL COMING.
"A SLEEPER AGENT FROM A FAMILY OF SLEEPER AGENTS..."
DID YOU EVEN KNOW SHE HAD ASSUMED THE MADAME HYDRA MANTLE, BARON?

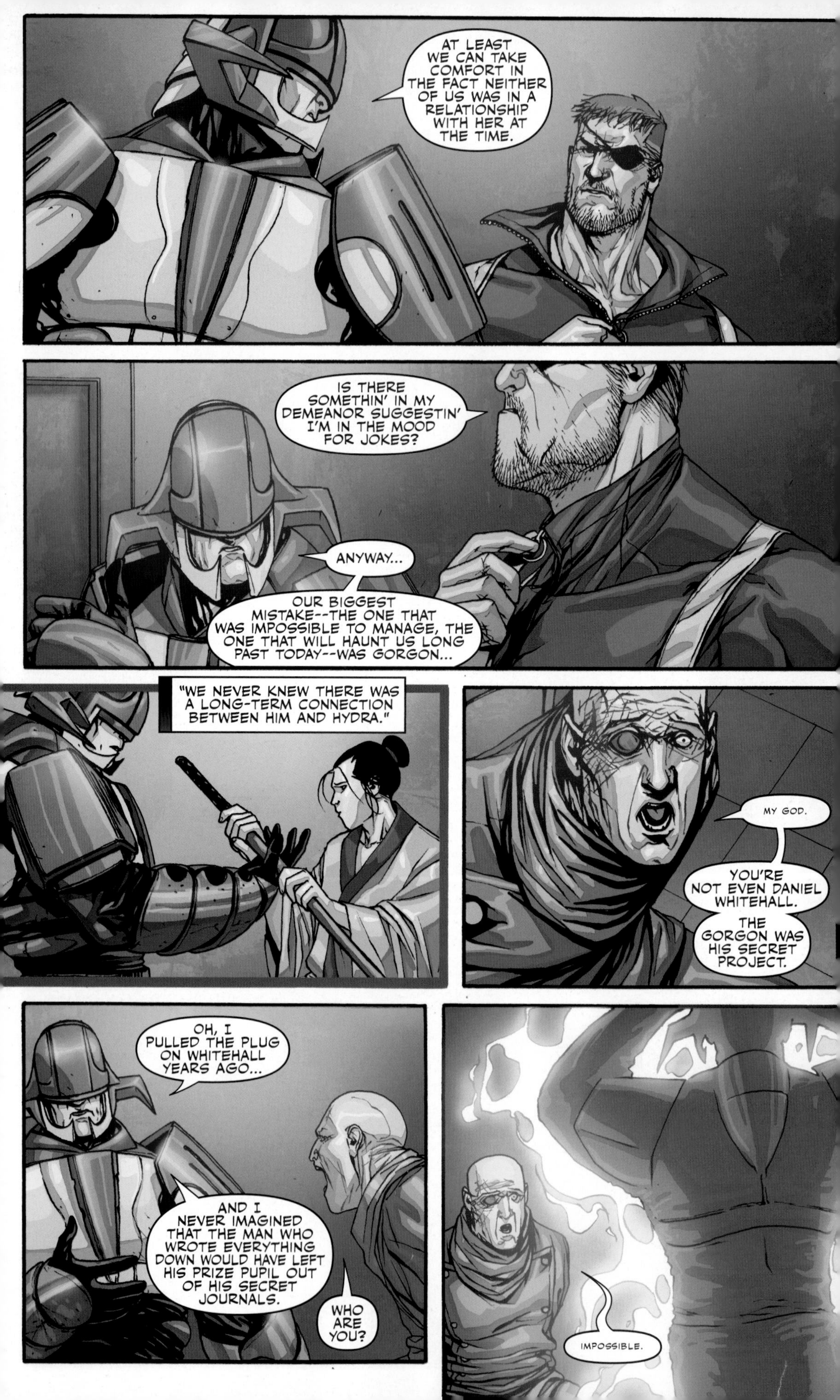
AT LEAST WE CAN TAKE COMFORT IN THE FACT NEITHER OF US WAS IN A RELATIONSHIP WITH HER AT THE TIME.
IS THERE SOMETHIN' IN MY DEMEANOR SUGGESTIN' I'M IN THE MOOD FOR JOKES?
ANYWAY...
OUR BIGGEST MISTAKE--THE ONE THAT WAS IMPOSSIBLE TO MANAGE, THE ONE THAT WILL HAUNT US LONG PAST TODAY--WAS GORGON...
"WE NEVER KNEW THERE WAS A LONG-TERM CONNECTION BETWEEN HIM AND HYDRA."
MY GOD.
YOU'RE NOT EVEN DANIEL WHITEHALL.
THE GORGON WAS HIS SECRET PROJECT.
OH, I PULLED THE PLUG ON WHITEHALL YEARS AGO...
AND I NEVER IMAGINED THAT THE MAN WHO WROTE EVERYTHING DOWN WOULD HAVE LEFT HIS PRIZE PUPIL OUT OF HIS SECRET JOURNALS.
WHO ARE YOU?
IMPOSSIBLE.

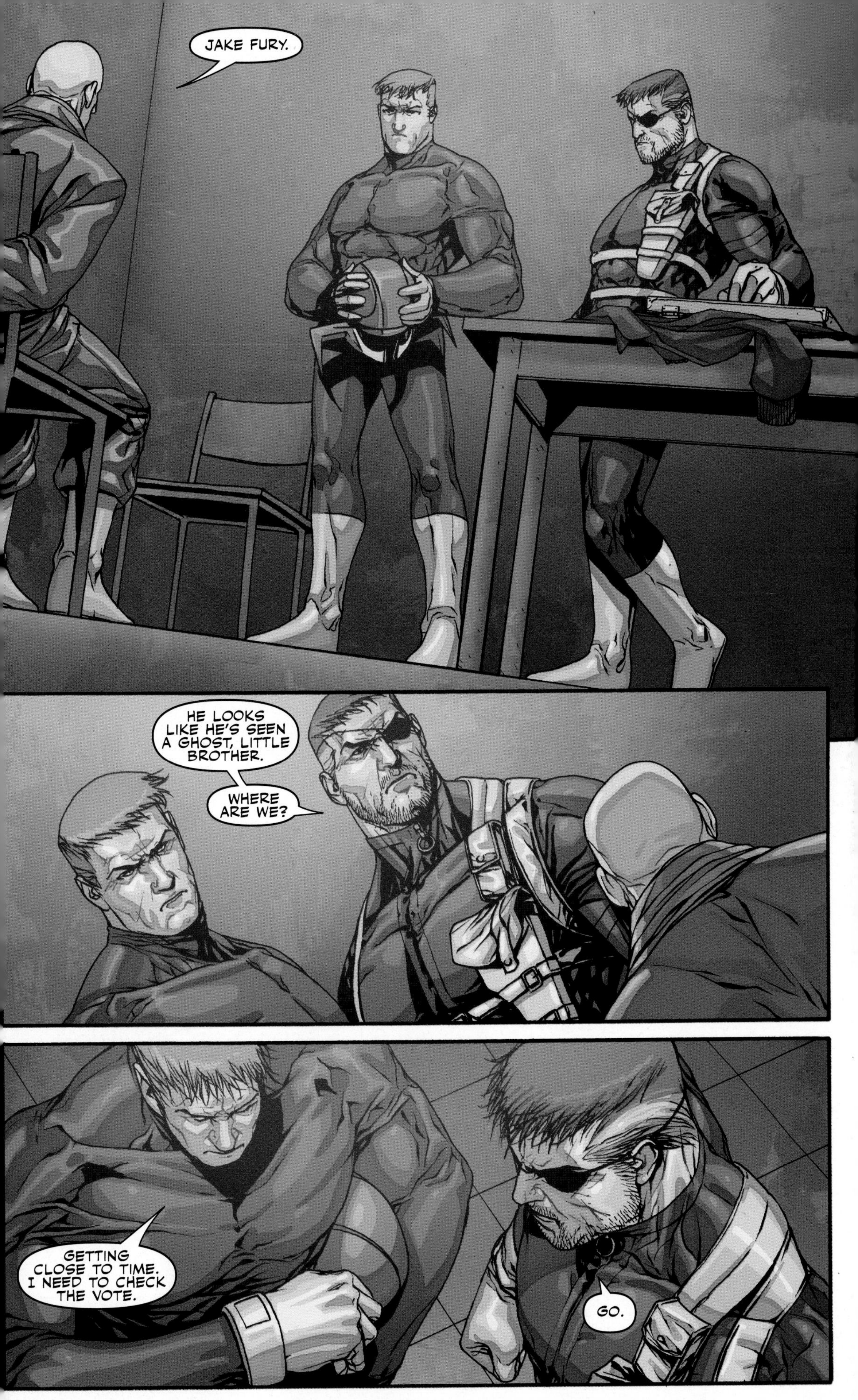
JAKE FURY.
HE LOOKS LIKE HE'S SEEN A GHOST, LITTLE BROTHER.
WHERE ARE WE?
GETTING CLOSE TO TIME. I NEED TO CHECK THE VOTE.
GO.

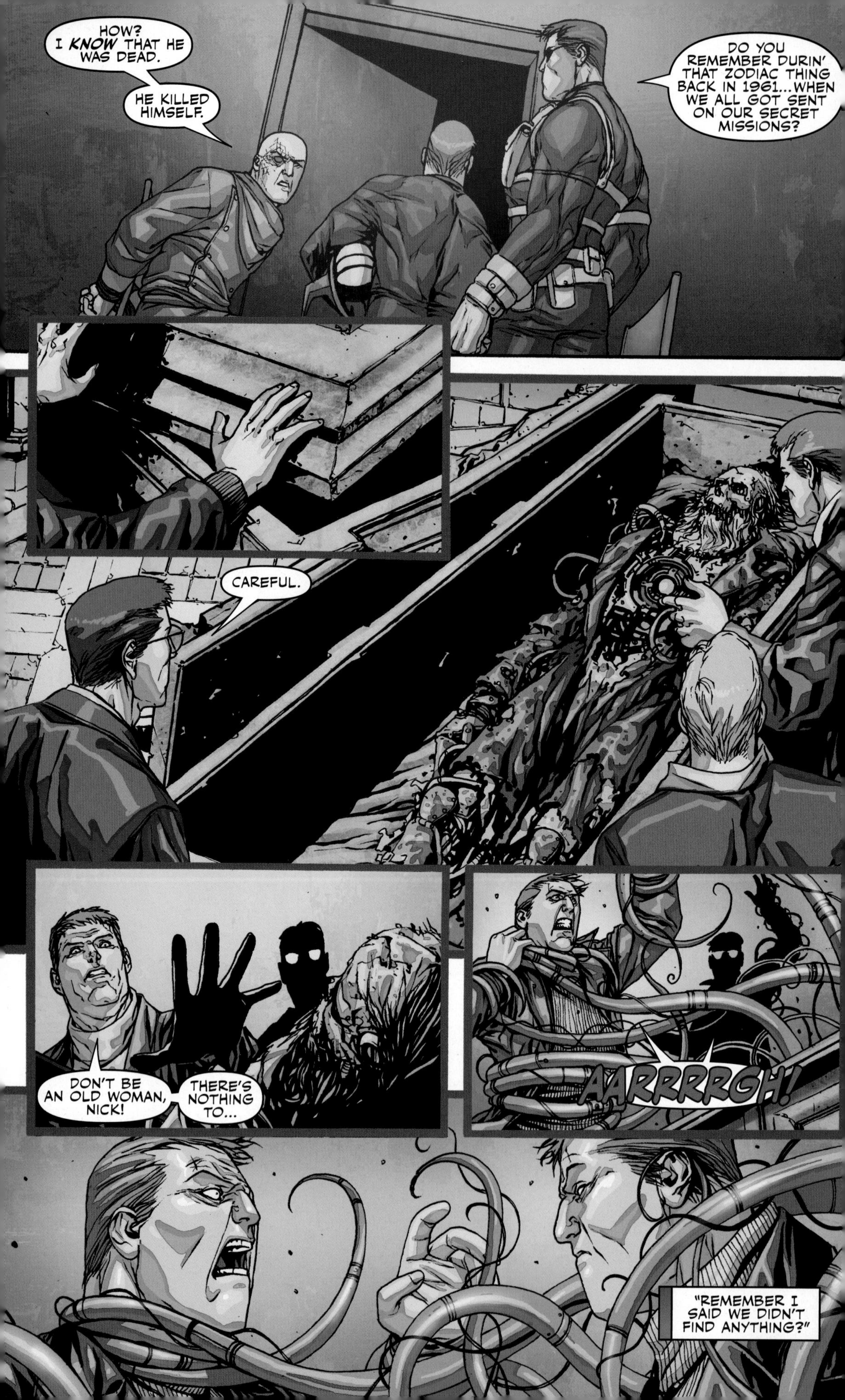
HOW? I KNOW THAT HE WAS DEAD.
HE KILLED HIMSELF.
DO YOU REMEMBER DURIN' THAT ZODIAC THING BACK IN 1961...WHEN WE ALL GOT SENT ON OUR SECRET MISSIONS?
CAREFUL.
DON'T BE AN OLD WOMAN, NICK!
THERE'S NOTHING TO...
AARRRRGH!
"REMEMBER I SAID WE DIDN'T FIND ANYTHING?"

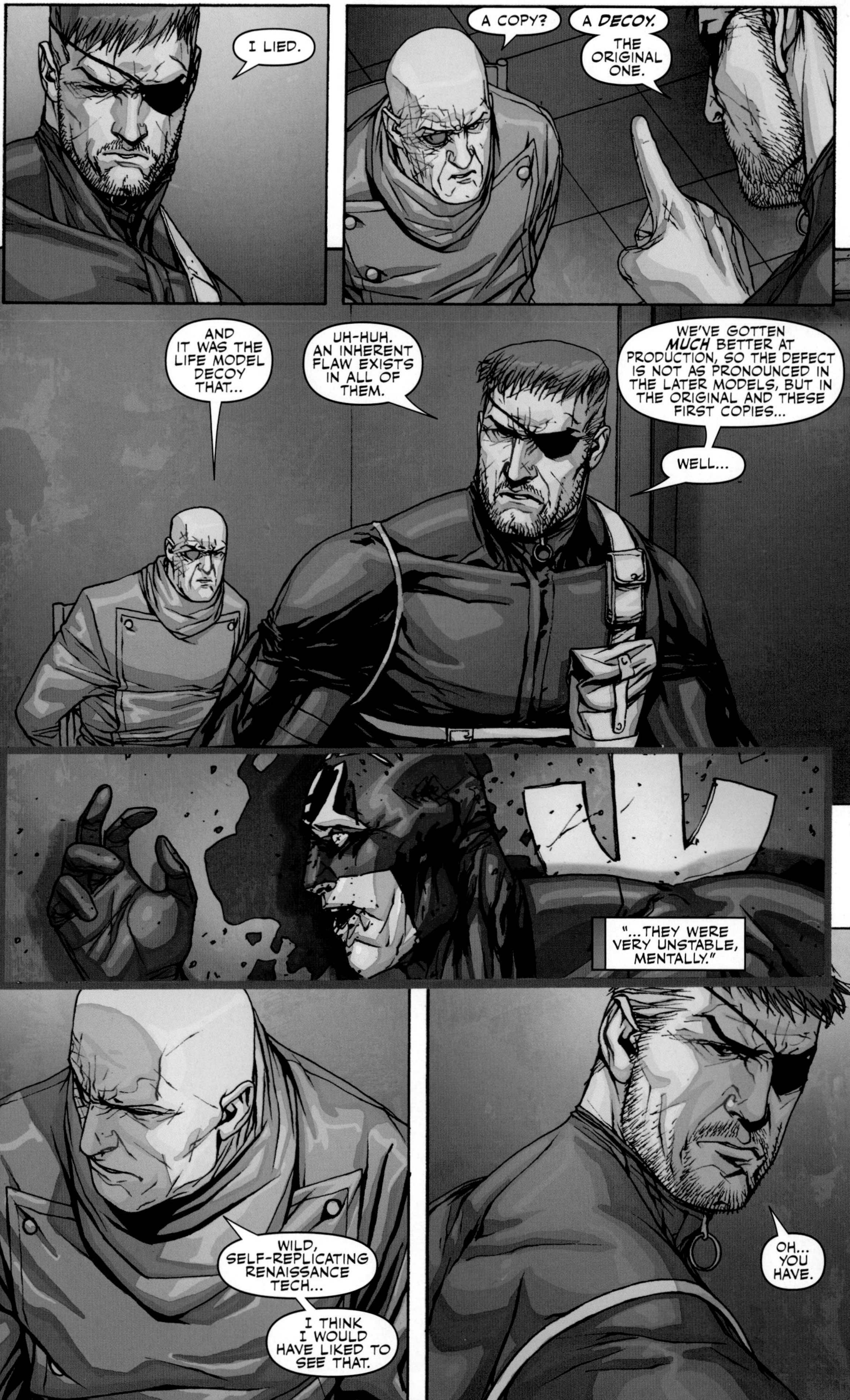
I LIED.
A COPY?
A DECOY.
THE ORIGINAL ONE.
AND IT WAS THE LIFE MODEL DECOY THAT...
UH-HUH. AN INHERENT FLAW EXISTS IN ALL OF THEM.
WE'VE GOTTEN MUCH BETTER AT PRODUCTION, SO THE DEFECT IS NOT AS PRONOUNCED IN THE LATER MODELS, BUT IN THE ORIGINAL AND THESE FIRST COPIES...
WELL...
"...THEY WERE VERY UNSTABLE, MENTALLY."
WILD, SELF-REPLICATING RENAISSANCE TECH...
I THINK I WOULD HAVE LIKED TO SEE THAT.
OH... YOU HAVE.

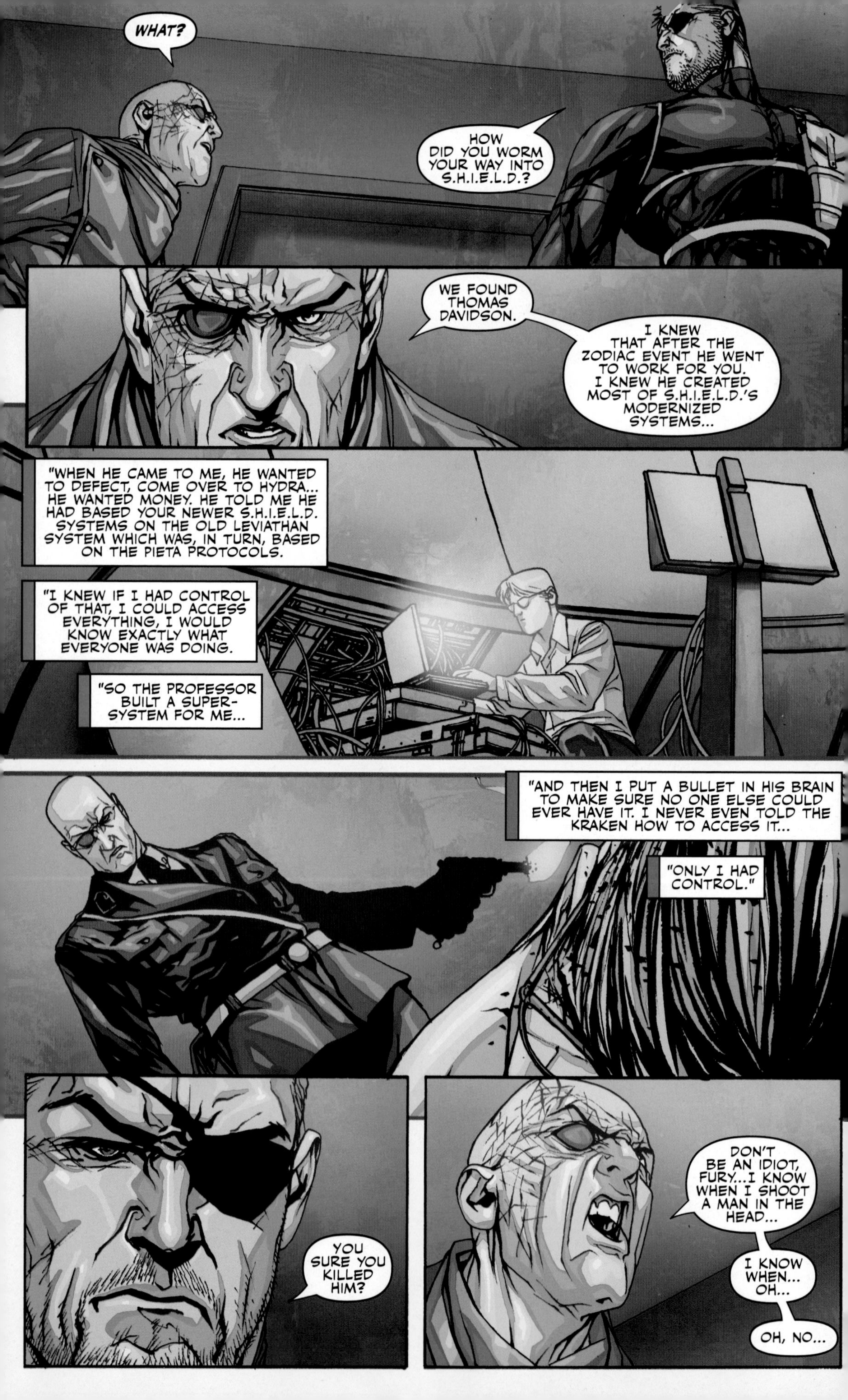
WHAT?
HOW DID YOU WORM YOUR WAY INTO S.H.I.E.L.D.?
WE FOUND THOMAS DAVIDSON.
I KNEW THAT AFTER THE ZODIAC EVENT HE WENT TO WORK FOR YOU. I KNEW HE CREATED MOST OF S.H.I.E.L.D.'S MODERNIZED SYSTEMS...
"WHEN HE CAME TO ME, HE WANTED TO DEFECT, COME OVER TO HYDRA... HE WANTED MONEY. HE TOLD ME HE HAD BASED YOUR NEWER S.H.I.E.L.D. SYSTEMS ON THE OLD LEVIATHAN SYSTEM WHICH WAS, IN TURN, BASED ON THE PIETA PROTOCOLS.
"I KNEW IF I HAD CONTROL OF THAT, I COULD ACCESS EVERYTHING, I WOULD KNOW EXACTLY WHAT EVERYONE WAS DOING.
"SO THE PROFESSOR BUILT A SUPER-SYSTEM FOR ME...
"AND THEN I PUT A BULLET IN HIS BRAIN TO MAKE SURE NO ONE ELSE COULD EVER HAVE IT. I NEVER EVEN TOLD THE KRAKEN HOW TO ACCESS IT...
"ONLY I HAD CONTROL."
YOU SURE YOU KILLED HIM?
DON'T BE AN IDIOT, FURY...I KNOW WHEN I SHOOT A MAN IN THE HEAD...
I KNOW WHEN... OH...
OH, NO...

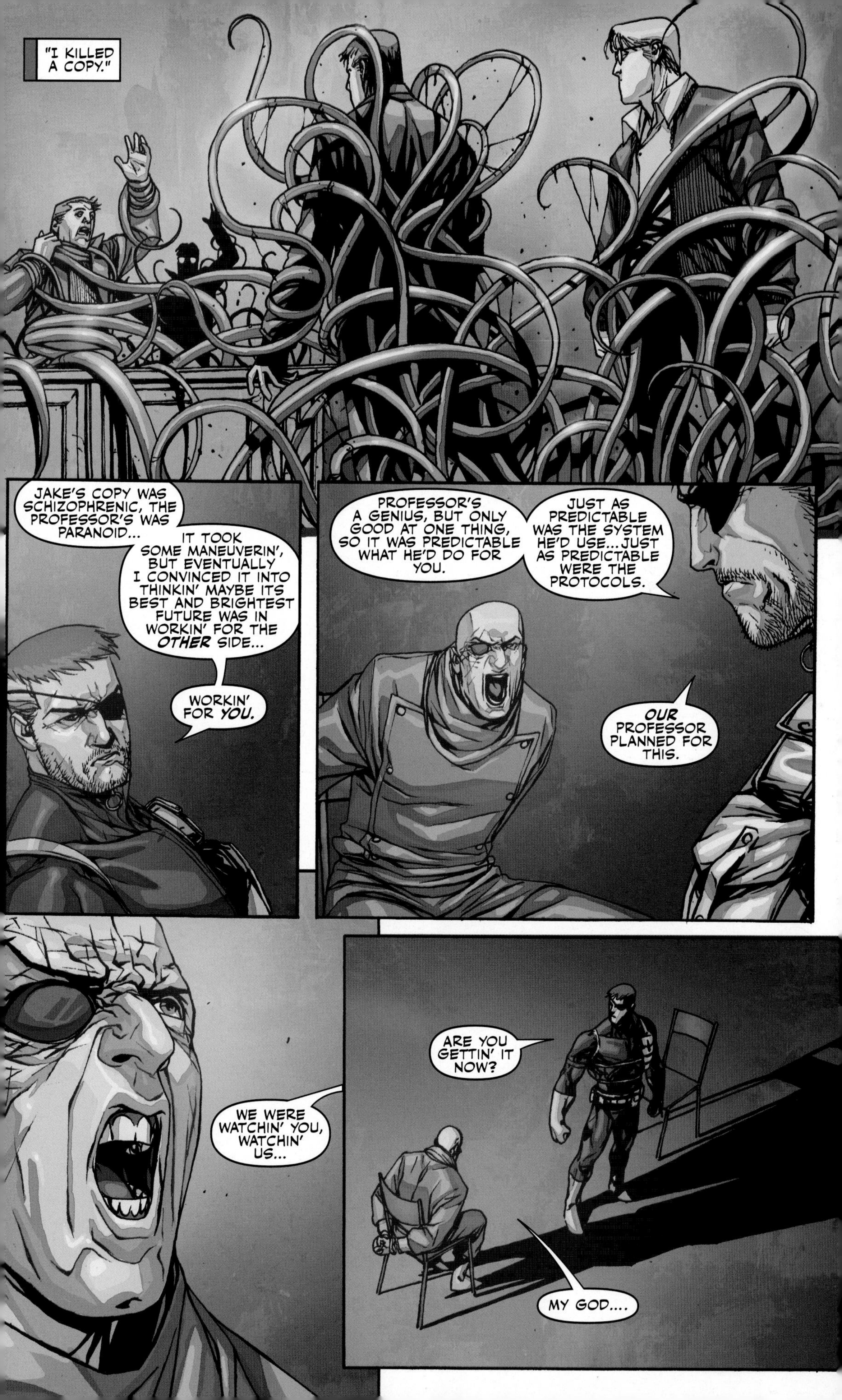
"I KILLED A COPY."
JAKE'S COPY WAS SCHIZOPHRENIC, THE PROFESSOR'S WAS PARANOID...
IT TOOK SOME MANEUVERIN', BUT EVENTUALLY I CONVINCED IT INTO THINKIN' MAYBE ITS BEST AND BRIGHTEST FUTURE WAS IN WORKIN' FOR THE *OTHER* SIDE...
WORKIN' FOR *YOU.*
PROFESSOR'S A GENIUS, BUT ONLY GOOD AT ONE THING, SO IT WAS PREDICTABLE WHAT HE'D DO FOR YOU.
JUST AS PREDICTABLE WAS THE SYSTEM HE'D USE...JUST AS PREDICTABLE WERE THE PROTOCOLS.
OUR PROFESSOR PLANNED FOR THIS.
ARE YOU GETTIN' IT NOW?
WE WERE WATCHIN' YOU, WATCHIN' US...
MY GOD....

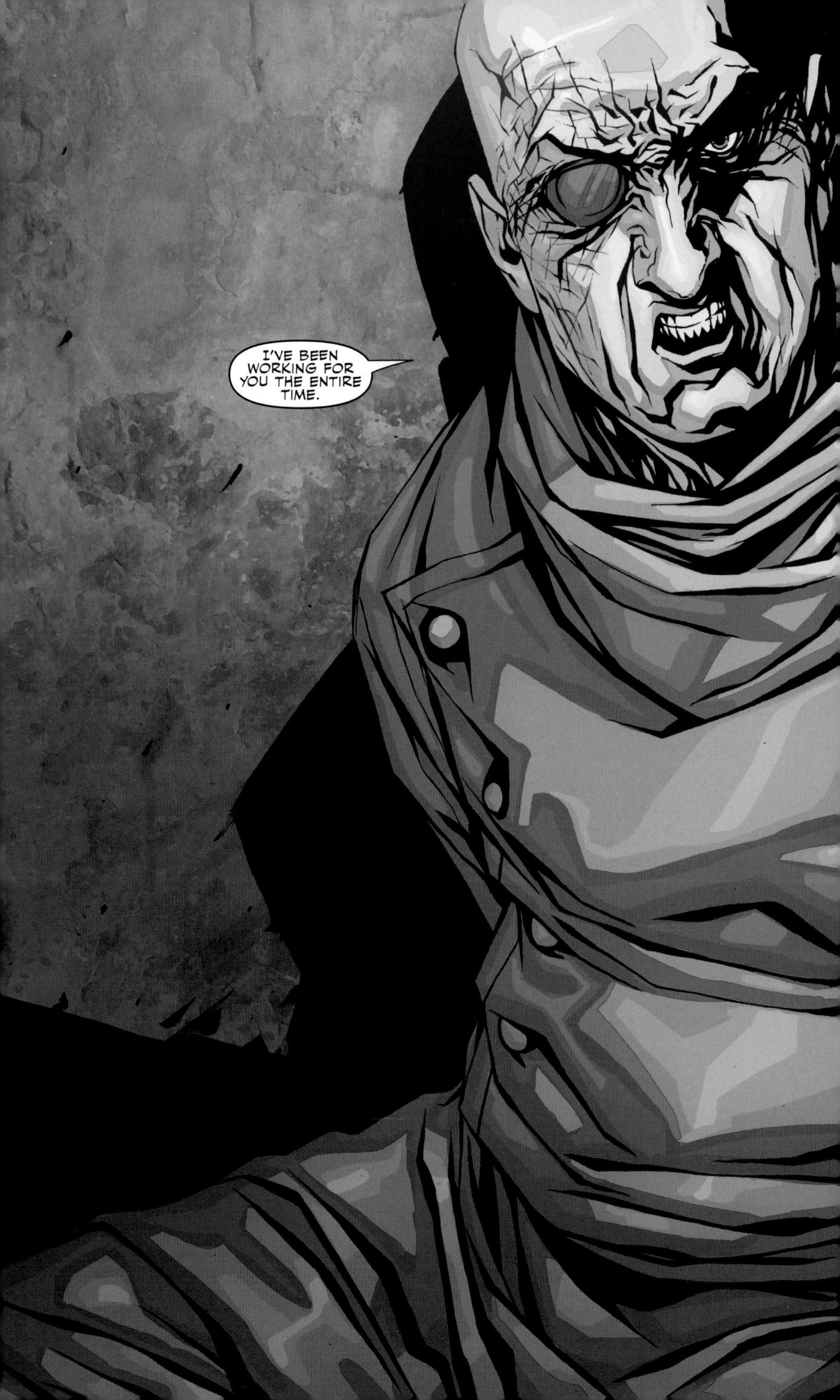
I'VE BEEN WORKING FOR YOU THE ENTIRE TIME.

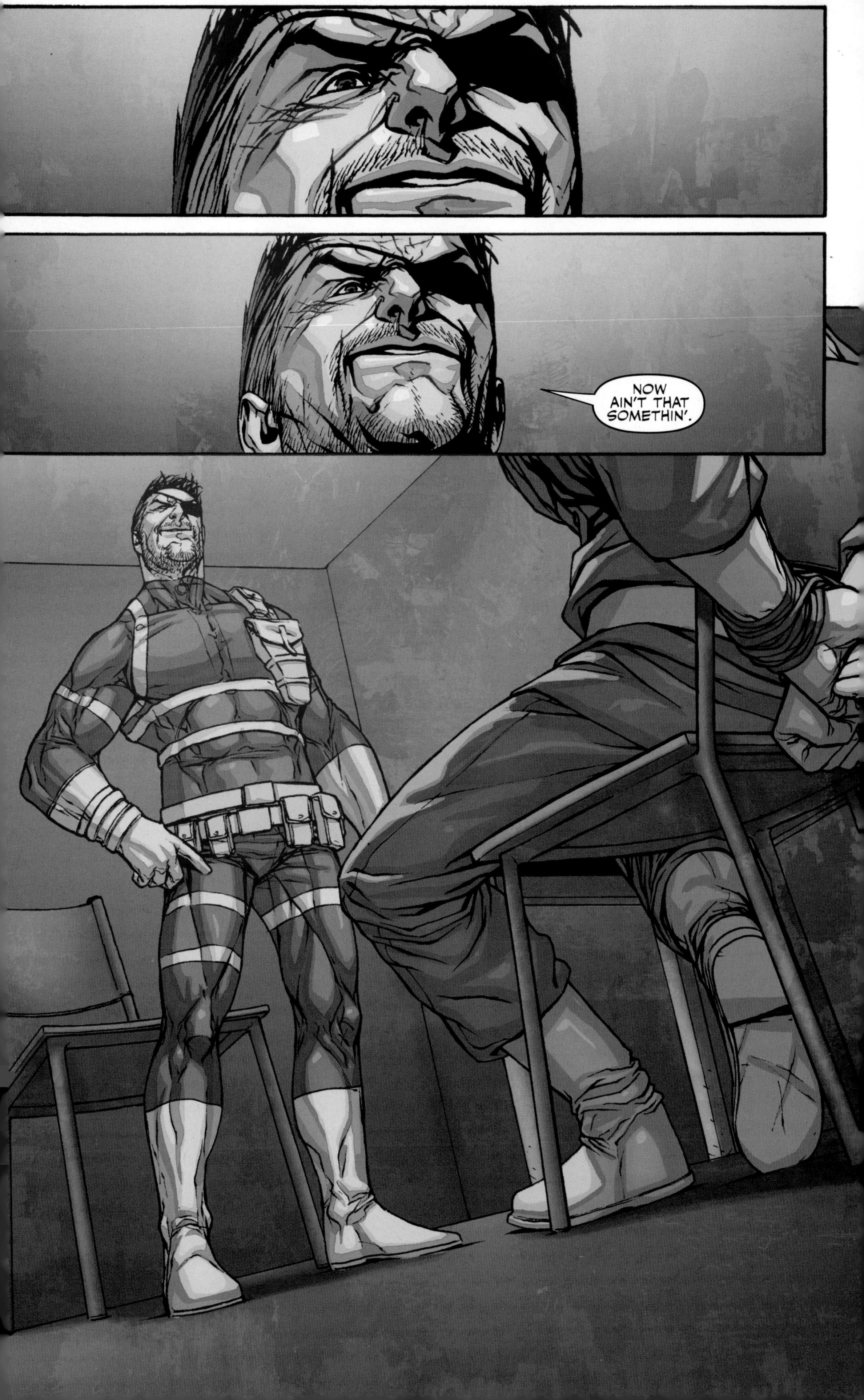
NOW AIN'T THAT SOMETHIN'.

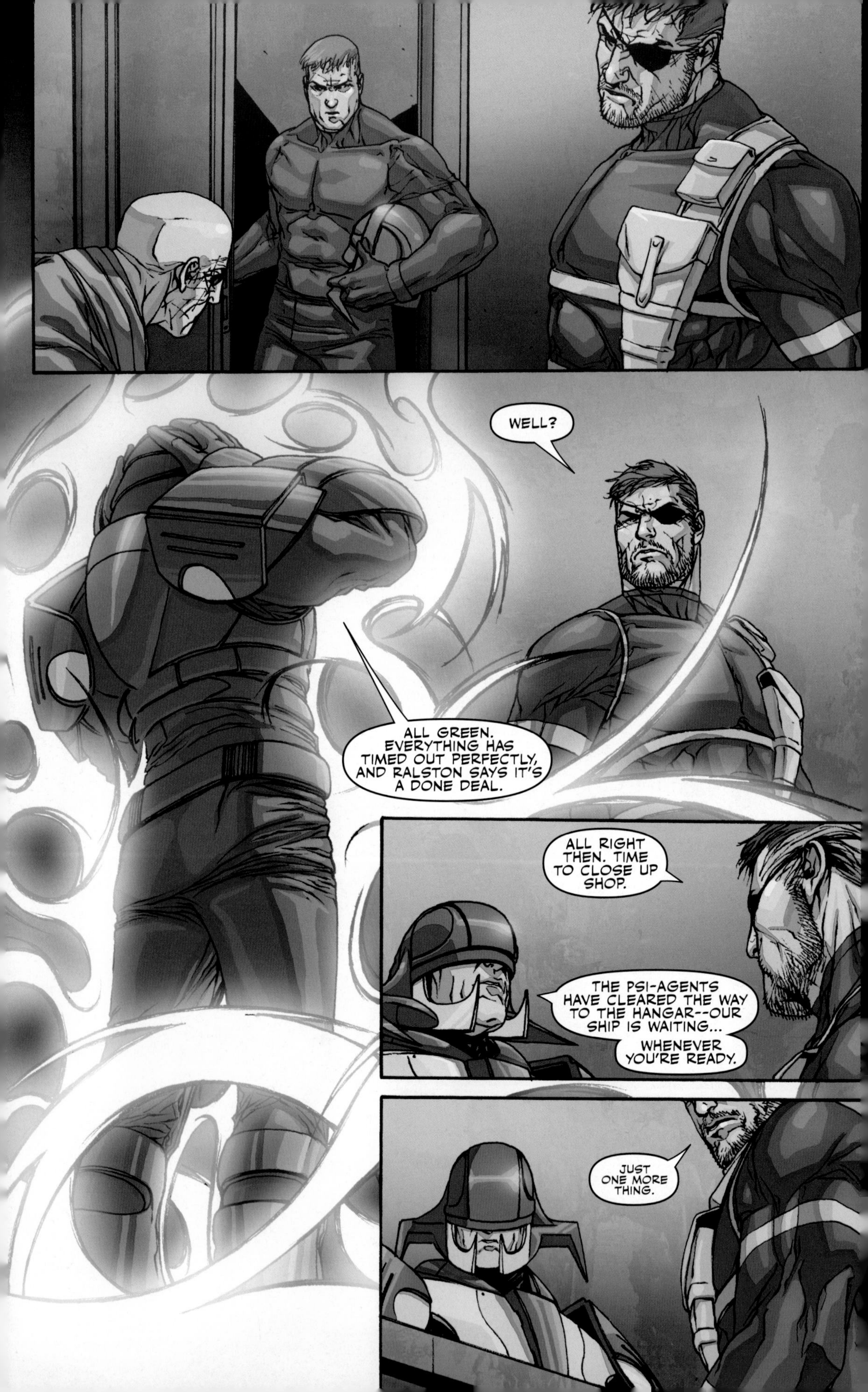
WELL?
ALL GREEN. EVERYTHING HAS TIMED OUT PERFECTLY, AND RALSTON SAYS IT'S A DONE DEAL.
ALL RIGHT THEN. TIME TO CLOSE UP SHOP.
THE PSI-AGENTS HAVE CLEARED THE WAY TO THE HANGAR--OUR SHIP IS WAITING...
WHENEVER YOU'RE READY.
JUST ONE MORE THING.

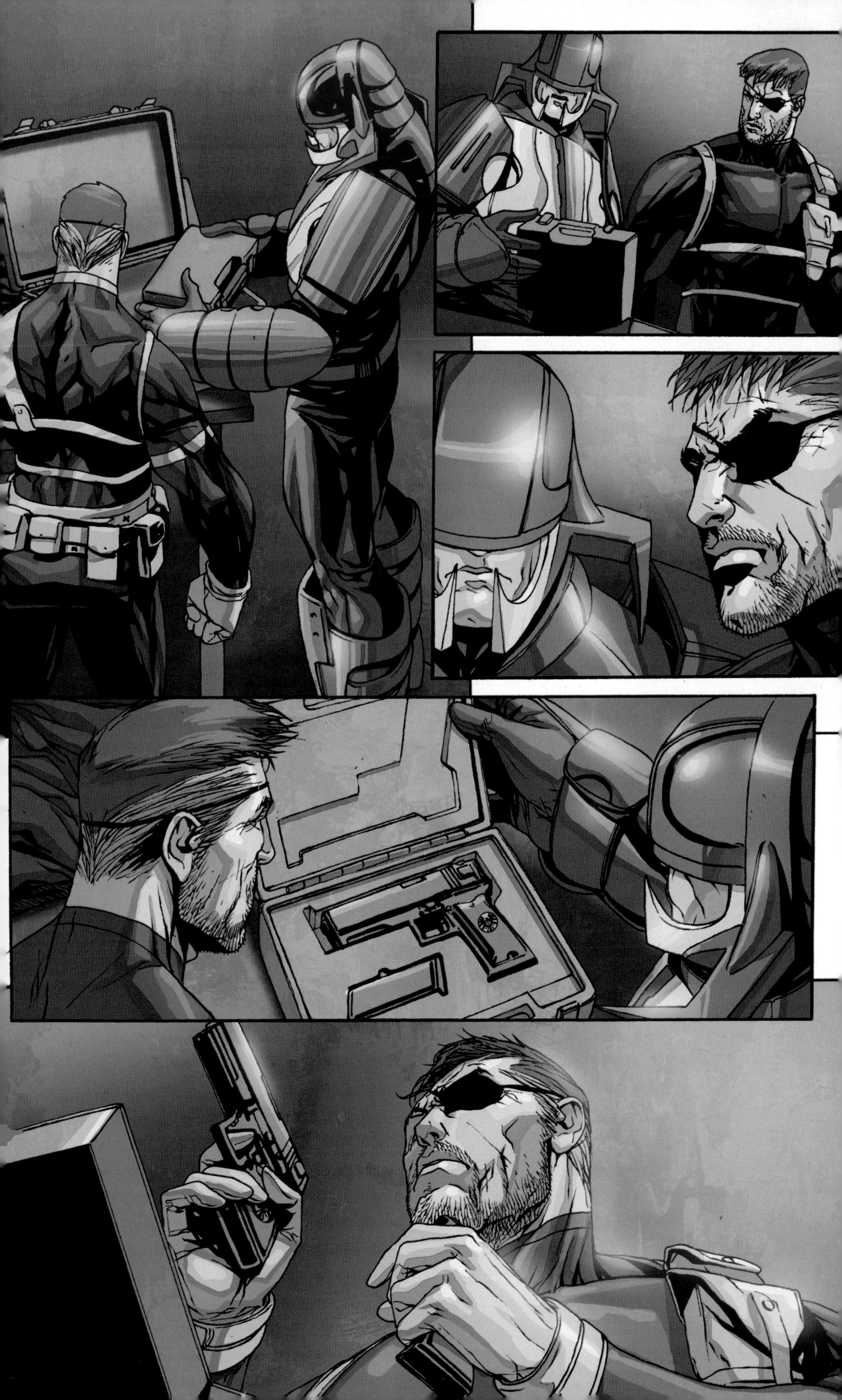

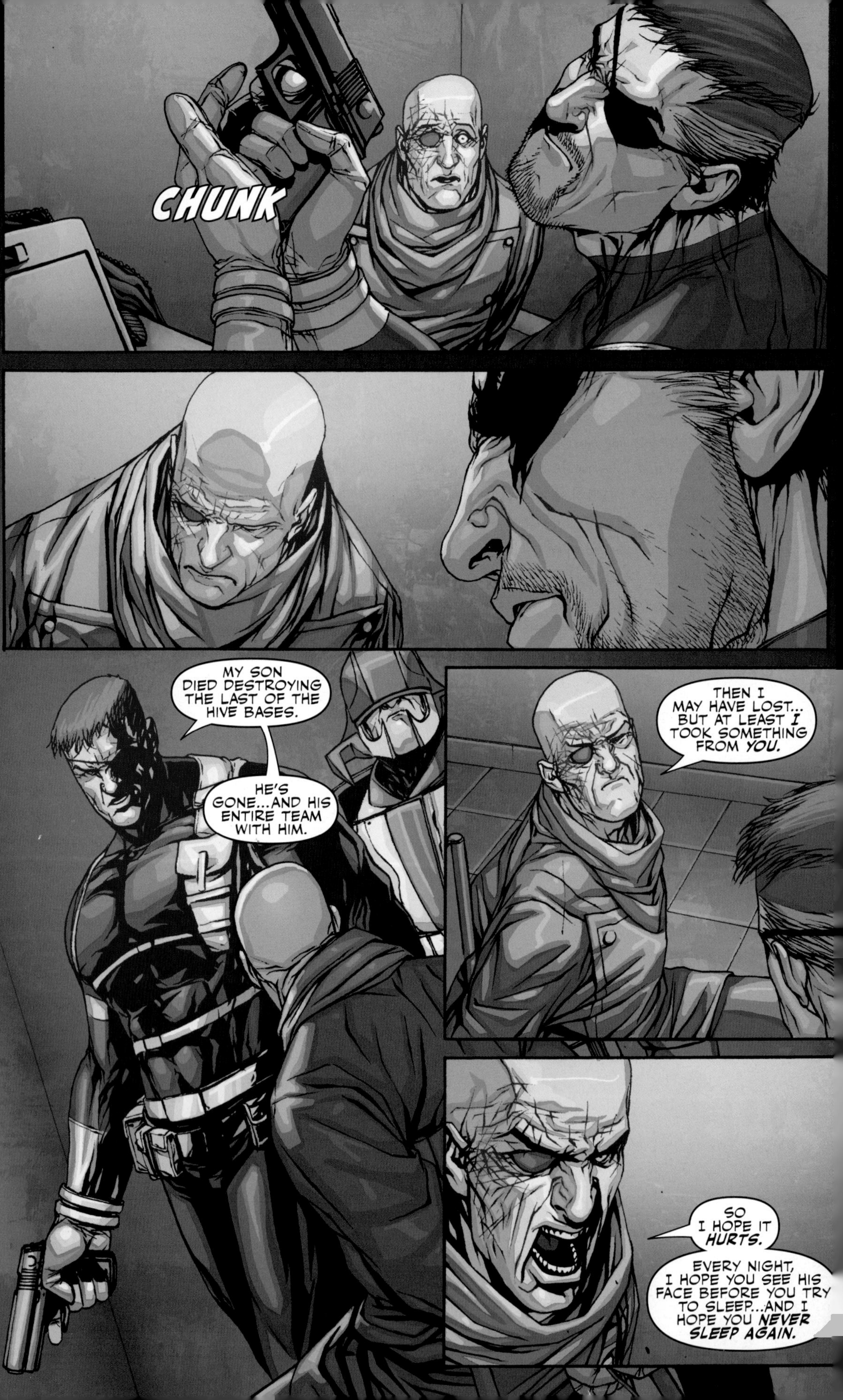
CHUNK
MY SON DIED DESTROYING THE LAST OF THE HIVE BASES.
HE'S GONE...AND HIS ENTIRE TEAM WITH HIM.
THEN I MAY HAVE LOST... BUT AT LEAST I TOOK SOMETHING FROM YOU.
SO I HOPE IT HURTS.
EVERY NIGHT, I HOPE YOU SEE HIS FACE BEFORE YOU TRY TO SLEEP...AND I HOPE YOU NEVER SLEEP AGAIN.

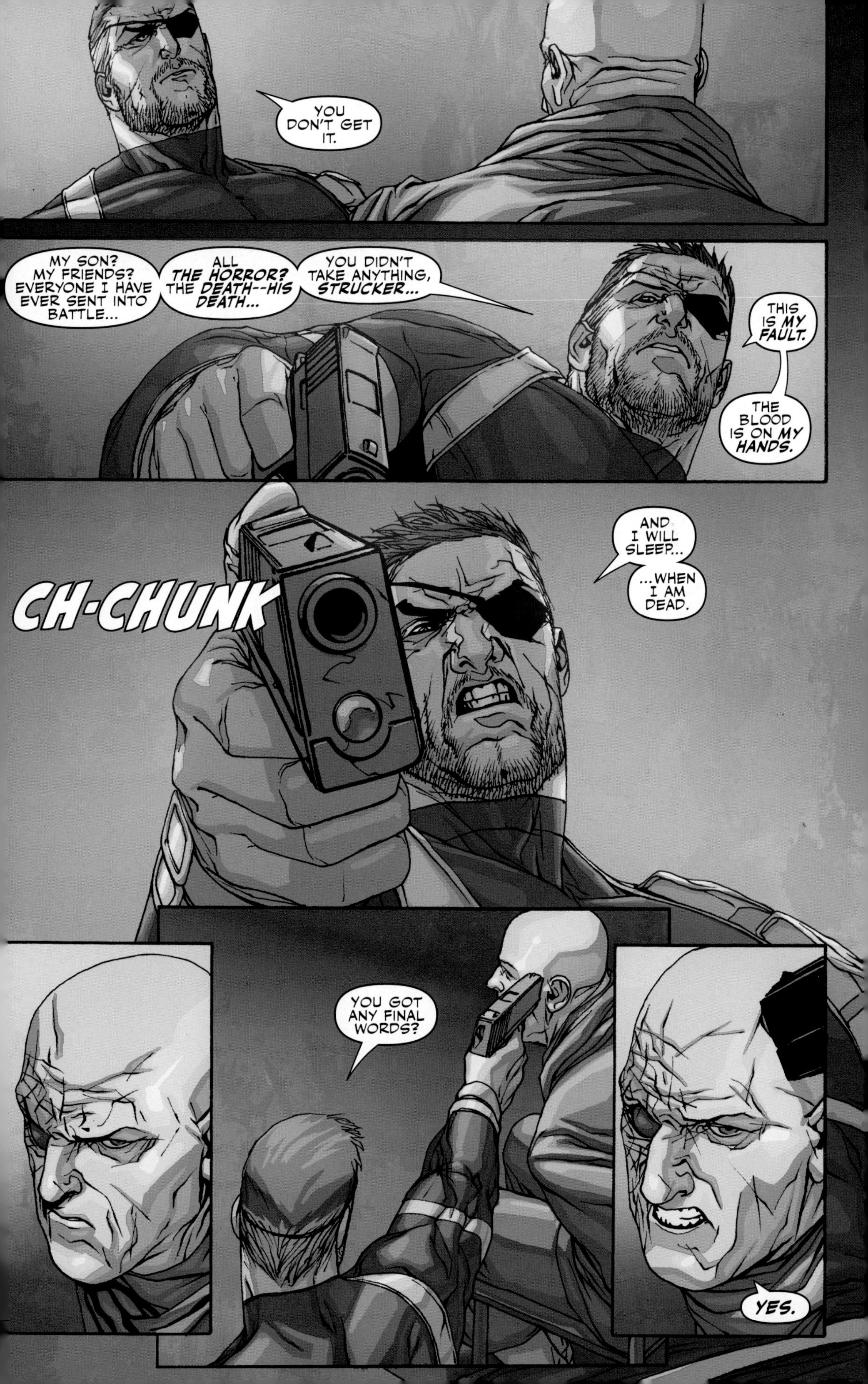
YOU DON'T GET IT.
MY SON? MY FRIENDS? EVERYONE I HAVE EVER SENT INTO BATTLE...
ALL THE HORROR? THE DEATH--HIS DEATH...
YOU DIDN'T TAKE ANYTHING, STRUCKER...
THIS IS MY FAULT.
THE BLOOD IS ON MY HANDS.
CH-CHUNK
AND I WILL SLEEP...
...WHEN I AM DEAD.
YOU GOT ANY FINAL WORDS?
YES.

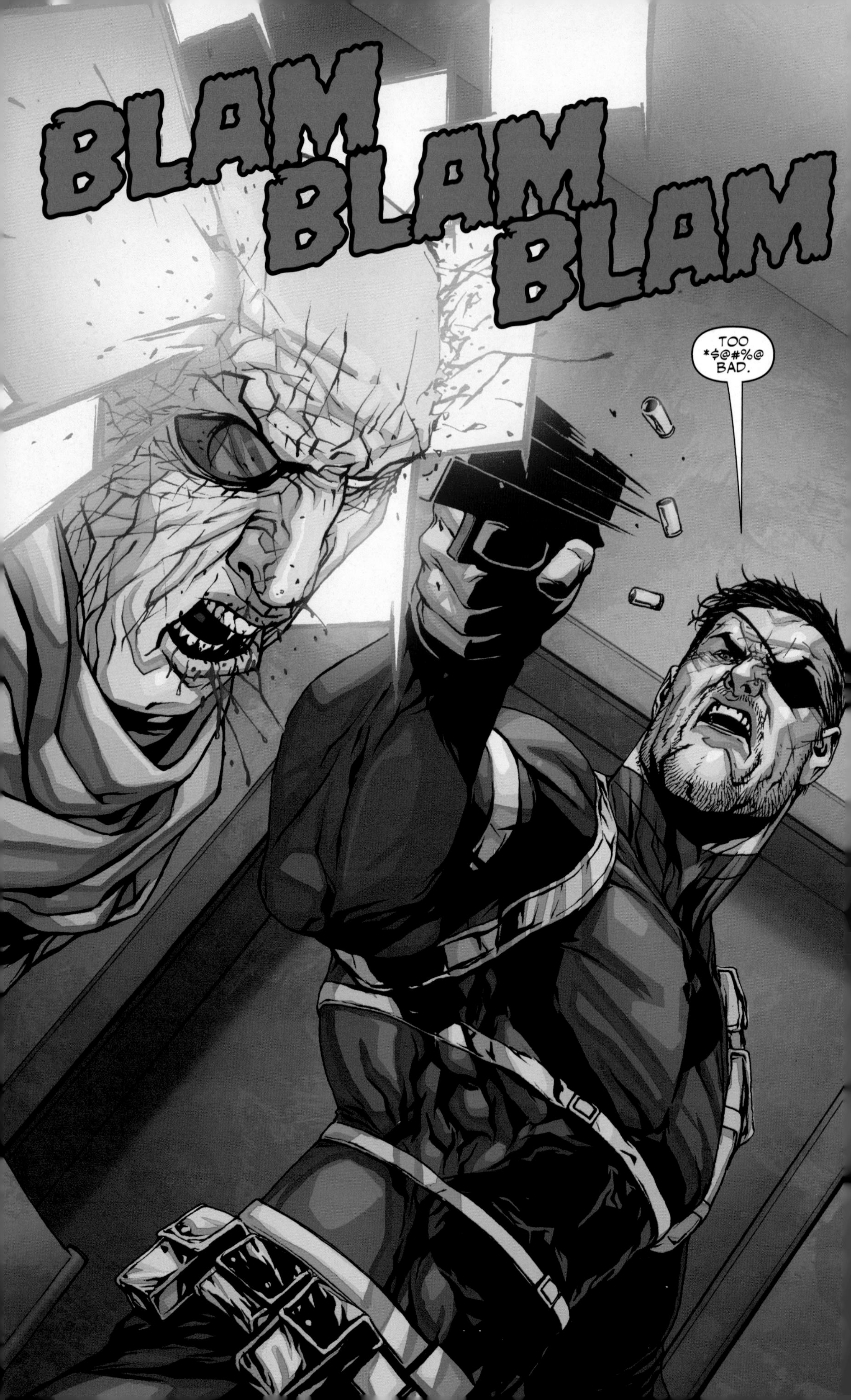
BLAM BLAM BLAM
TOO *$@#%@ BAD.

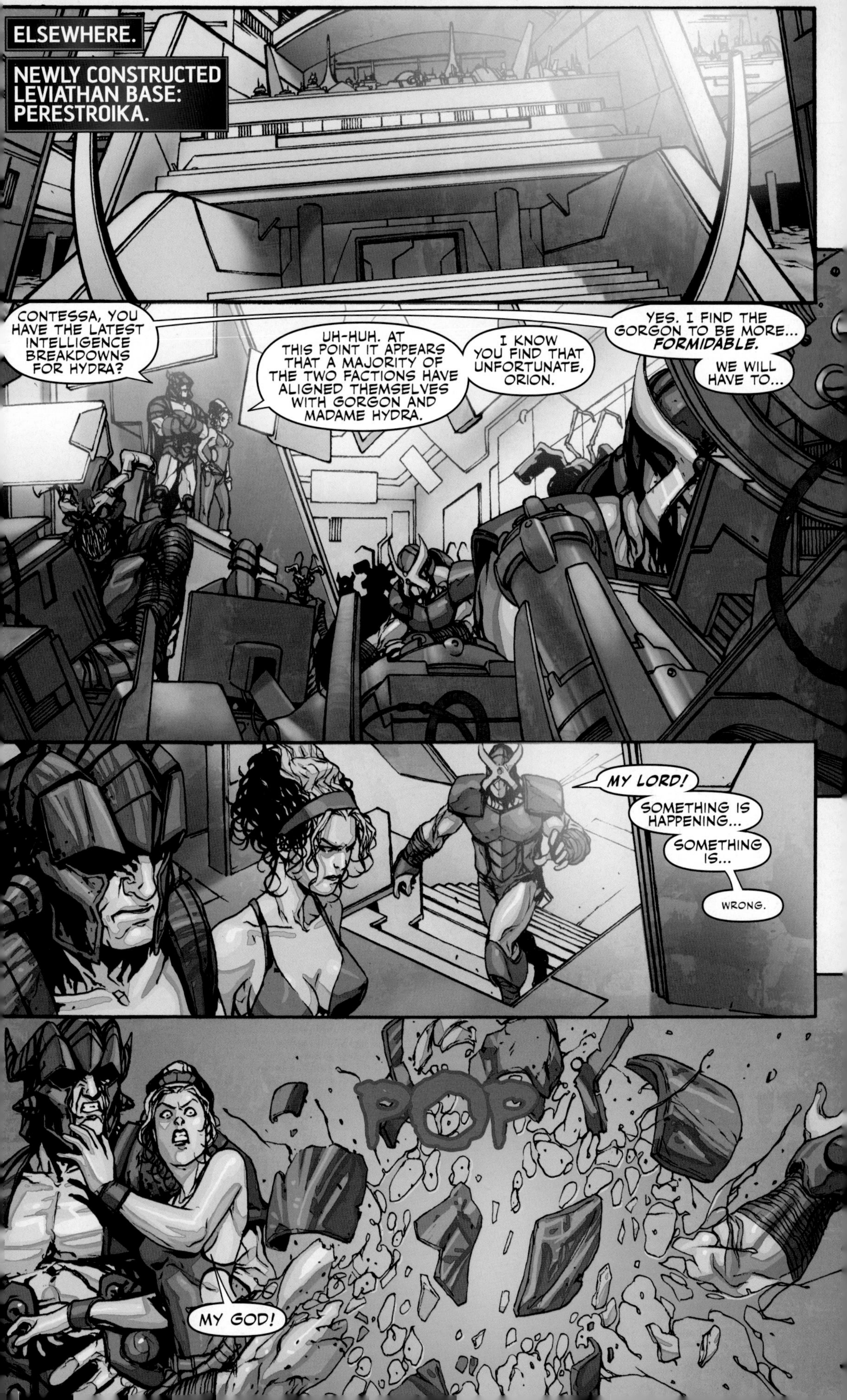
ELSEWHERE.
NEWLY CONSTRUCTED LEVIATHAN BASE: PERESTROIKA.
CONTESSA, YOU HAVE THE LATEST INTELLIGENCE BREAKDOWNS FOR HYDRA?
UH-HUH. AT THIS POINT IT APPEARS THAT A MAJORITY OF THE TWO FACTIONS HAVE ALIGNED THEMSELVES WITH GORGON AND MADAME HYDRA.
I KNOW YOU FIND THAT UNFORTUNATE, ORION.
YES. I FIND THE GORGON TO BE MORE... *FORMIDABLE.*
WE WILL HAVE TO...
MY LORD!
SOMETHING IS HAPPENING...
SOMETHING IS...
WRONG.
POP
MY GOD!

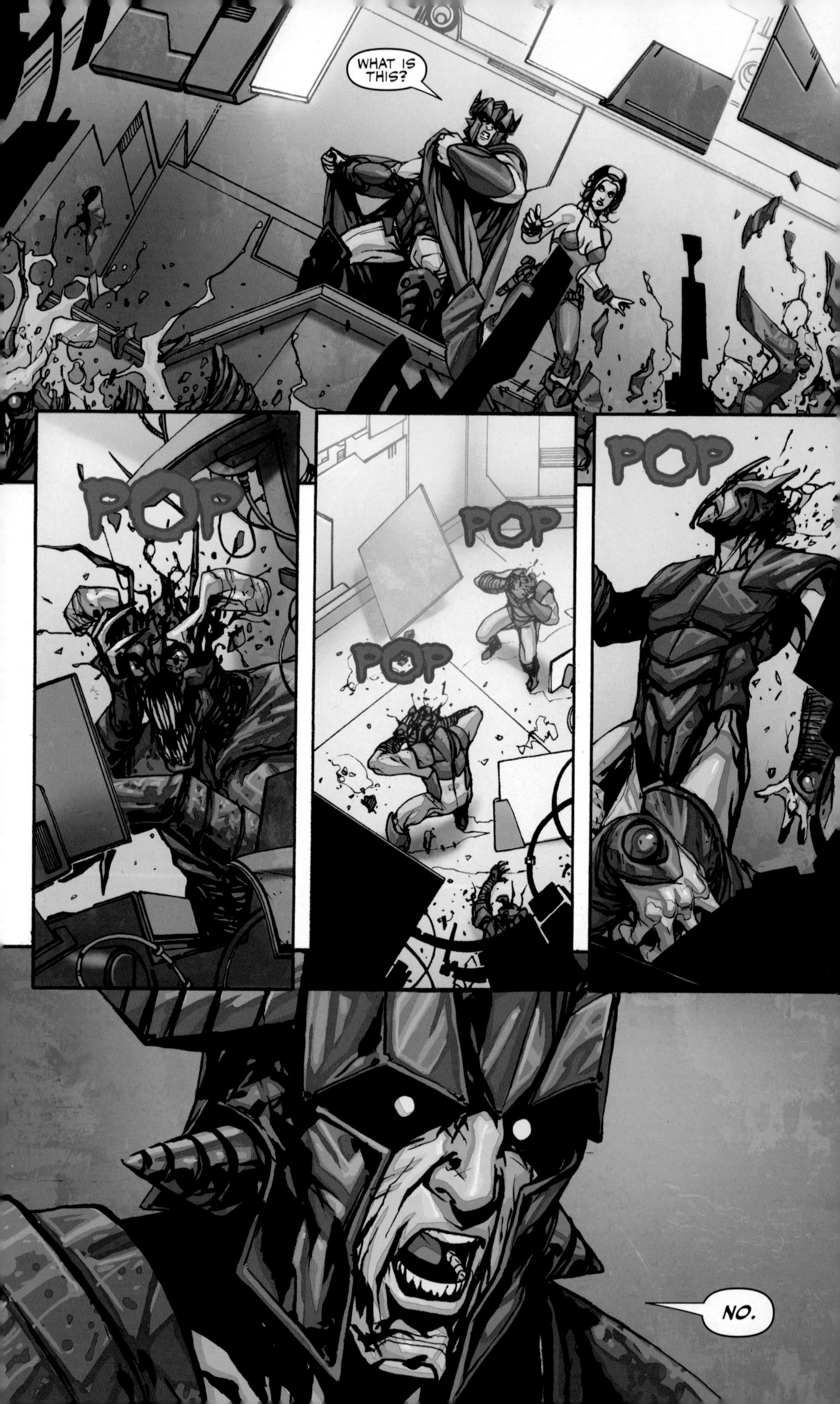
WHAT IS THIS?
POP
POP
POP
POP
NO.

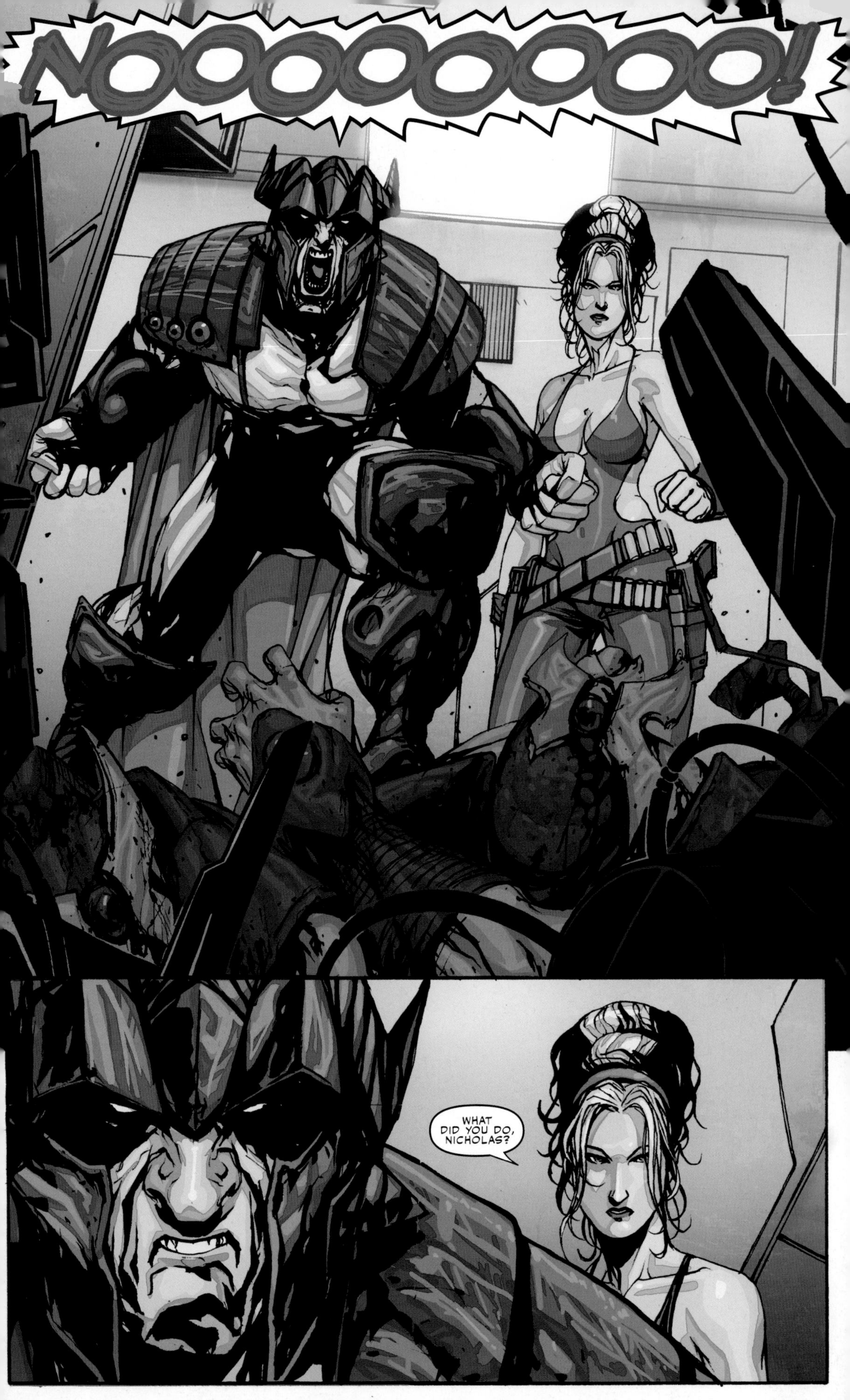
NOOOOOOOO!
WHAT DID YOU DO, NICHOLAS?

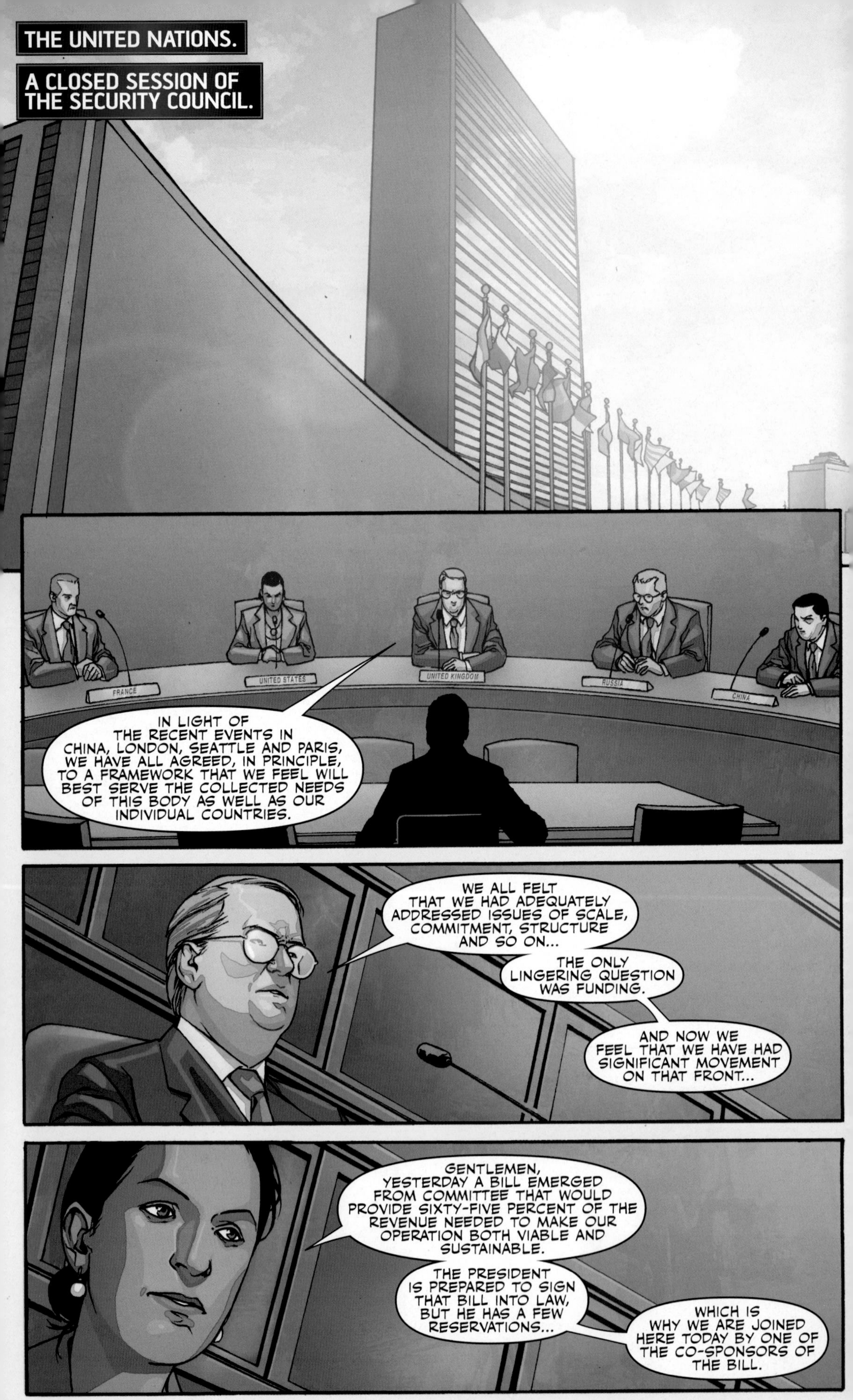
THE UNITED NATIONS.
A CLOSED SESSION OF THE SECURITY COUNCIL.
FRANCE
UNITED STATES
UNITED KINGDOM
RUSSIA
CHINA
IN LIGHT OF THE RECENT EVENTS IN CHINA, LONDON, SEATTLE AND PARIS, WE HAVE ALL AGREED, IN PRINCIPLE, TO A FRAMEWORK THAT WE FEEL WILL BEST SERVE THE COLLECTED NEEDS OF THIS BODY AS WELL AS OUR INDIVIDUAL COUNTRIES.
WE ALL FELT THAT WE HAD ADEQUATELY ADDRESSED ISSUES OF SCALE, COMMITMENT, STRUCTURE AND SO ON...
THE ONLY LINGERING QUESTION WAS FUNDING.
AND NOW WE FEEL THAT WE HAVE HAD SIGNIFICANT MOVEMENT ON THAT FRONT...
GENTLEMEN, YESTERDAY A BILL EMERGED FROM COMMITTEE THAT WOULD PROVIDE SIXTY-FIVE PERCENT OF THE REVENUE NEEDED TO MAKE OUR OPERATION BOTH VIABLE AND SUSTAINABLE.
THE PRESIDENT IS PREPARED TO SIGN THAT BILL INTO LAW, BUT HE HAS A FEW RESERVATIONS...
WHICH IS WHY WE ARE JOINED HERE TODAY BY ONE OF THE CO-SPONSORS OF THE BILL.

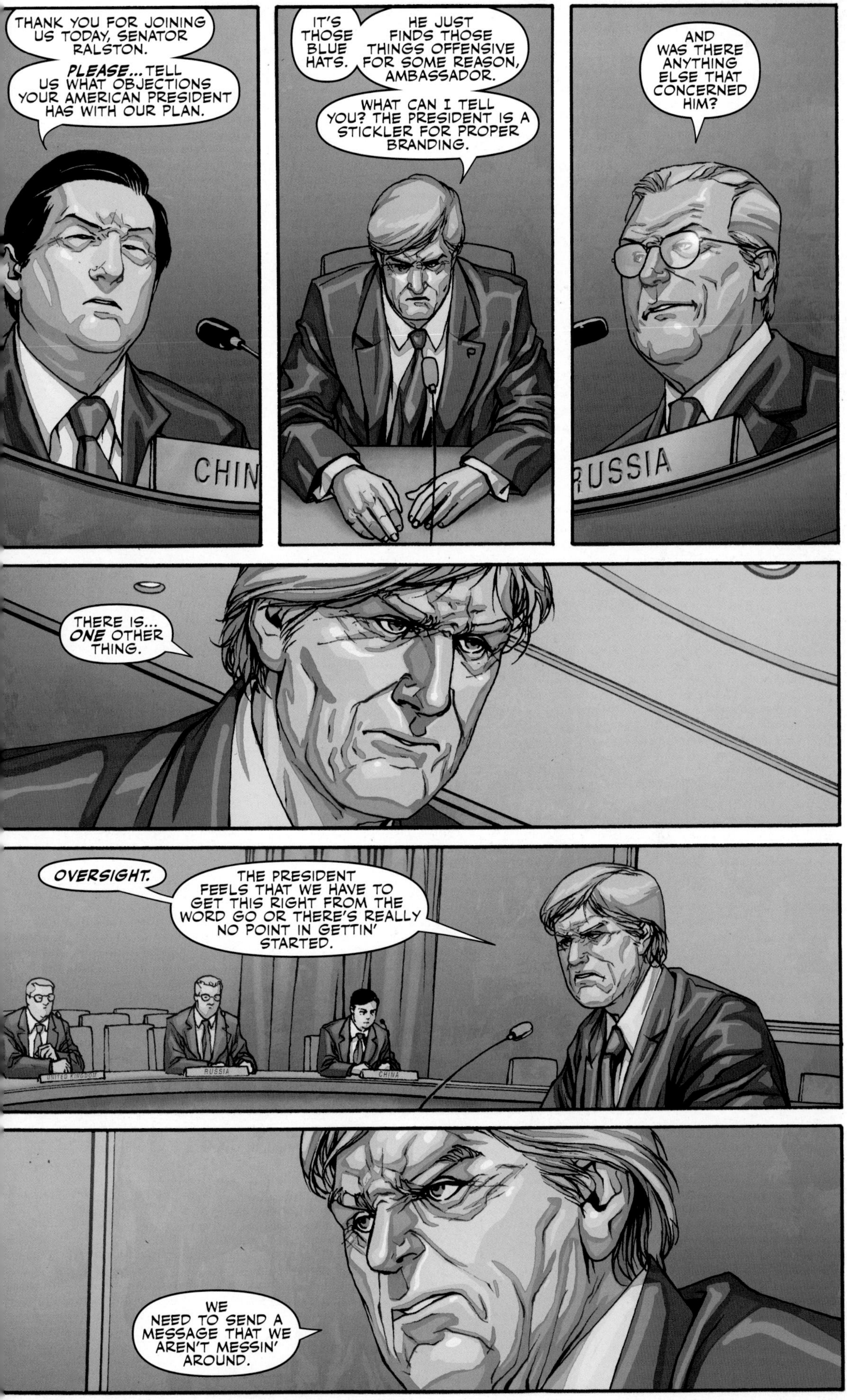
THANK YOU FOR JOINING US TODAY, SENATOR RALSTON.
PLEASE... TELL US WHAT OBJECTIONS YOUR AMERICAN PRESIDENT HAS WITH OUR PLAN.
CHIN
IT'S THOSE BLUE HATS.
HE JUST FINDS THOSE THINGS OFFENSIVE FOR SOME REASON, AMBASSADOR.
WHAT CAN I TELL YOU? THE PRESIDENT IS A STICKLER FOR PROPER BRANDING.
AND WAS THERE ANYTHING ELSE THAT CONCERNED HIM?
RUSSIA
THERE IS... ONE OTHER THING.
OVERSIGHT.
THE PRESIDENT FEELS THAT WE HAVE TO GET THIS RIGHT FROM THE WORD GO OR THERE'S REALLY NO POINT IN GETTIN' STARTED.
RUSSIA
CHINA
WE NEED TO SEND A MESSAGE THAT WE AREN'T MESSIN' AROUND.

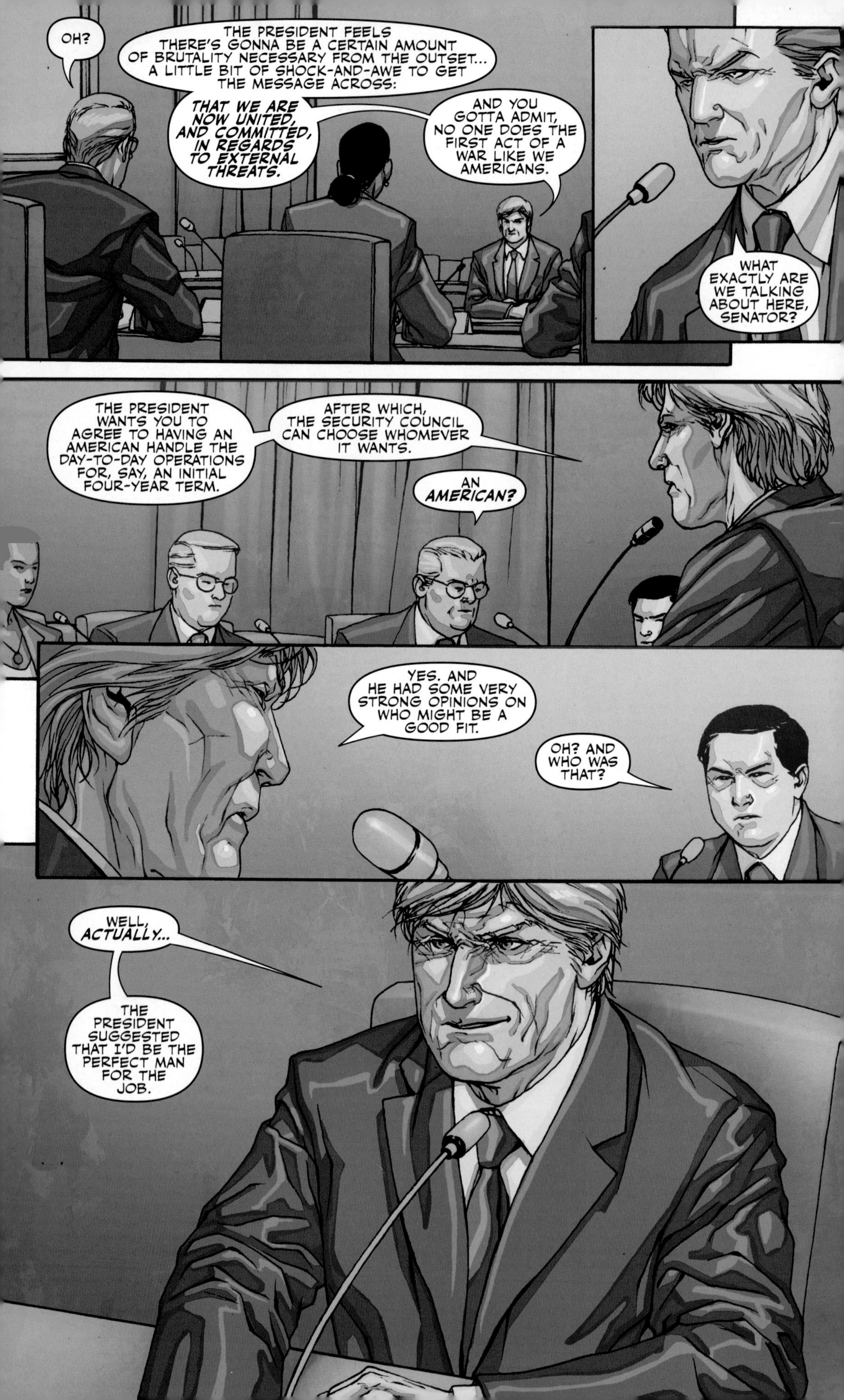
OH?
THE PRESIDENT FEELS THERE'S GONNA BE A CERTAIN AMOUNT OF BRUTALITY NECESSARY FROM THE OUTSET... A LITTLE BIT OF SHOCK-AND-AWE TO GET THE MESSAGE ACROSS:
THAT WE ARE NOW UNITED, AND COMMITTED, IN REGARDS TO EXTERNAL THREATS.
AND YOU GOTTA ADMIT, NO ONE DOES THE FIRST ACT OF A WAR LIKE WE AMERICANS.
WHAT EXACTLY ARE WE TALKING ABOUT HERE, SENATOR?
THE PRESIDENT WANTS YOU TO AGREE TO HAVING AN AMERICAN HANDLE THE DAY-TO-DAY OPERATIONS FOR, SAY, AN INITIAL FOUR-YEAR TERM.
AFTER WHICH, THE SECURITY COUNCIL CAN CHOOSE WHOMEVER IT WANTS.
AN AMERICAN?
YES. AND HE HAD SOME VERY STRONG OPINIONS ON WHO MIGHT BE A GOOD FIT.
OH? AND WHO WAS THAT?
WELL, ACTUALLY...
THE PRESIDENT SUGGESTED THAT I'D BE THE PERFECT MAN FOR THE JOB.

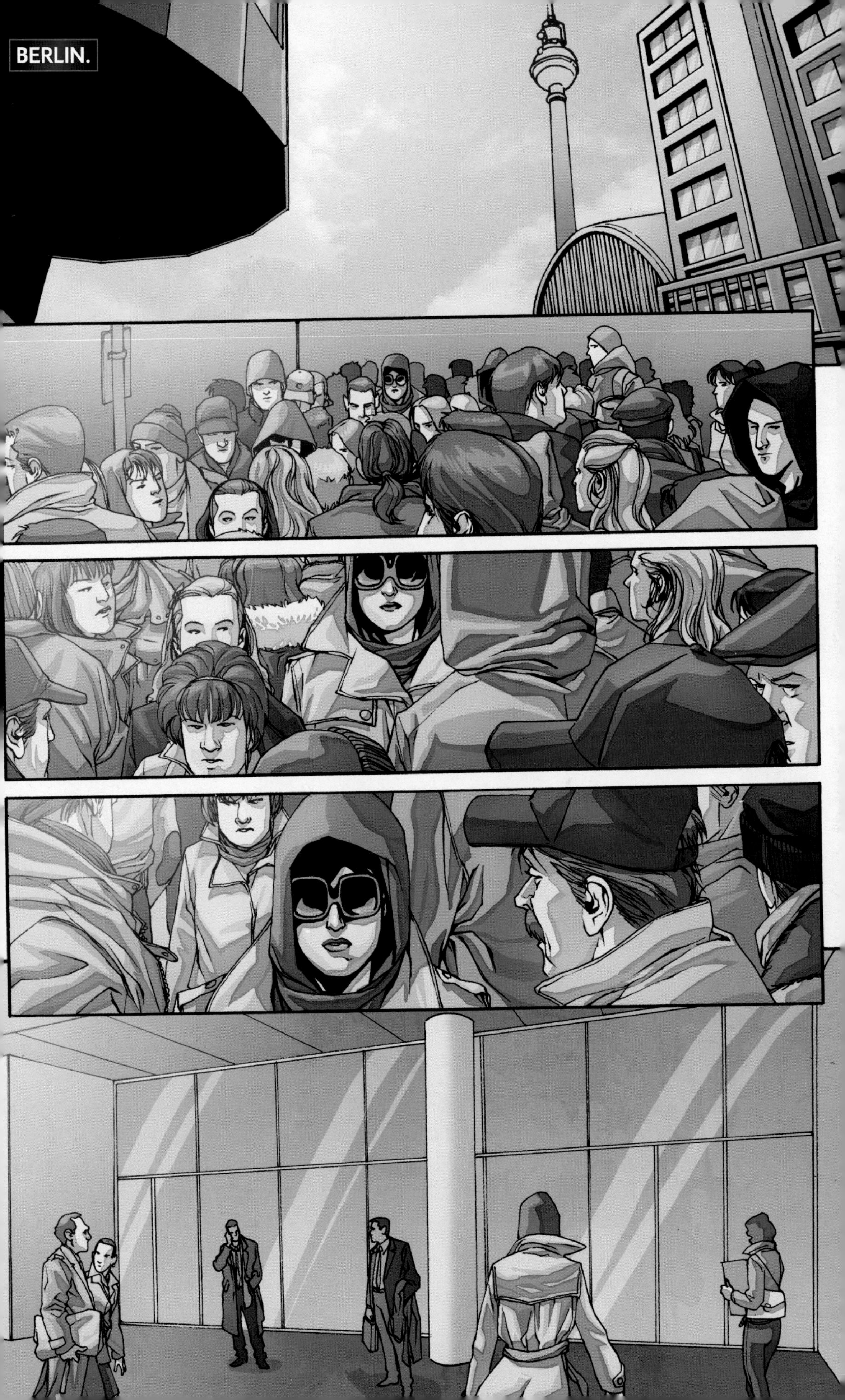
BERLIN.

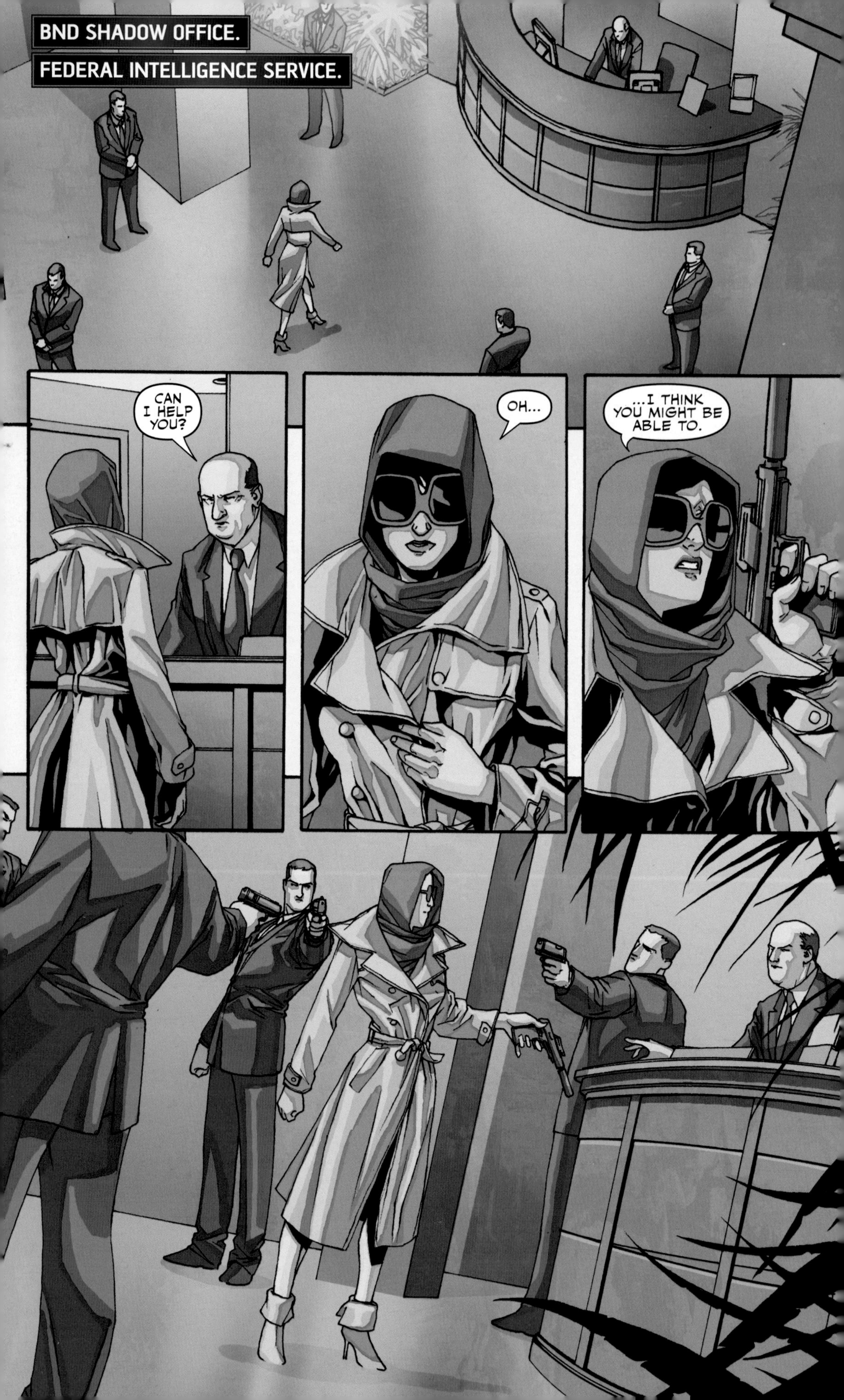
BND SHADOW OFFICE.
FEDERAL INTELLIGENCE SERVICE.
CAN I HELP YOU?
OH...
...I THINK YOU MIGHT BE ABLE TO.

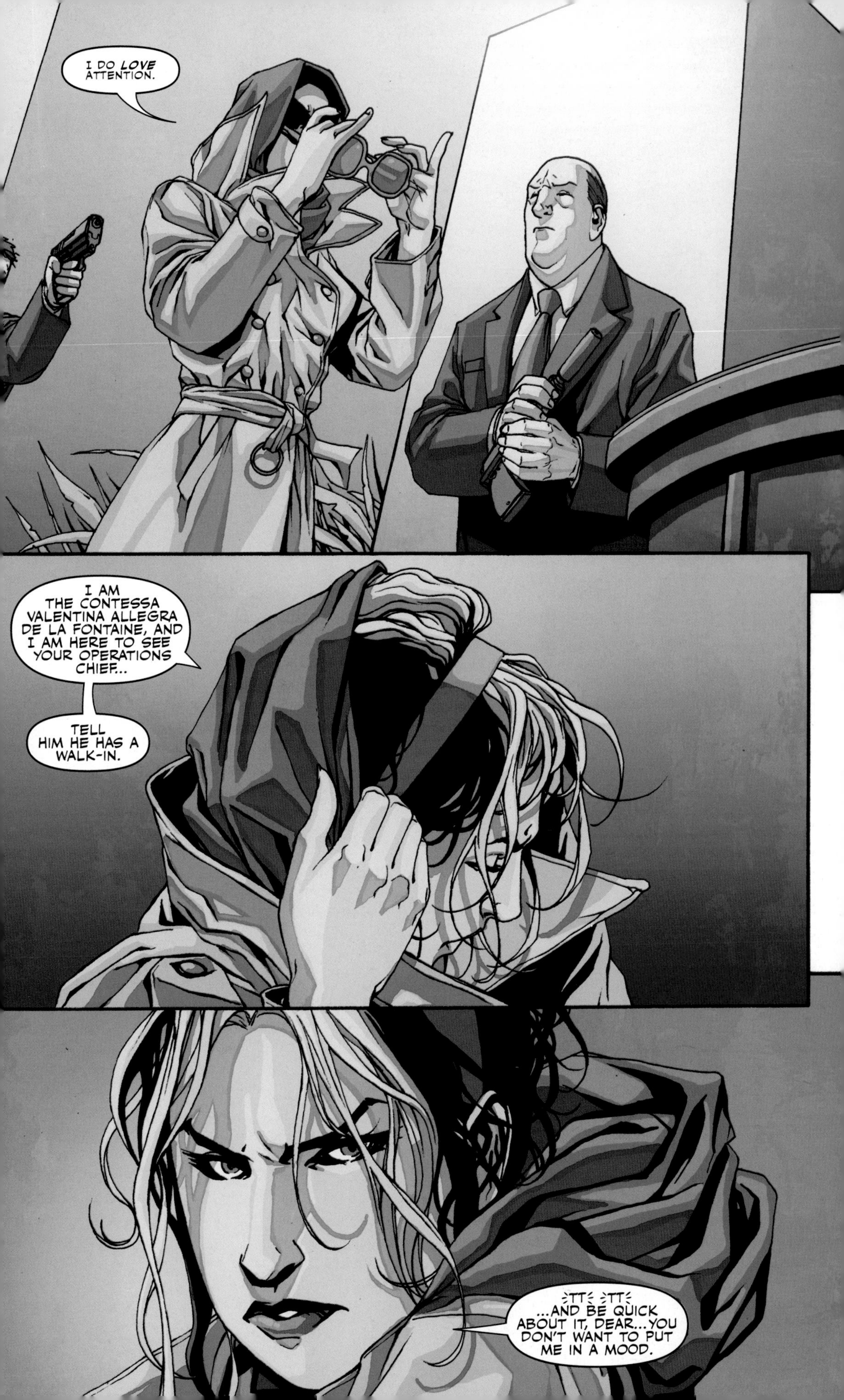
I DO LOVE ATTENTION.
I AM THE CONTESSA VALENTINA ALLEGRA DE LA FONTAINE, AND I AM HERE TO SEE YOUR OPERATIONS CHIEF...
TELL HIM HE HAS A WALK-IN.
TT TT
...AND BE QUICK ABOUT IT, DEAR...YOU DON'T WANT TO PUT ME IN A MOOD.

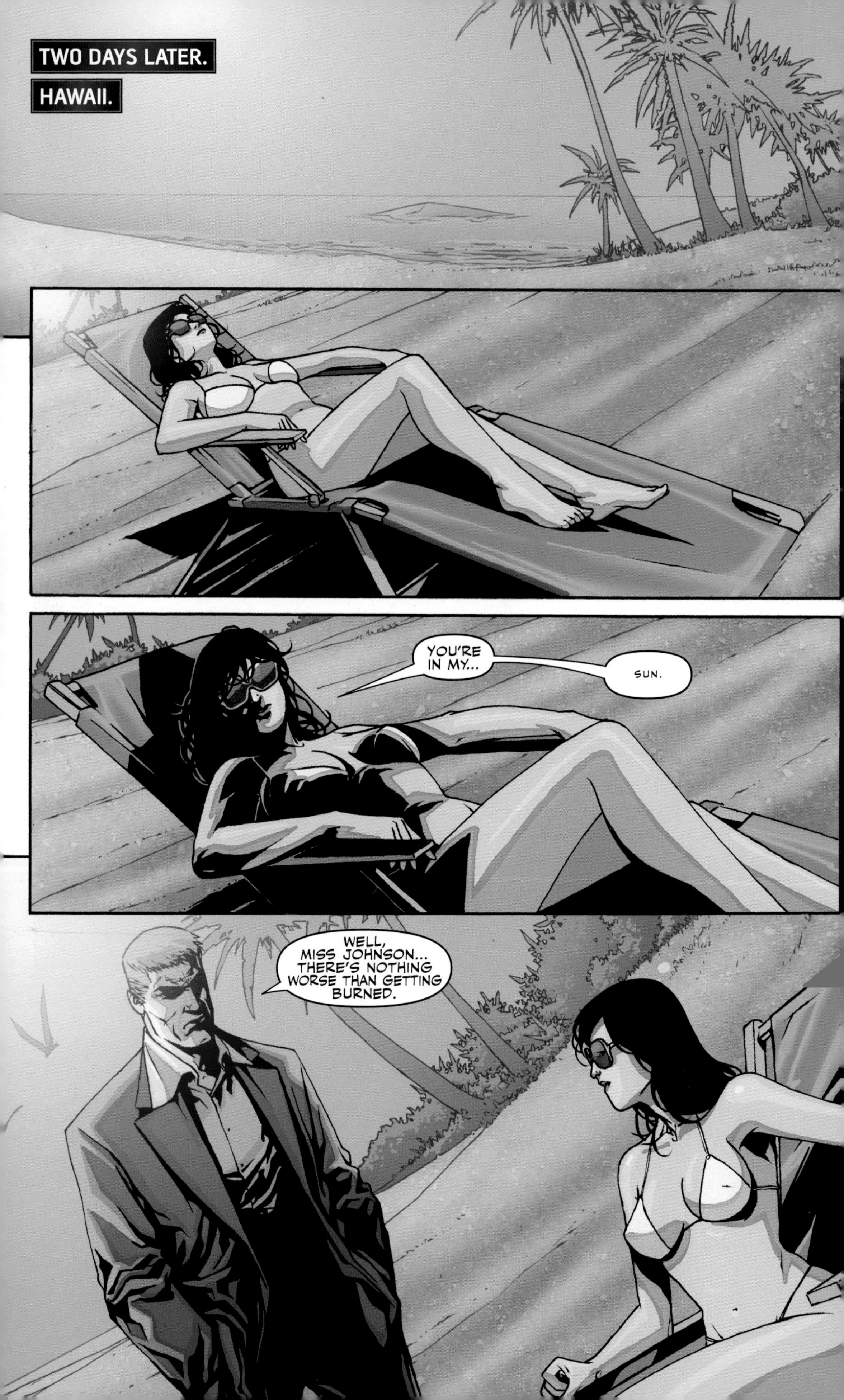
TWO DAYS LATER.
HAWAII.
YOU'RE IN MY...
SUN.
WELL, MISS JOHNSON... THERE'S NOTHING WORSE THAN GETTING BURNED.

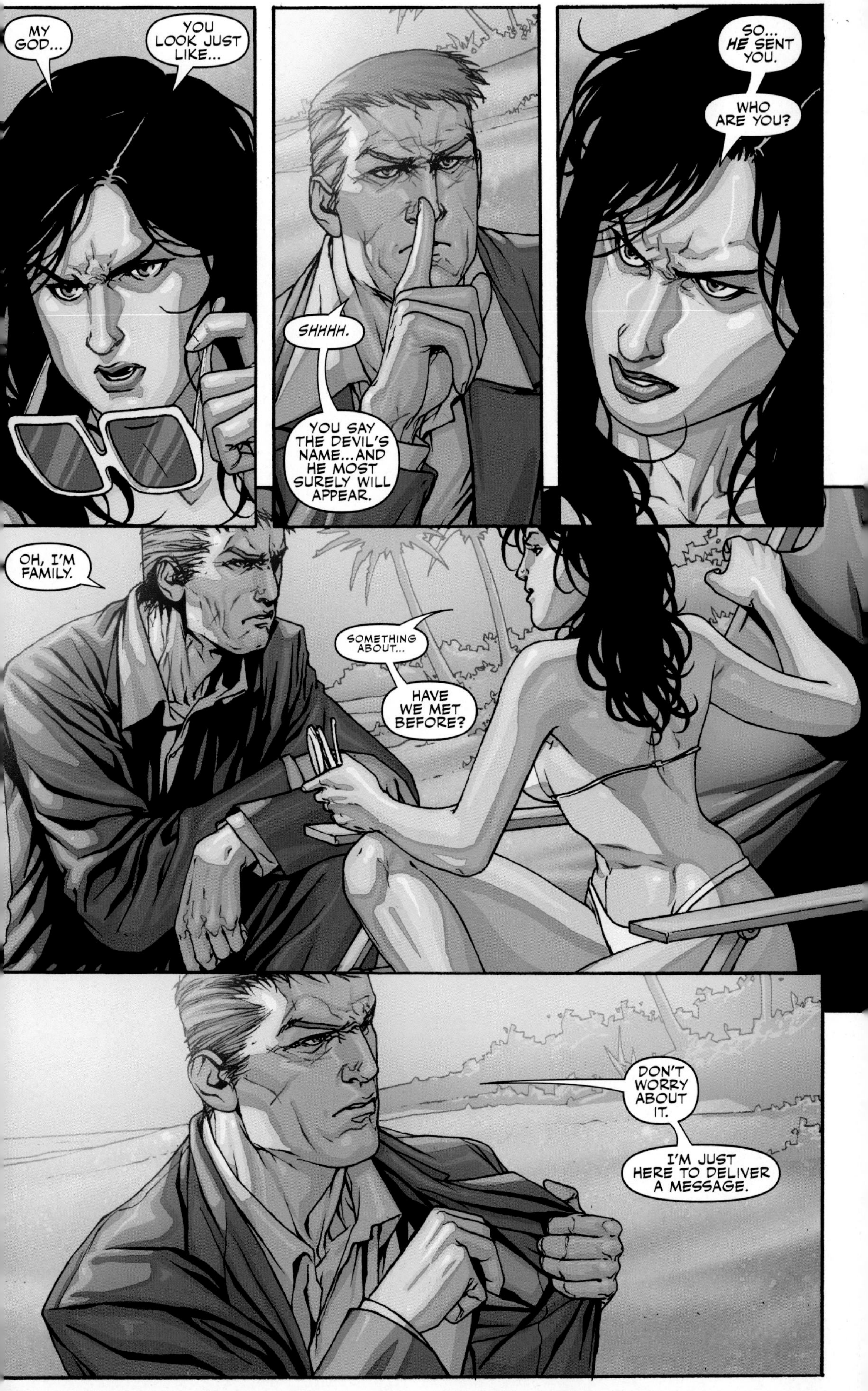
MY GOD...
YOU LOOK JUST LIKE...
SHHHH.
YOU SAY THE DEVIL'S NAME...AND HE MOST SURELY WILL APPEAR.
SO... HE SENT YOU.
WHO ARE YOU?
OH, I'M FAMILY.
SOMETHING ABOUT...
HAVE WE MET BEFORE?
DON'T WORRY ABOUT IT.
I'M JUST HERE TO DELIVER A MESSAGE.

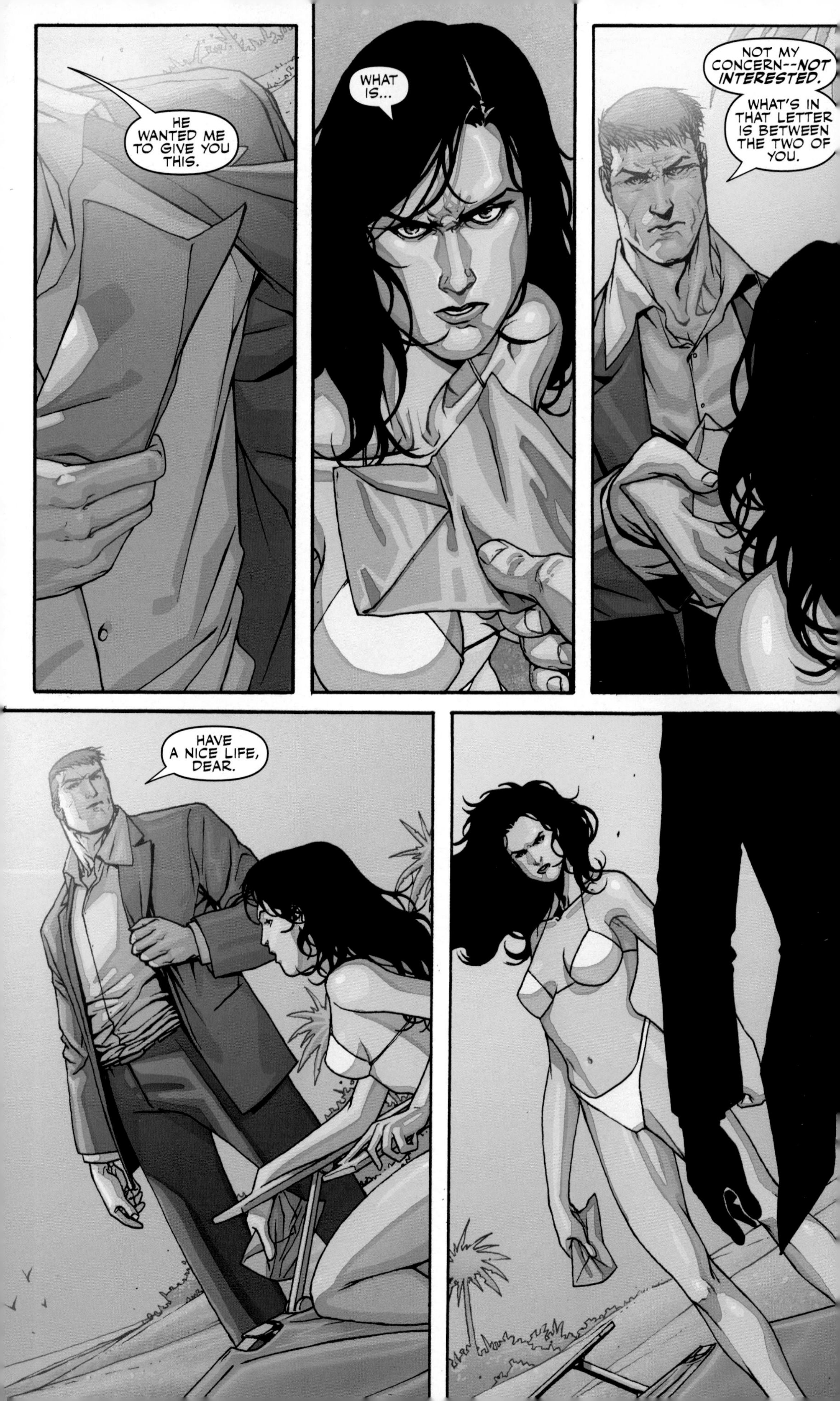
HE WANTED ME TO GIVE YOU THIS.
WHAT IS...
NOT MY CONCERN--*NOT INTERESTED.*
WHAT'S IN THAT LETTER IS BETWEEN THE TWO OF YOU.
HAVE A NICE LIFE, DEAR.

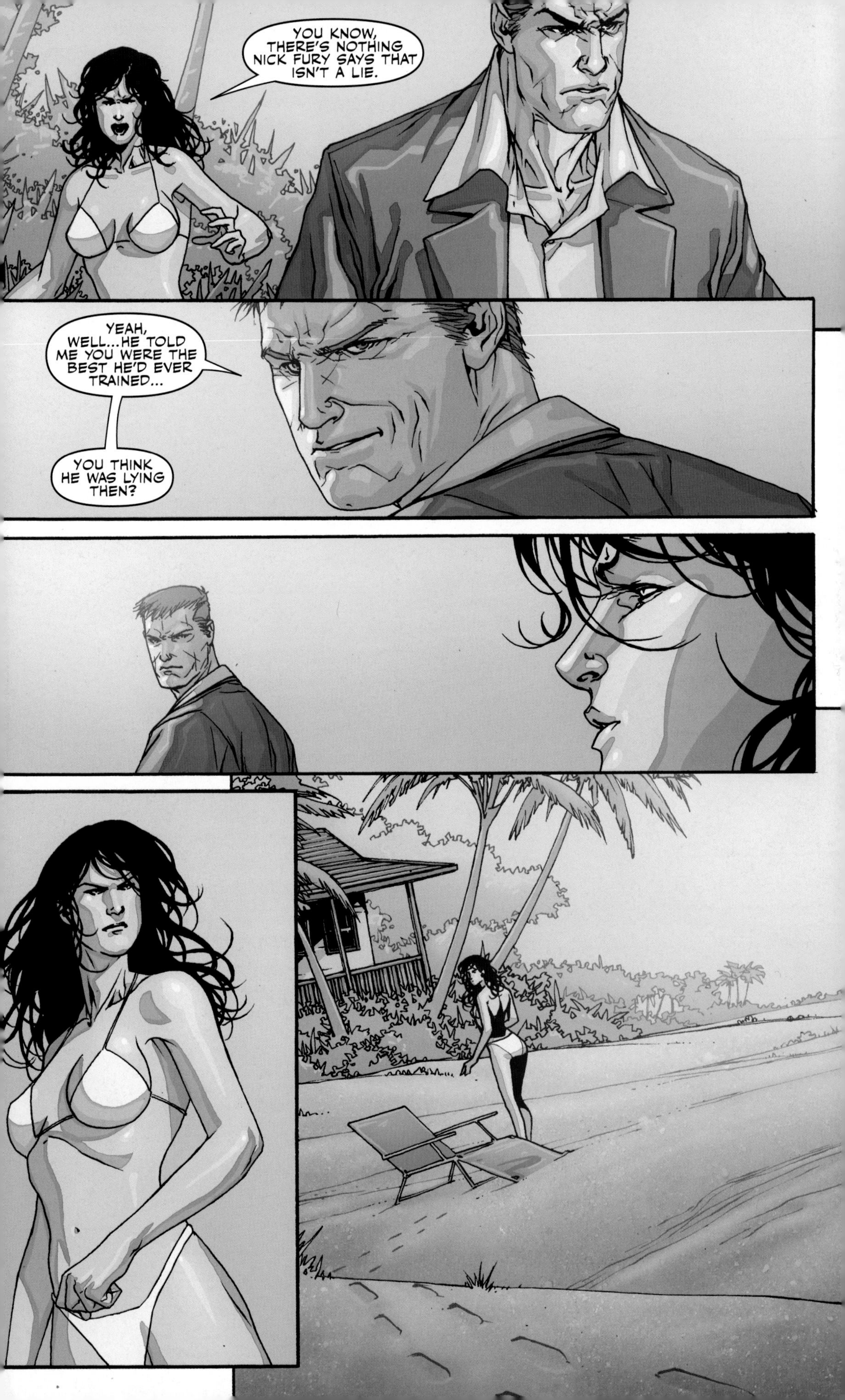
YOU KNOW, THERE'S NOTHING NICK FURY SAYS THAT ISN'T A LIE.
YEAH, WELL...HE TOLD ME YOU WERE THE BEST HE'D EVER TRAINED...
YOU THINK HE WAS LYING THEN?

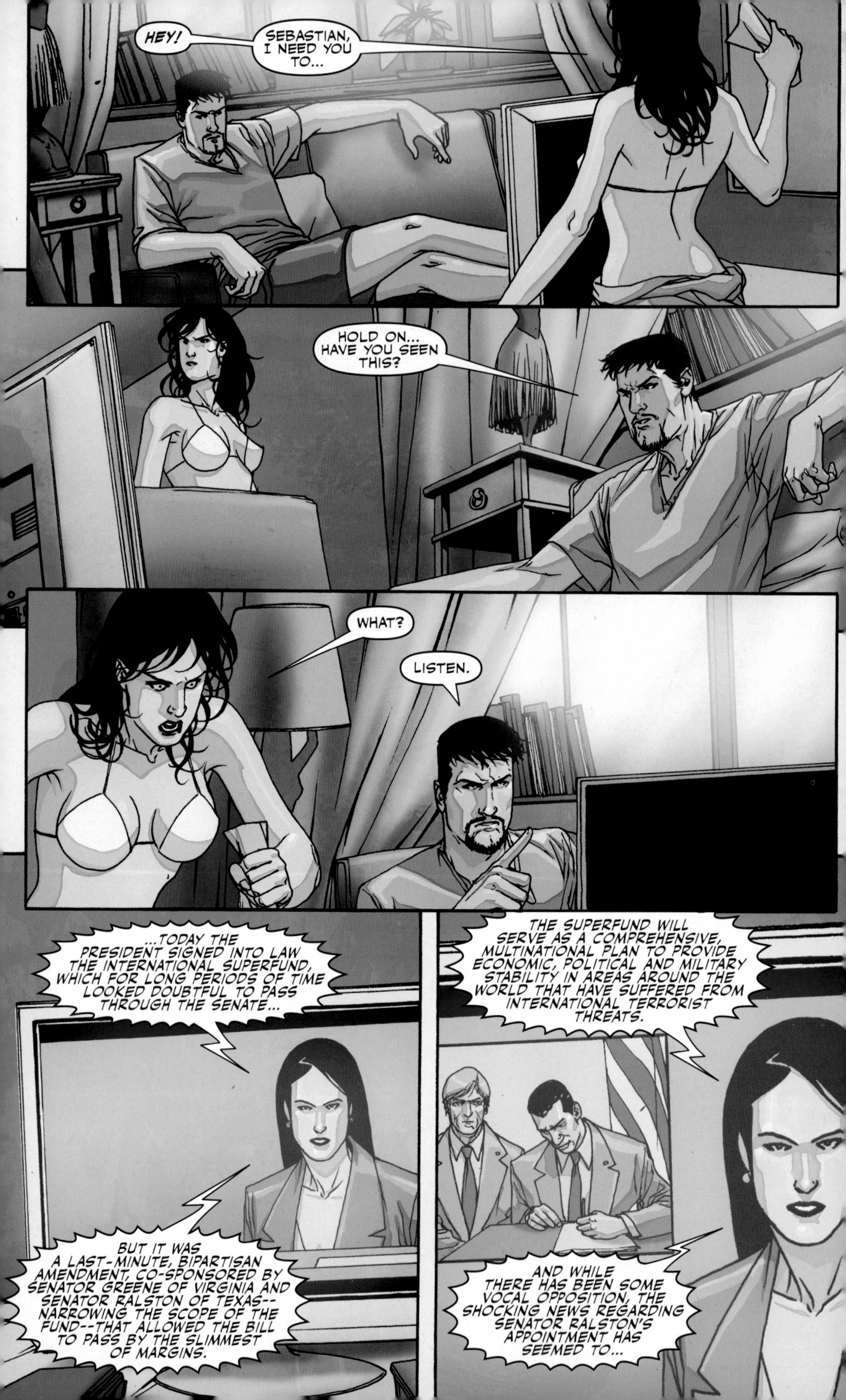
HEY!
SEBASTIAN, I NEED YOU TO...
HOLD ON... HAVE YOU SEEN THIS?
WHAT?
LISTEN.
...TODAY THE PRESIDENT SIGNED INTO LAW THE INTERNATIONAL SUPERFUND, WHICH FOR LONG PERIODS OF TIME LOOKED DOUBTFUL TO PASS THROUGH THE SENATE...
BUT IT WAS A LAST-MINUTE, BIPARTISAN AMENDMENT, CO-SPONSORED BY SENATOR GREENE OF VIRGINIA AND SENATOR RALSTON OF TEXAS--NARROWING THE SCOPE OF THE FUND--THAT ALLOWED THE BILL TO PASS BY THE SLIMMEST OF MARGINS.
THE SUPERFUND WILL SERVE AS A COMPREHENSIVE, MULTINATIONAL PLAN TO PROVIDE ECONOMIC, POLITICAL AND MILITARY STABILITY IN AREAS AROUND THE WORLD THAT HAVE SUFFERED FROM INTERNATIONAL TERRORIST THREATS.
AND WHILE THERE HAS BEEN SOME VOCAL OPPOSITION, THE SHOCKING NEWS REGARDING SENATOR RALSTON'S APPOINTMENT HAS SEEMED TO...

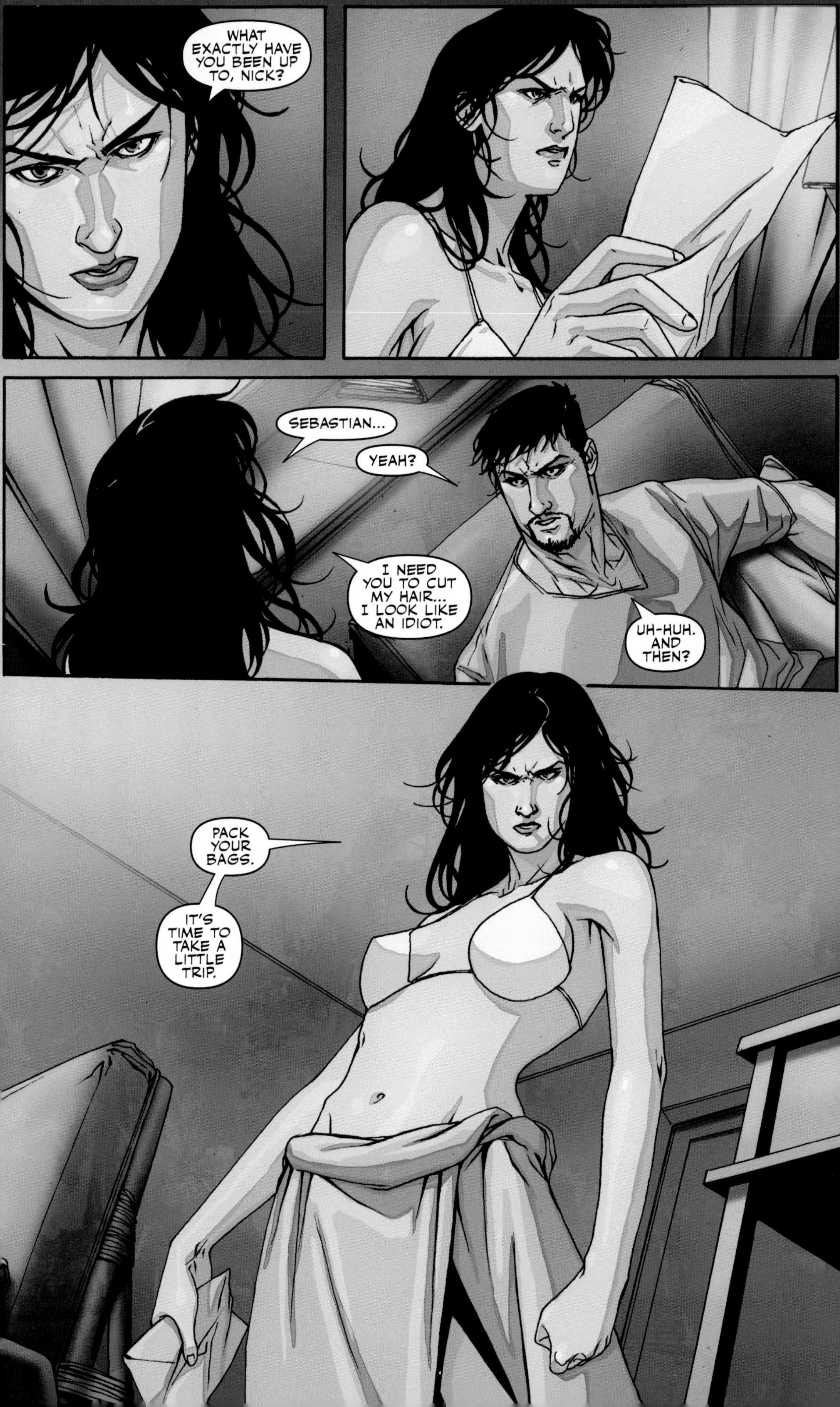
WHAT EXACTLY HAVE YOU BEEN UP TO, NICK?
SEBASTIAN...
YEAH?
I NEED YOU TO CUT MY HAIR... I LOOK LIKE AN IDIOT.
UH-HUH. AND THEN?
PACK YOUR BAGS.
IT'S TIME TO TAKE A LITTLE TRIP.

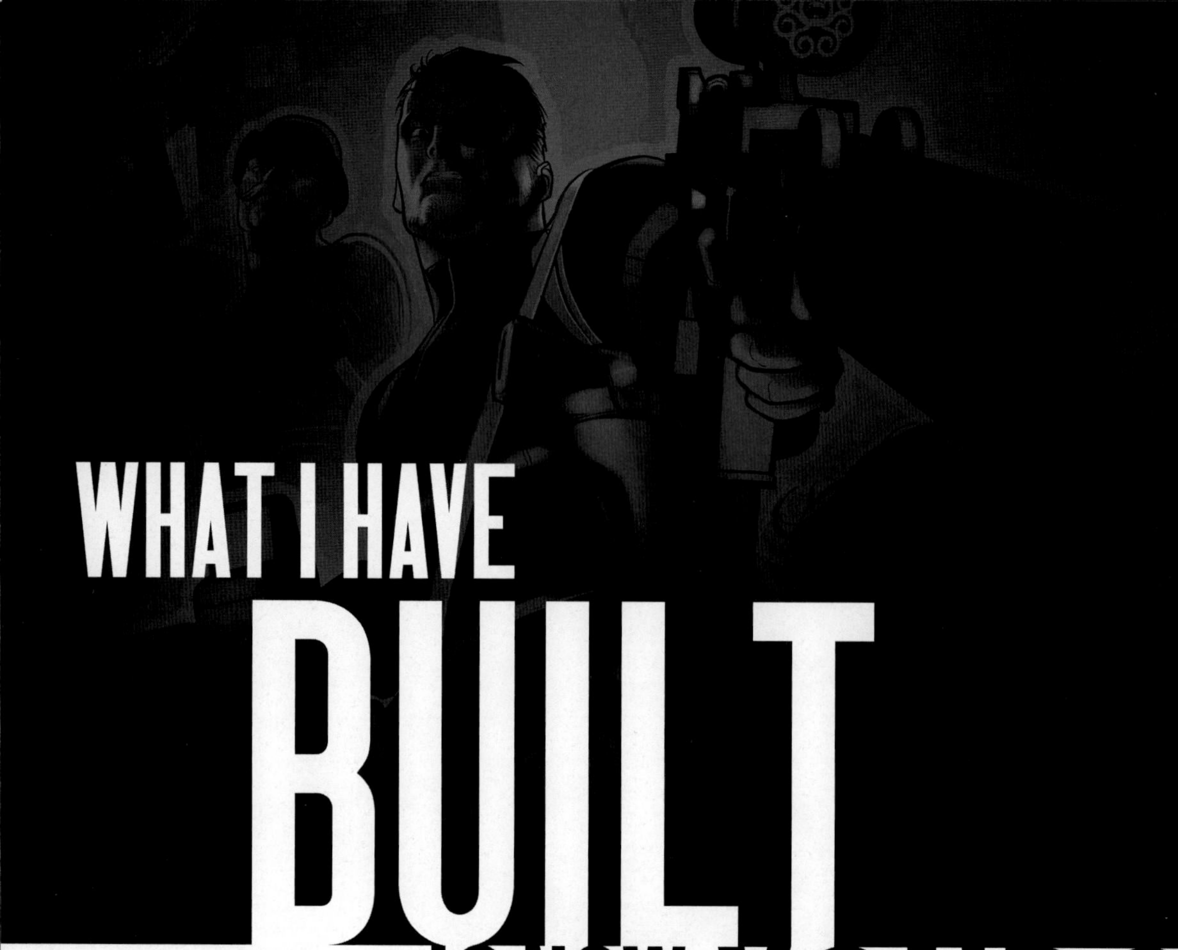
WHAT I HAVE
BUILT
IS NOW YOURS

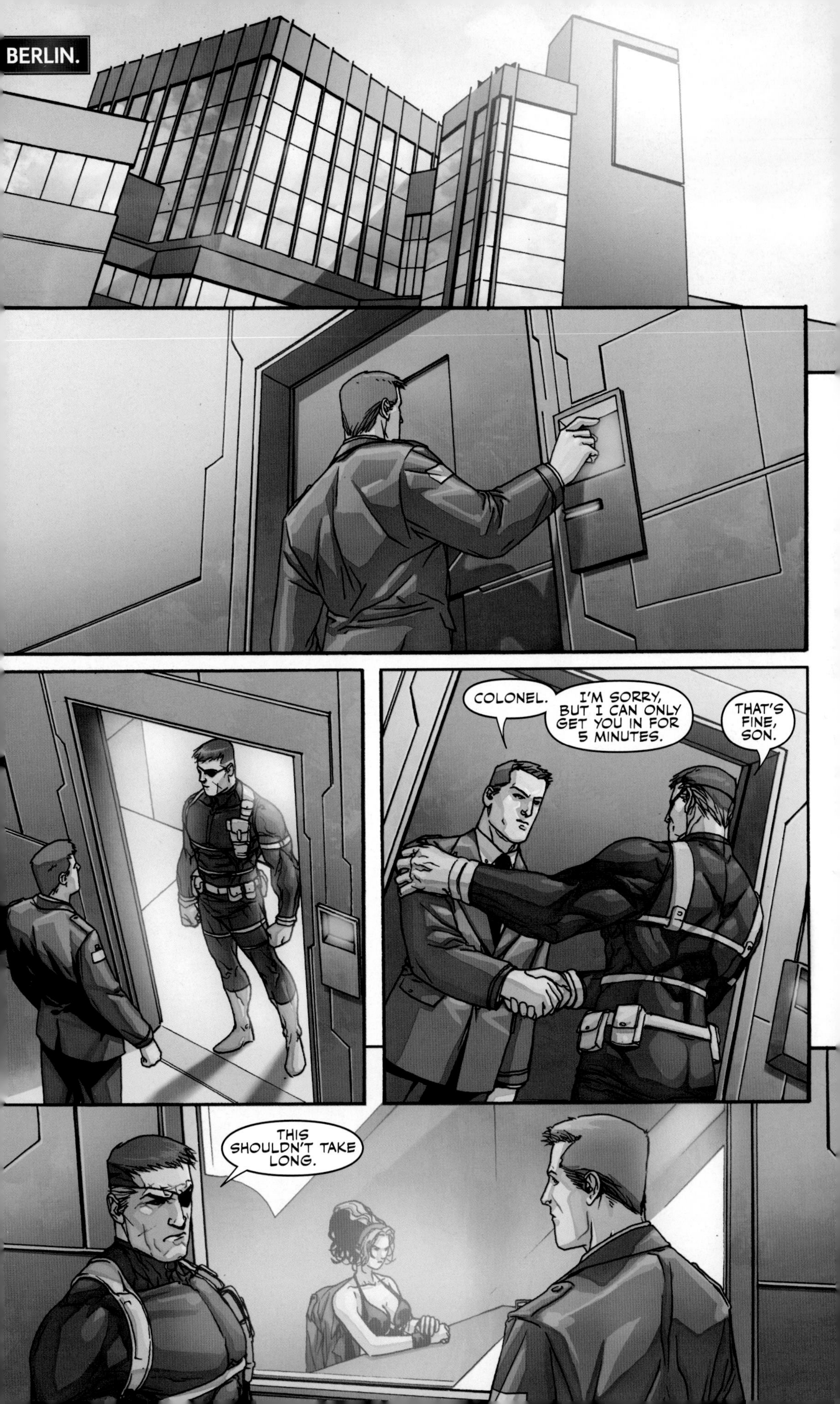
BERLIN.
COLONEL.
I'M SORRY, BUT I CAN ONLY GET YOU IN FOR 5 MINUTES.
THAT'S FINE, SON.
THIS SHOULDN'T TAKE LONG.

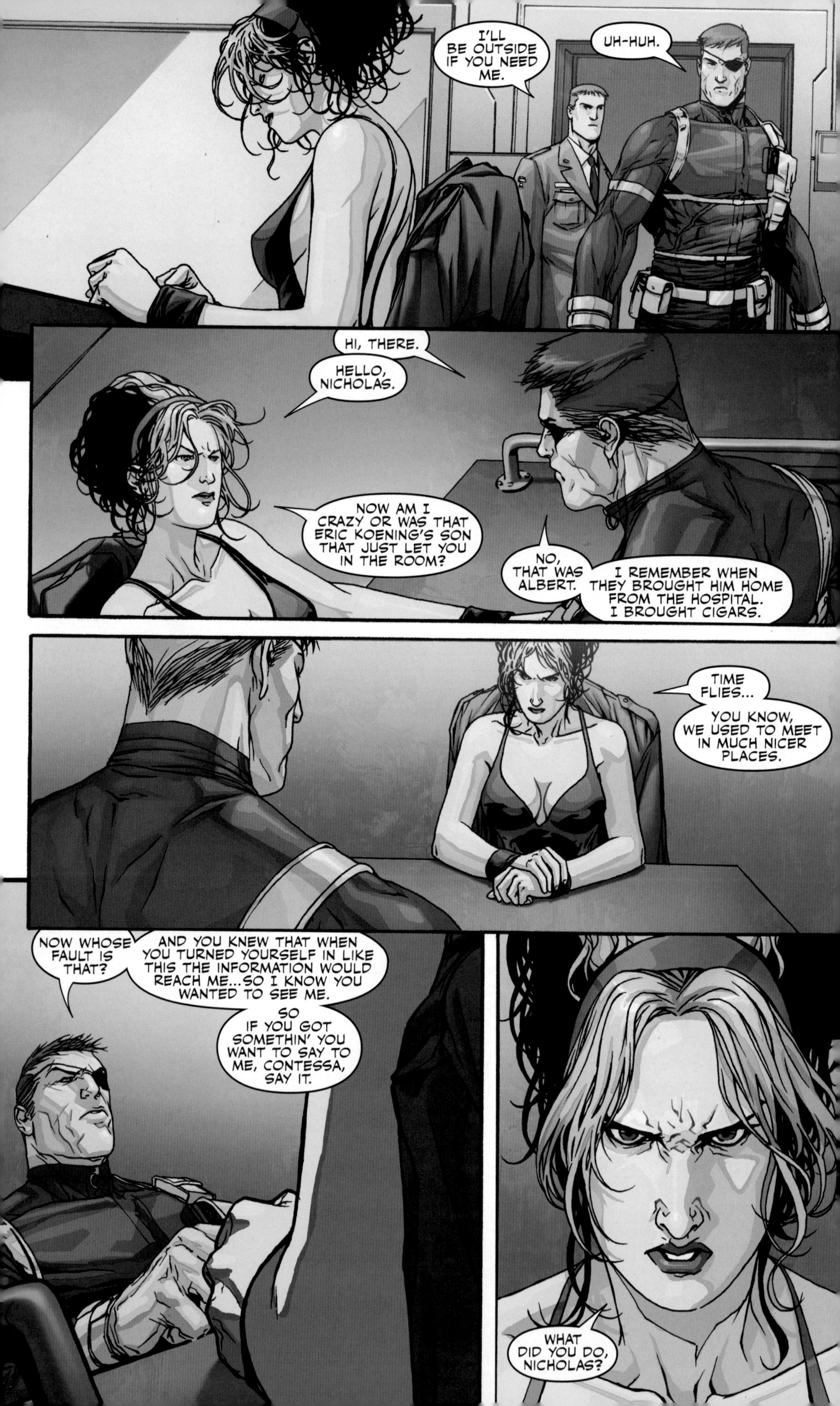
I'LL BE OUTSIDE IF YOU NEED ME.
UH-HUH.
HI, THERE.
HELLO, NICHOLAS.
NOW AM I CRAZY OR WAS THAT ERIC KOENING'S SON THAT JUST LET YOU IN THE ROOM?
NO, THAT WAS ALBERT.
I REMEMBER WHEN THEY BROUGHT HIM HOME FROM THE HOSPITAL. I BROUGHT CIGARS.
TIME FLIES...
YOU KNOW, WE USED TO MEET IN MUCH NICER PLACES.
NOW WHOSE FAULT IS THAT?
AND YOU KNEW THAT WHEN YOU TURNED YOURSELF IN LIKE THIS THE INFORMATION WOULD REACH ME...SO I KNOW YOU WANTED TO SEE ME.
SO IF YOU GOT SOMETHIN' YOU WANT TO SAY TO ME, CONTESSA, SAY IT.
WHAT DID YOU DO, NICHOLAS?

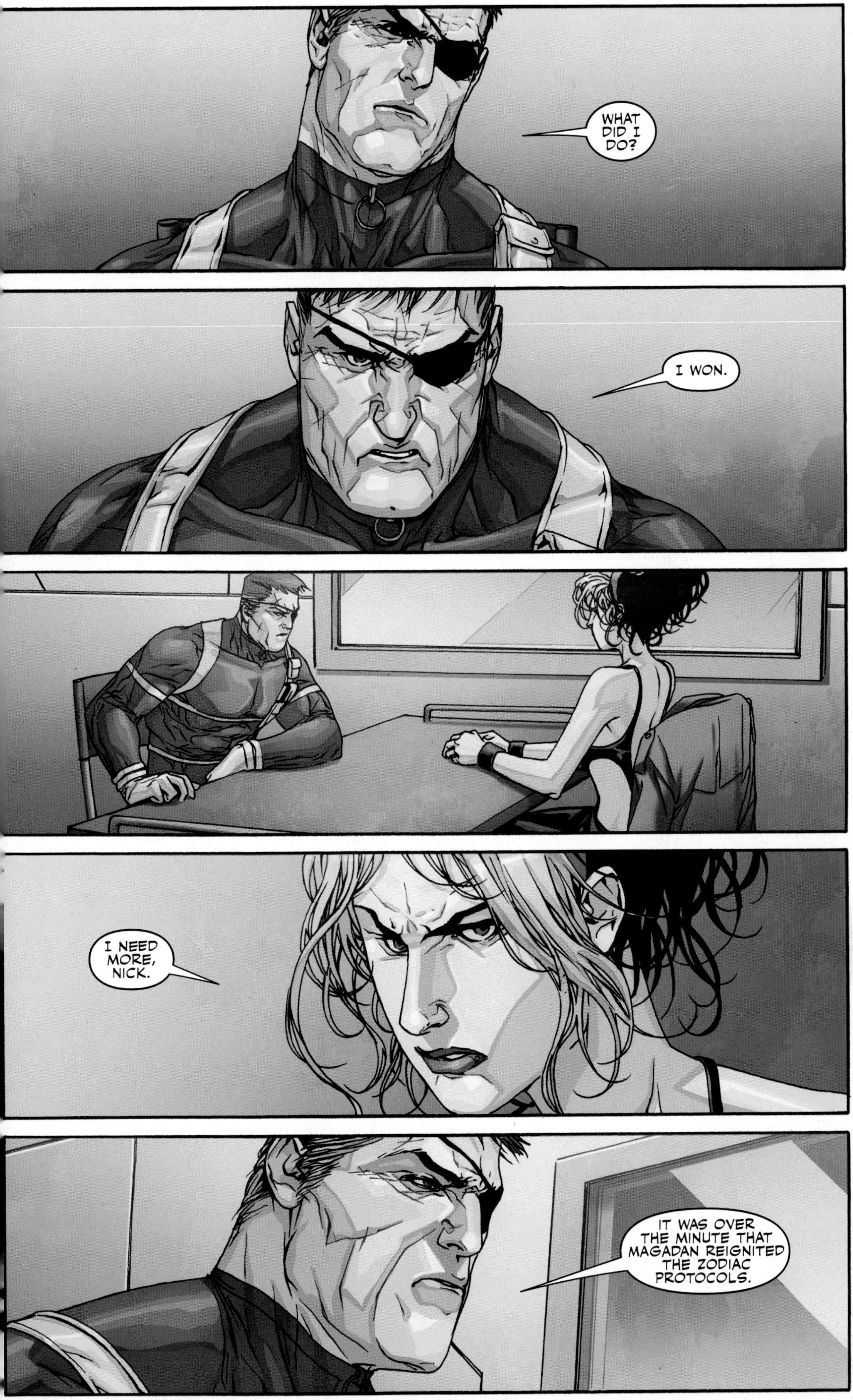
WHAT DID I DO?
I WON.
I NEED MORE, NICK.
IT WAS OVER THE MINUTE THAT MAGADAN REIGNITED THE ZODIAC PROTOCOLS.

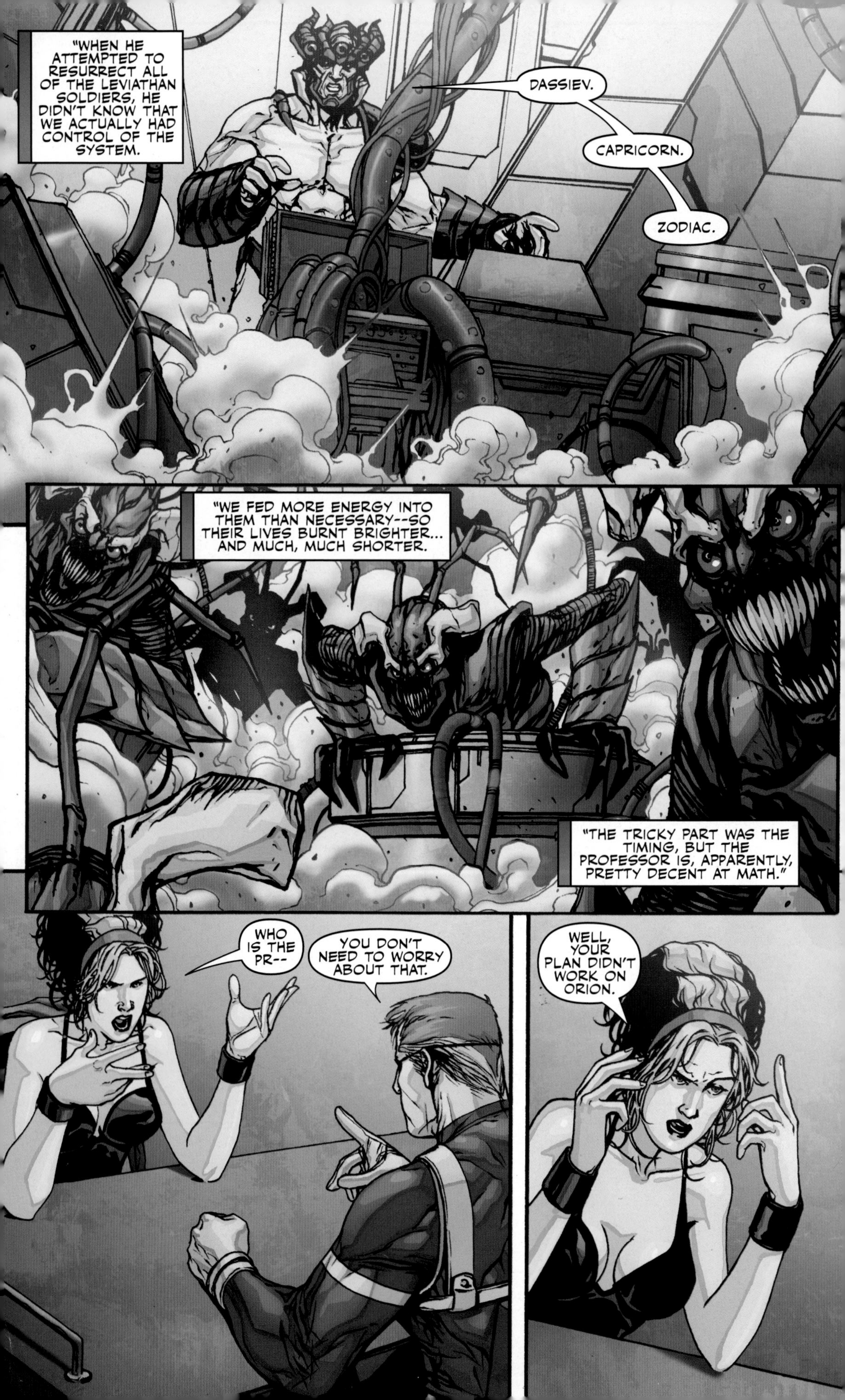
"WHEN HE ATTEMPTED TO RESURRECT ALL OF THE LEVIATHAN SOLDIERS, HE DIDN'T KNOW THAT WE ACTUALLY HAD CONTROL OF THE SYSTEM.
DASSIEV.
CAPRICORN.
ZODIAC.
"WE FED MORE ENERGY INTO THEM THAN NECESSARY--SO THEIR LIVES BURNT BRIGHTER... AND MUCH, MUCH SHORTER.
"THE TRICKY PART WAS THE TIMING, BUT THE PROFESSOR IS, APPARENTLY, PRETTY DECENT AT MATH."
WHO IS THE PR--
YOU DON'T NEED TO WORRY ABOUT THAT.
WELL, YOUR PLAN DIDN'T WORK ON ORION.

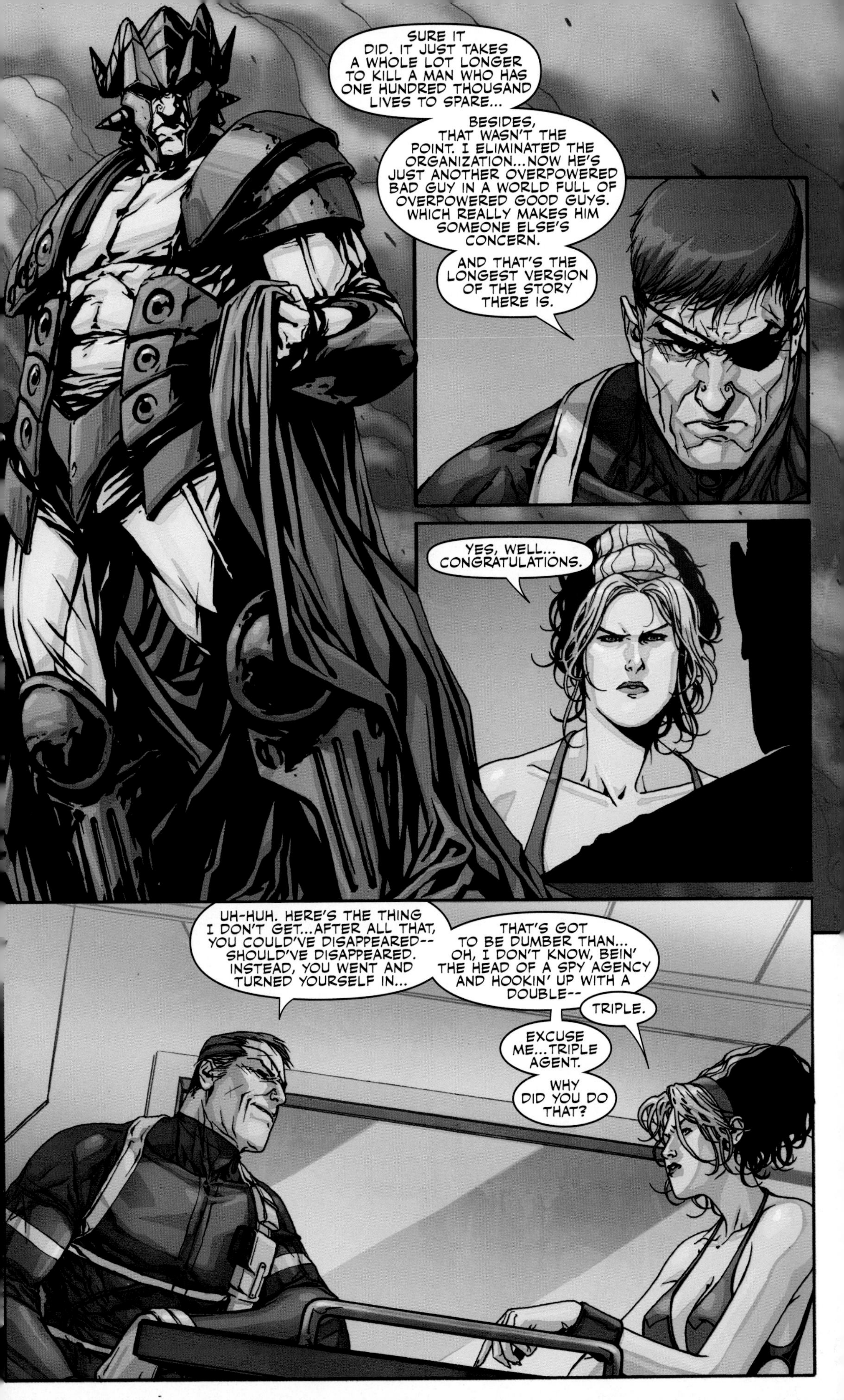

SURE IT DID. IT JUST TAKES A WHOLE LOT LONGER TO KILL A MAN WHO HAS ONE HUNDRED THOUSAND LIVES TO SPARE...
BESIDES, THAT WASN'T THE POINT. I ELIMINATED THE ORGANIZATION...NOW HE'S JUST ANOTHER OVERPOWERED BAD GUY IN A WORLD FULL OF OVERPOWERED GOOD GUYS. WHICH REALLY MAKES HIM SOMEONE ELSE'S CONCERN.
AND THAT'S THE LONGEST VERSION OF THE STORY THERE IS.
YES, WELL... CONGRATULATIONS.
UH-HUH. HERE'S THE THING I DON'T GET...AFTER ALL THAT, YOU COULD'VE DISAPPEARED-- SHOULD'VE DISAPPEARED. INSTEAD, YOU WENT AND TURNED YOURSELF IN...
THAT'S GOT TO BE DUMBER THAN... OH, I DON'T KNOW, BEIN' THE HEAD OF A SPY AGENCY AND HOOKIN' UP WITH A DOUBLE--
TRIPLE.
EXCUSE ME...TRIPLE AGENT.
WHY DID YOU DO THAT?

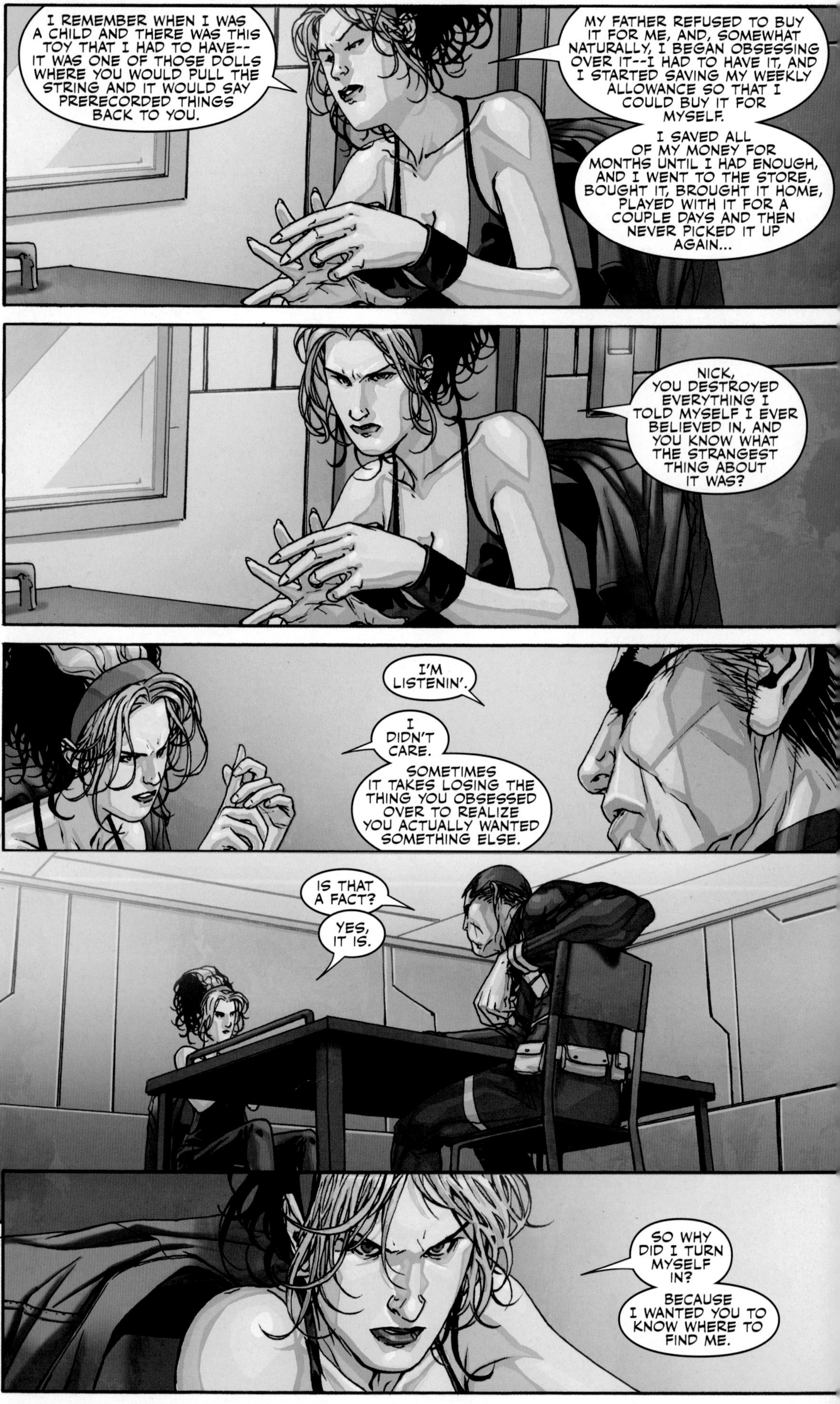
I REMEMBER WHEN I WAS A CHILD AND THERE WAS THIS TOY THAT I HAD TO HAVE-- IT WAS ONE OF THOSE DOLLS WHERE YOU WOULD PULL THE STRING AND IT WOULD SAY PRERECORDED THINGS BACK TO YOU.
MY FATHER REFUSED TO BUY IT FOR ME, AND, SOMEWHAT NATURALLY, I BEGAN OBSESSING OVER IT--I HAD TO HAVE IT, AND I STARTED SAVING MY WEEKLY ALLOWANCE SO THAT I COULD BUY IT FOR MYSELF.
I SAVED ALL OF MY MONEY FOR MONTHS UNTIL I HAD ENOUGH, AND I WENT TO THE STORE, BOUGHT IT, BROUGHT IT HOME, PLAYED WITH IT FOR A COUPLE DAYS AND THEN NEVER PICKED IT UP AGAIN...
NICK, YOU DESTROYED EVERYTHING I TOLD MYSELF I EVER BELIEVED IN, AND YOU KNOW WHAT THE STRANGEST THING ABOUT IT WAS?
I'M LISTENIN'.
I DIDN'T CARE.
SOMETIMES IT TAKES LOSING THE THING YOU OBSESSED OVER TO REALIZE YOU ACTUALLY WANTED SOMETHING ELSE.
IS THAT A FACT?
YES, IT IS.
SO WHY DID I TURN MYSELF IN?
BECAUSE I WANTED YOU TO KNOW WHERE TO FIND ME.

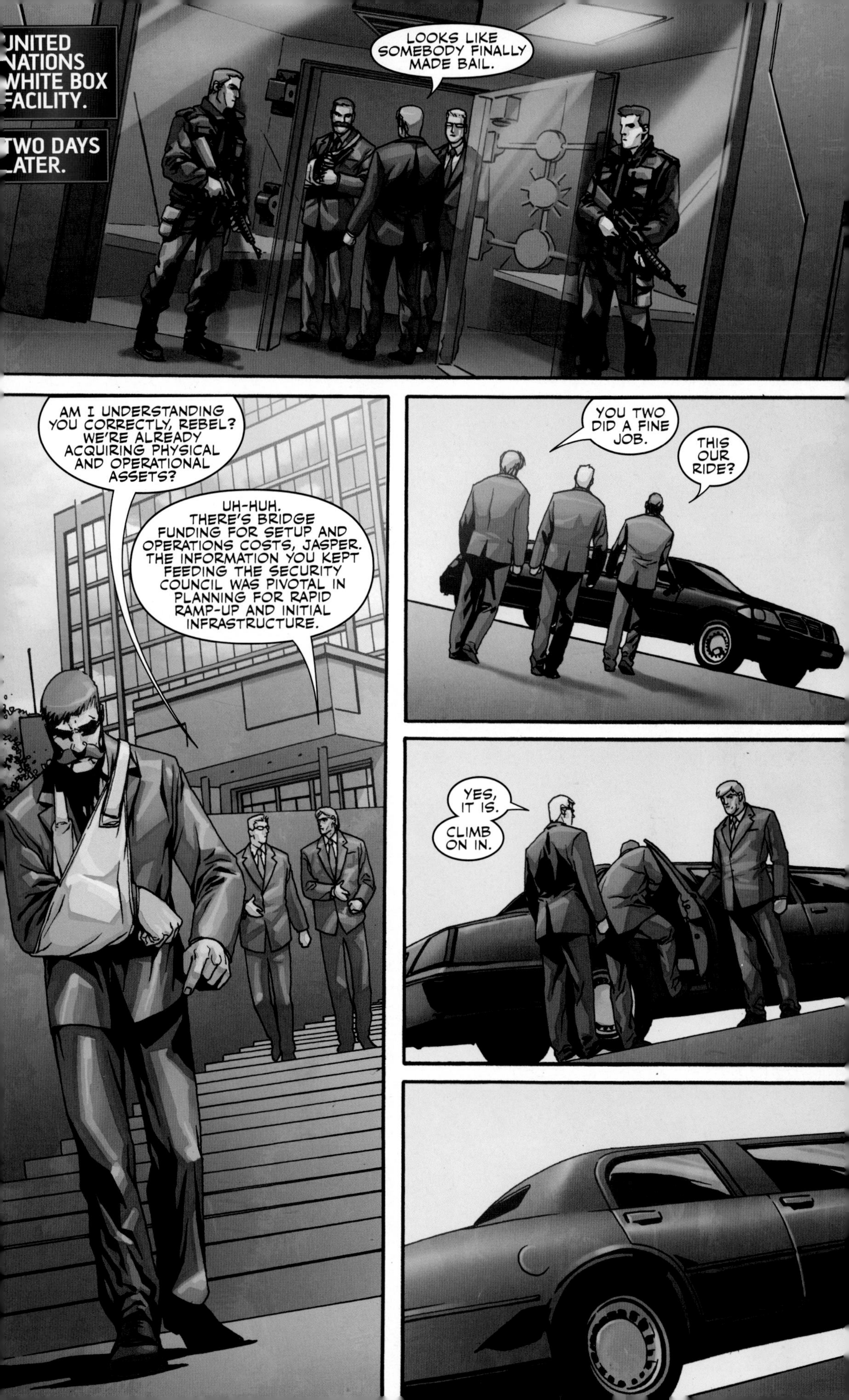
UNITED NATIONS WHITE BOX FACILITY.
TWO DAYS LATER.
LOOKS LIKE SOMEBODY FINALLY MADE BAIL.
AM I UNDERSTANDING YOU CORRECTLY, REBEL? WE'RE ALREADY ACQUIRING PHYSICAL AND OPERATIONAL ASSETS?
UH-HUH. THERE'S BRIDGE FUNDING FOR SETUP AND OPERATIONS COSTS, JASPER. THE INFORMATION YOU KEPT FEEDING THE SECURITY COUNCIL WAS PIVOTAL IN PLANNING FOR RAPID RAMP-UP AND INITIAL INFRASTRUCTURE.
YOU TWO DID A FINE JOB.
THIS OUR RIDE?
YES, IT IS.
CLIMB ON IN.

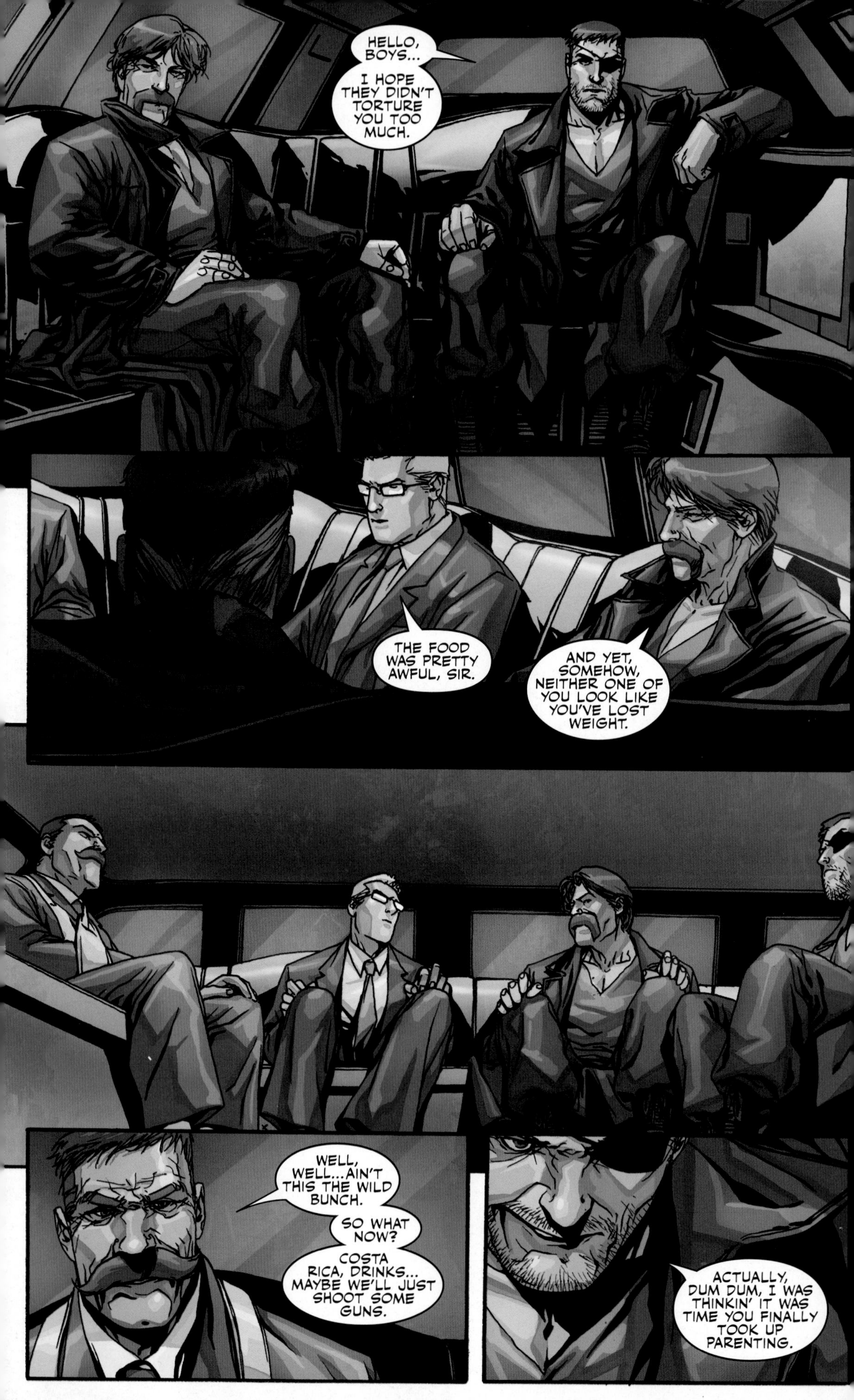
HELLO, BOYS...
I HOPE THEY DIDN'T TORTURE YOU TOO MUCH.
THE FOOD WAS PRETTY AWFUL, SIR.
AND YET, SOMEHOW, NEITHER ONE OF YOU LOOK LIKE YOU'VE LOST WEIGHT.
WELL, WELL...AIN'T THIS THE WILD BUNCH.
SO WHAT NOW?
COSTA RICA, DRINKS... MAYBE WE'LL JUST SHOOT SOME GUNS.
ACTUALLY, DUM DUM, I WAS THINKIN' IT WAS TIME YOU FINALLY TOOK UP PARENTING.

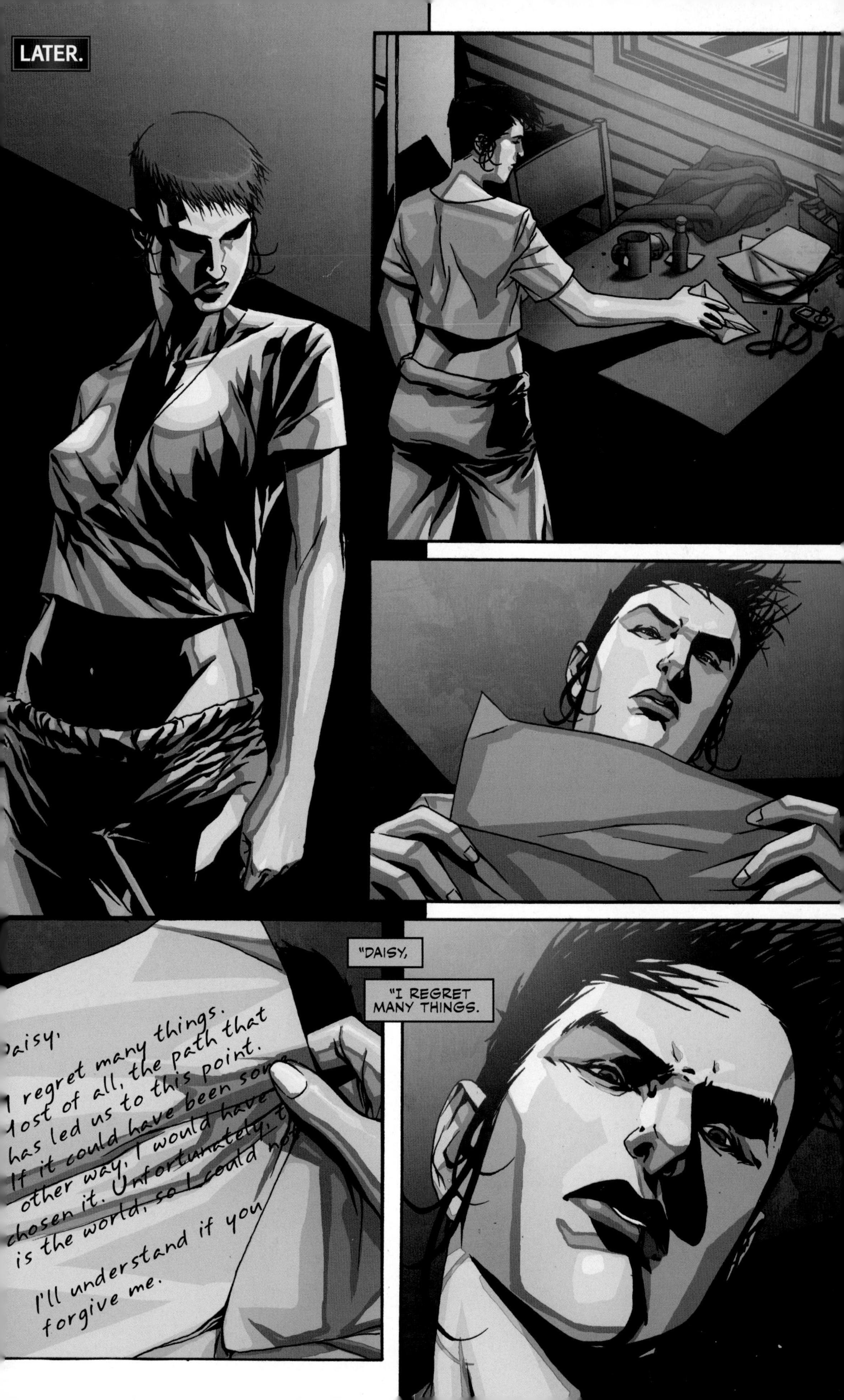
LATER.
"DAISY,
"I REGRET MANY THINGS.
Daisy,
I regret many things. Most of all, the path that has led us to this point. If it could have been some other way, I would have chosen it. Unfortunately, t is the world, so I could no
I'll understand if you forgive me.

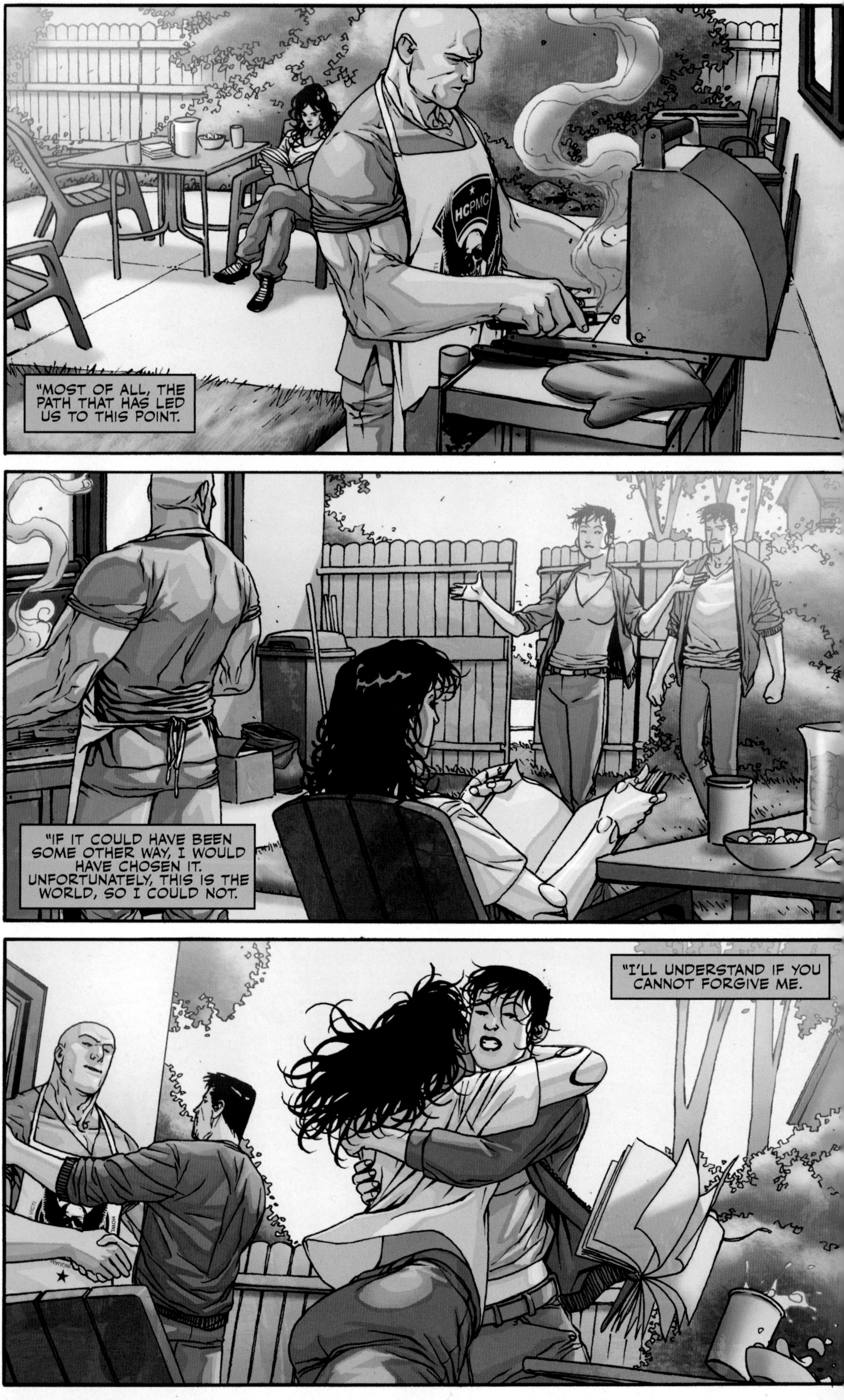
"MOST OF ALL, THE PATH THAT HAS LED US TO THIS POINT.
HCPMC
"IF IT COULD HAVE BEEN SOME OTHER WAY, I WOULD HAVE CHOSEN IT. UNFORTUNATELY, THIS IS THE WORLD, SO I COULD NOT.
"I'LL UNDERSTAND IF YOU CANNOT FORGIVE ME.

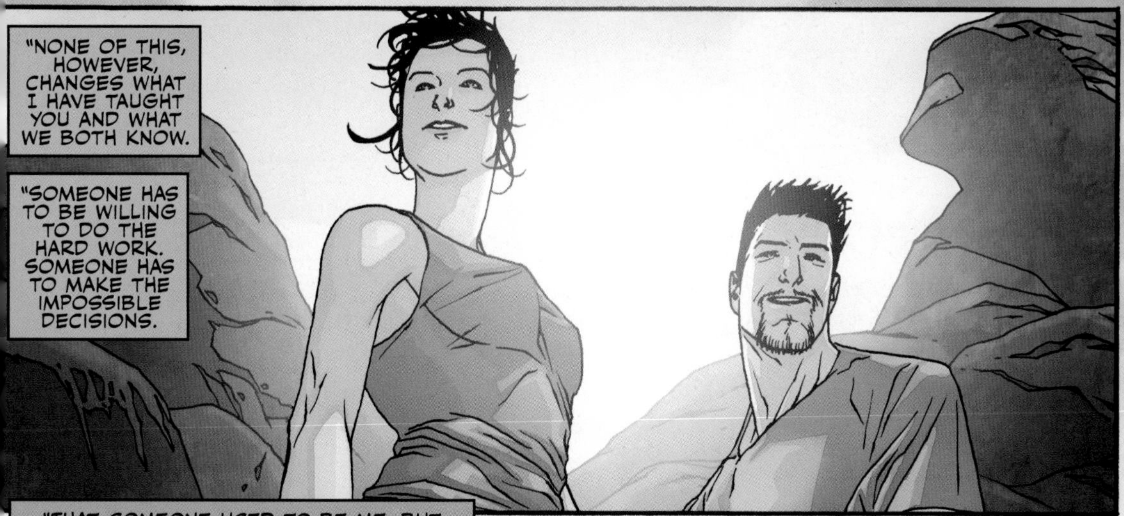
"NONE OF THIS, HOWEVER, CHANGES WHAT I HAVE TAUGHT YOU AND WHAT WE BOTH KNOW.
"SOMEONE HAS TO BE WILLING TO DO THE HARD WORK. SOMEONE HAS TO MAKE THE IMPOSSIBLE DECISIONS.

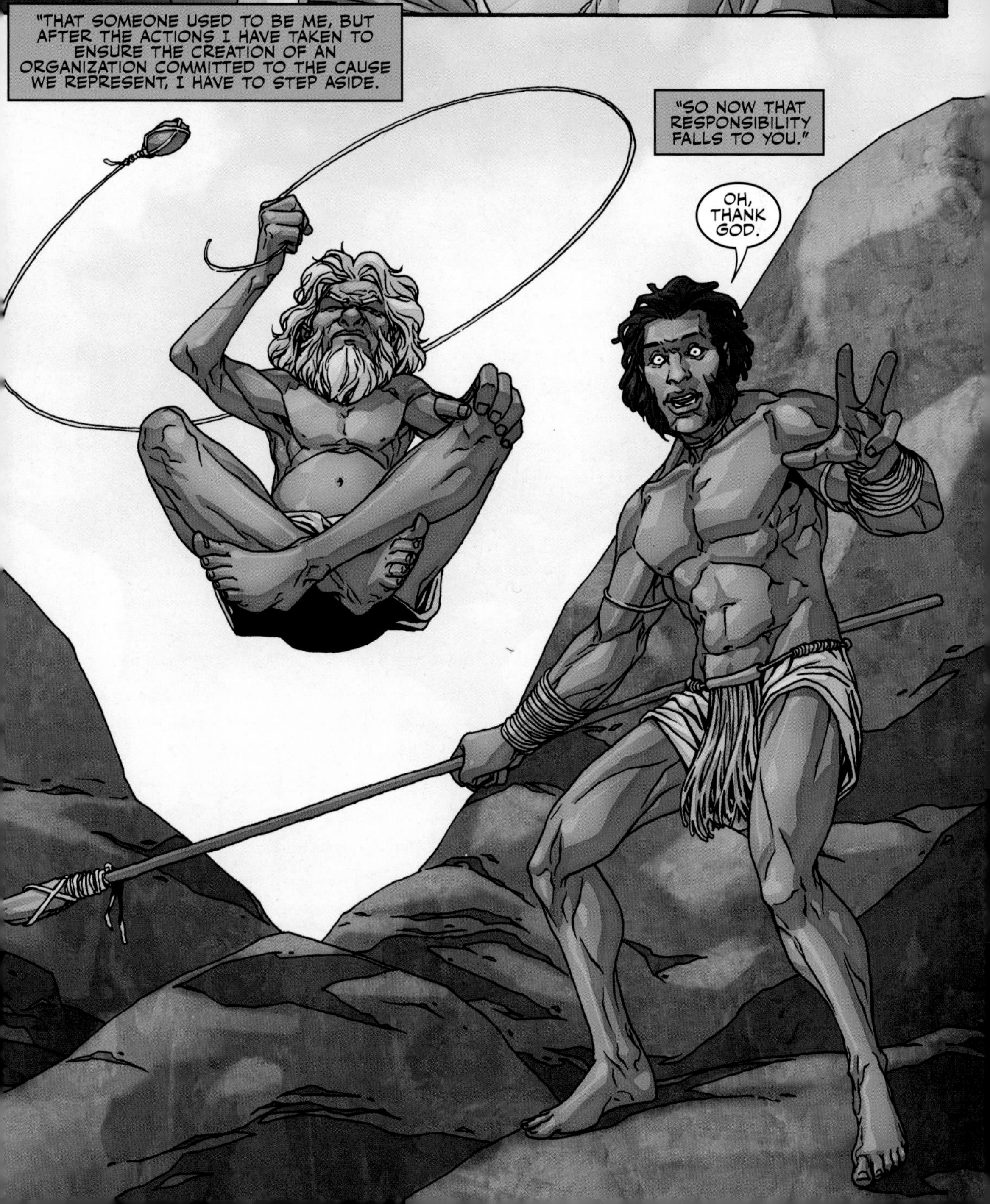
"THAT SOMEONE USED TO BE ME, BUT AFTER THE ACTIONS I HAVE TAKEN TO ENSURE THE CREATION OF AN ORGANIZATION COMMITTED TO THE CAUSE WE REPRESENT, I HAVE TO STEP ASIDE.
"SO NOW THAT RESPONSIBILITY FALLS TO YOU."
OH, THANK GOD.

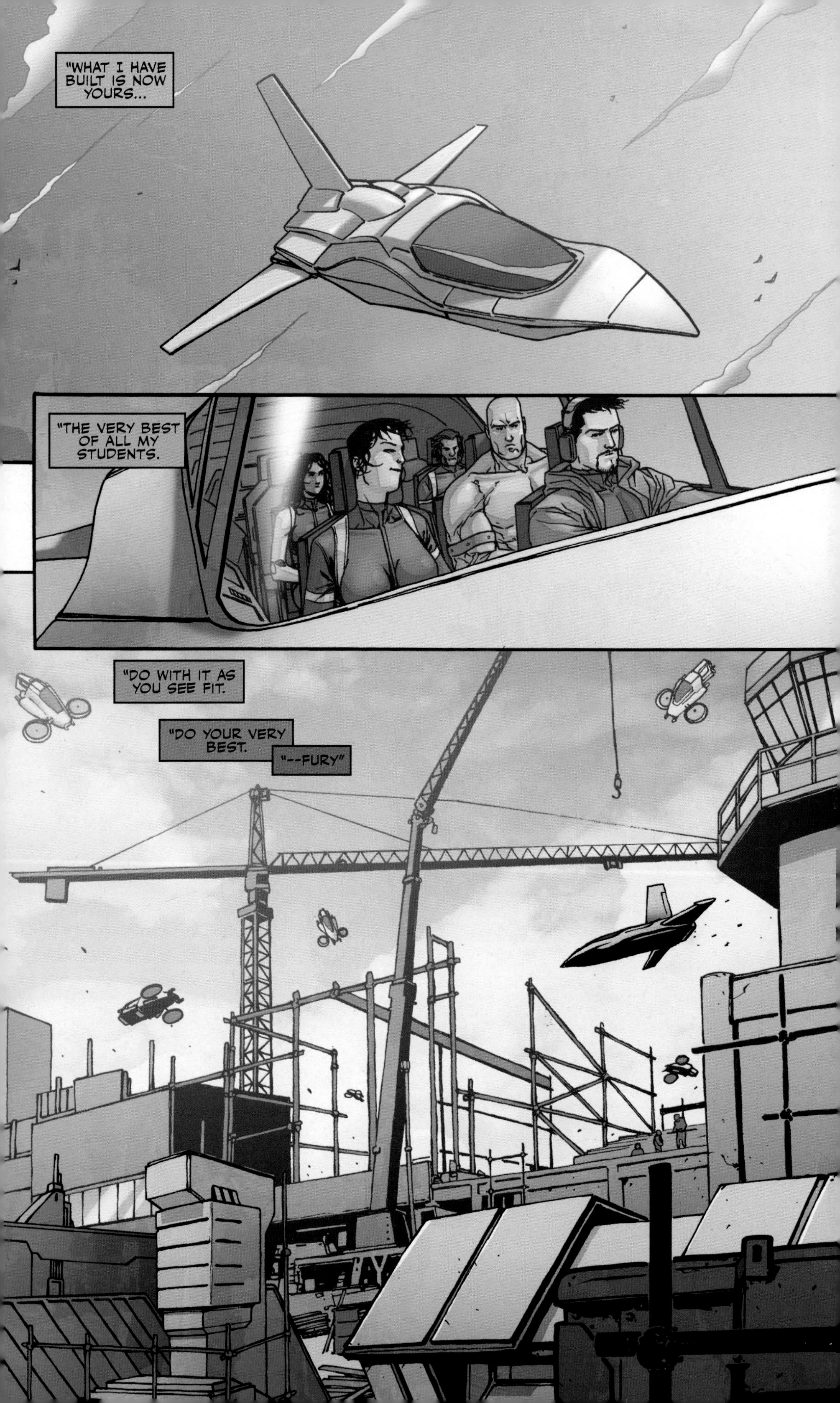
"WHAT I HAVE BUILT IS NOW YOURS...
"THE VERY BEST OF ALL MY STUDENTS.
"DO WITH IT AS YOU SEE FIT.
"DO YOUR VERY BEST.
"--FURY"

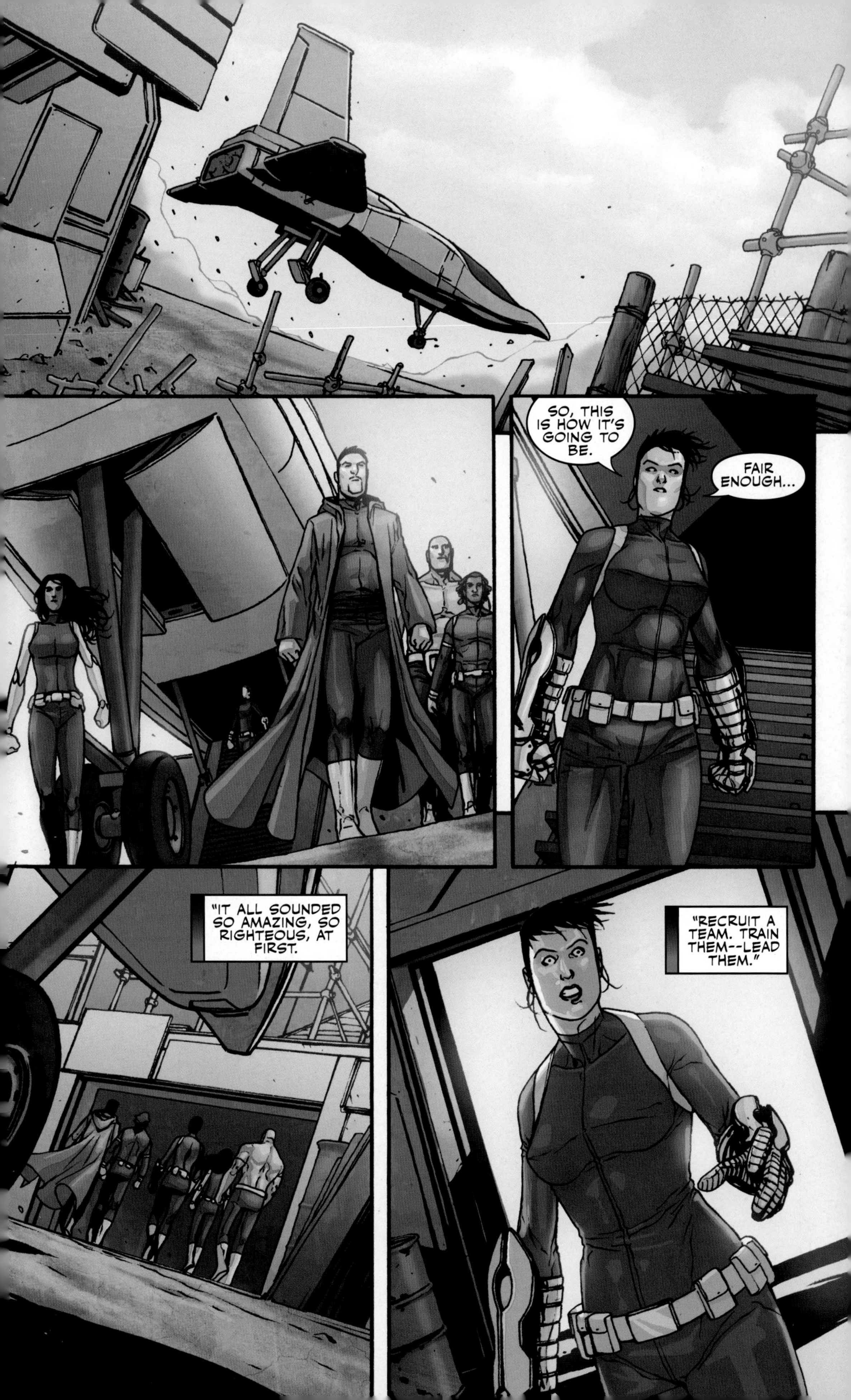
SO, THIS IS HOW IT'S GOING TO BE.
FAIR ENOUGH...
"IT ALL SOUNDED SO AMAZING, SO RIGHTEOUS, AT FIRST.
"RECRUIT A TEAM. TRAIN THEM--LEAD THEM."

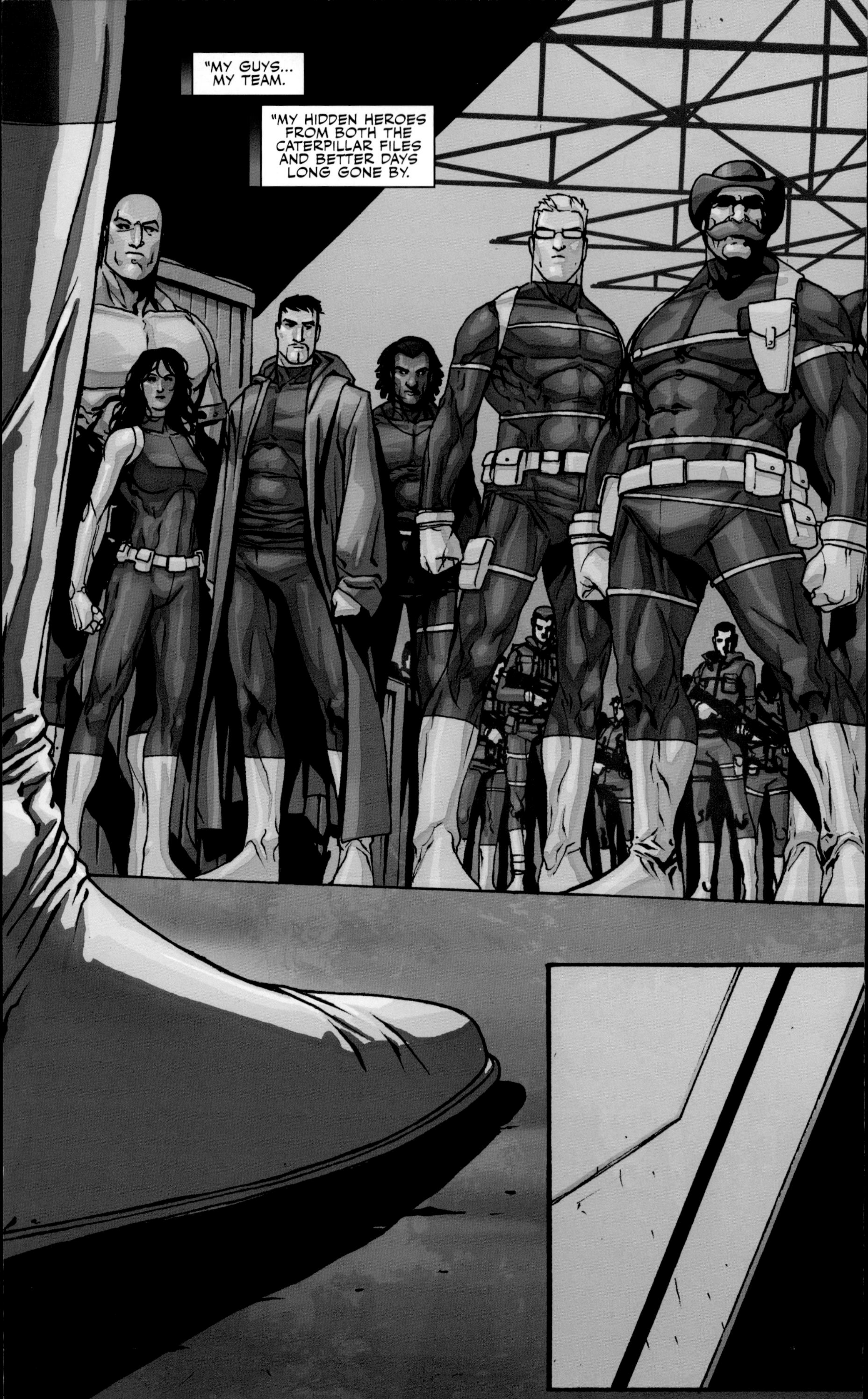
"MY GUYS... MY TEAM.
"MY HIDDEN HEROES FROM BOTH THE CATERPILLAR FILES AND BETTER DAYS LONG GONE BY.

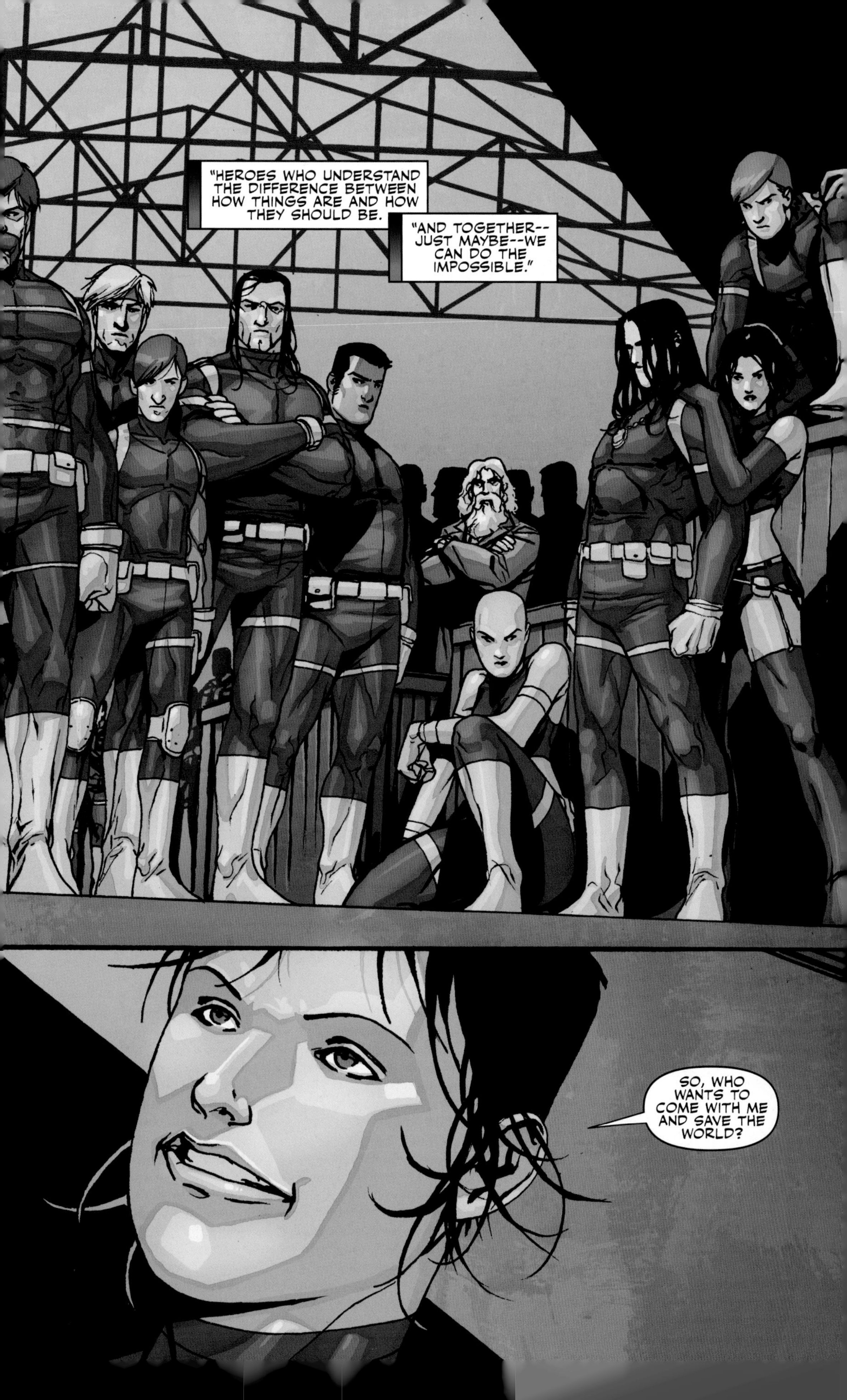
"HEROES WHO UNDERSTAND THE DIFFERENCE BETWEEN HOW THINGS ARE AND HOW THEY SHOULD BE.
"AND TOGETHER--JUST MAYBE--WE CAN DO THE IMPOSSIBLE."
SO, WHO WANTS TO COME WITH ME AND SAVE THE WORLD?

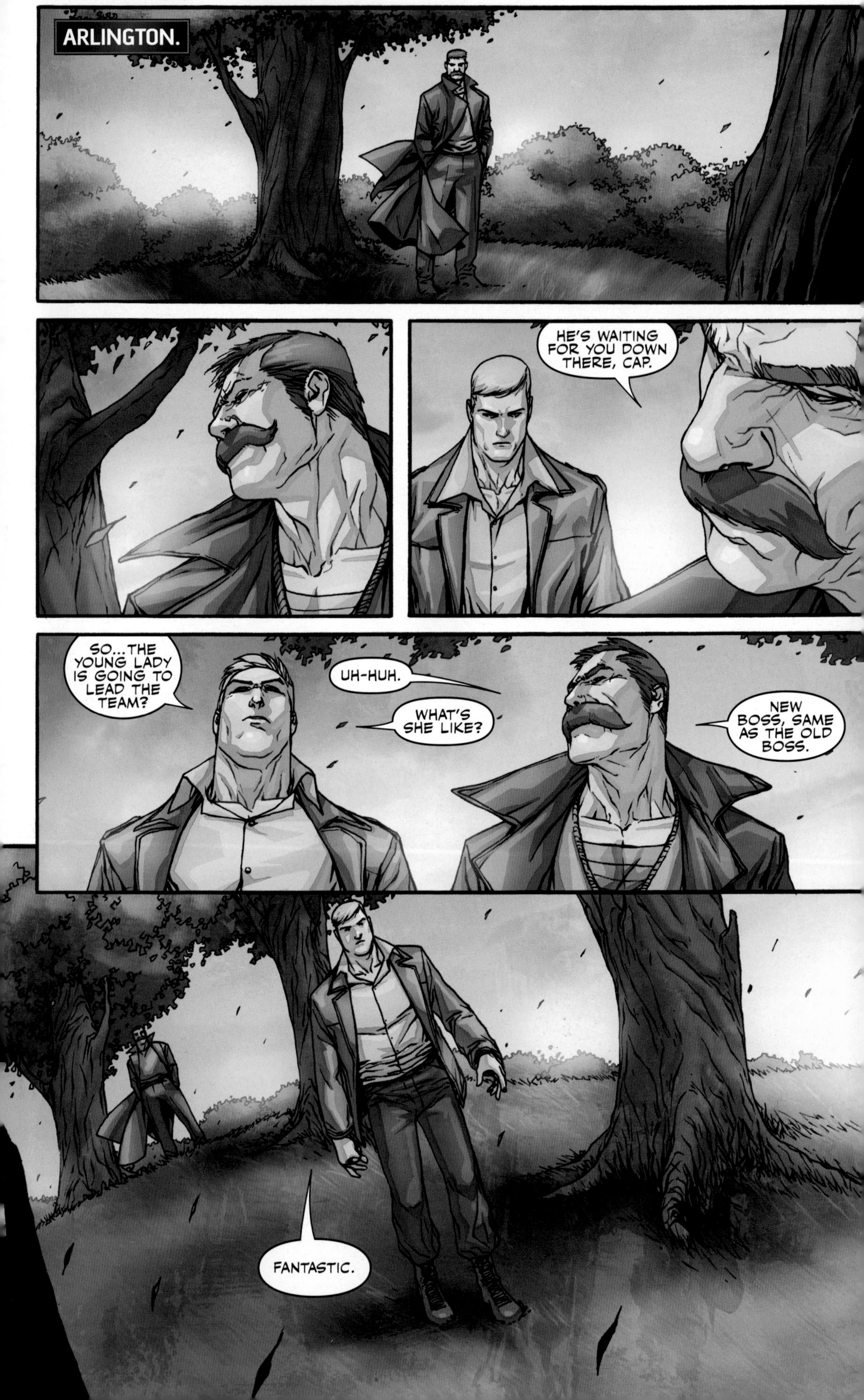
ARLINGTON.
HE'S WAITING FOR YOU DOWN THERE, CAP.
SO...THE YOUNG LADY IS GOING TO LEAD THE TEAM?
UH-HUH.
WHAT'S SHE LIKE?
NEW BOSS, SAME AS THE OLD BOSS.
FANTASTIC.

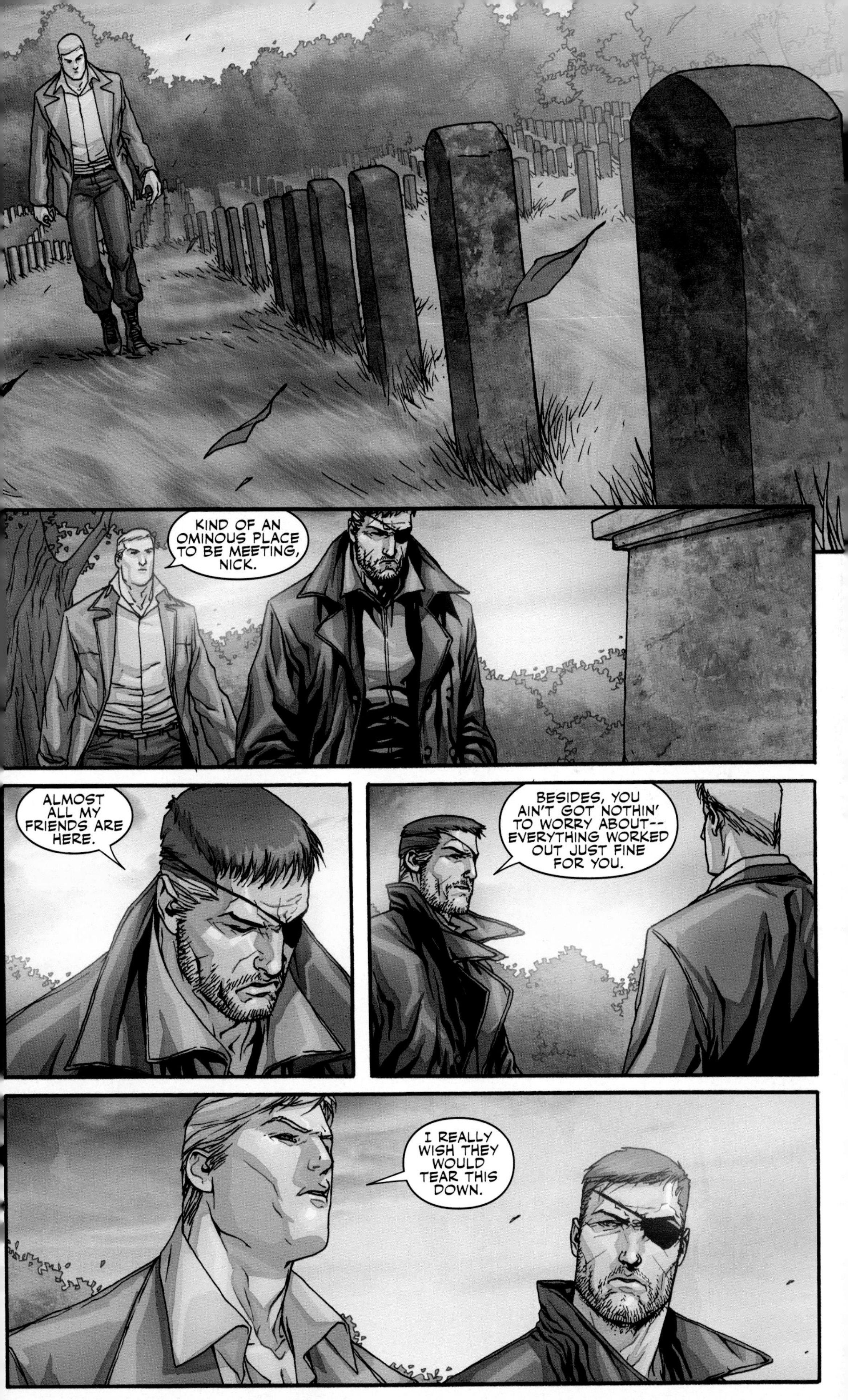
KIND OF AN OMINOUS PLACE TO BE MEETING, NICK.
ALMOST ALL MY FRIENDS ARE HERE.
BESIDES, YOU AIN'T GOT NOTHIN' TO WORRY ABOUT-- EVERYTHING WORKED OUT JUST FINE FOR YOU.
I REALLY WISH THEY WOULD TEAR THIS DOWN.

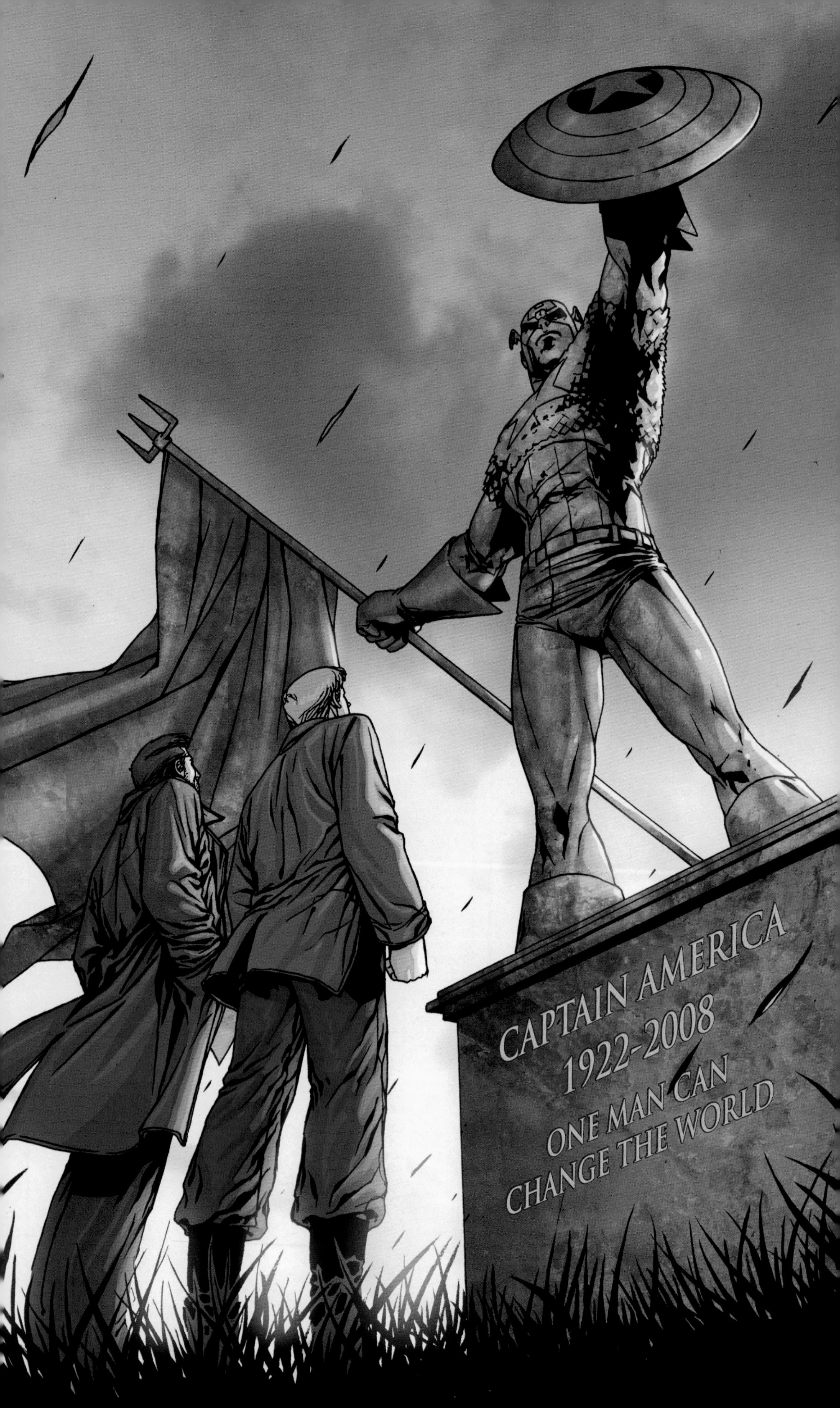
CAPTAIN AMERICA
1922-2008
ONE MAN CAN
CHANGE THE WORLD

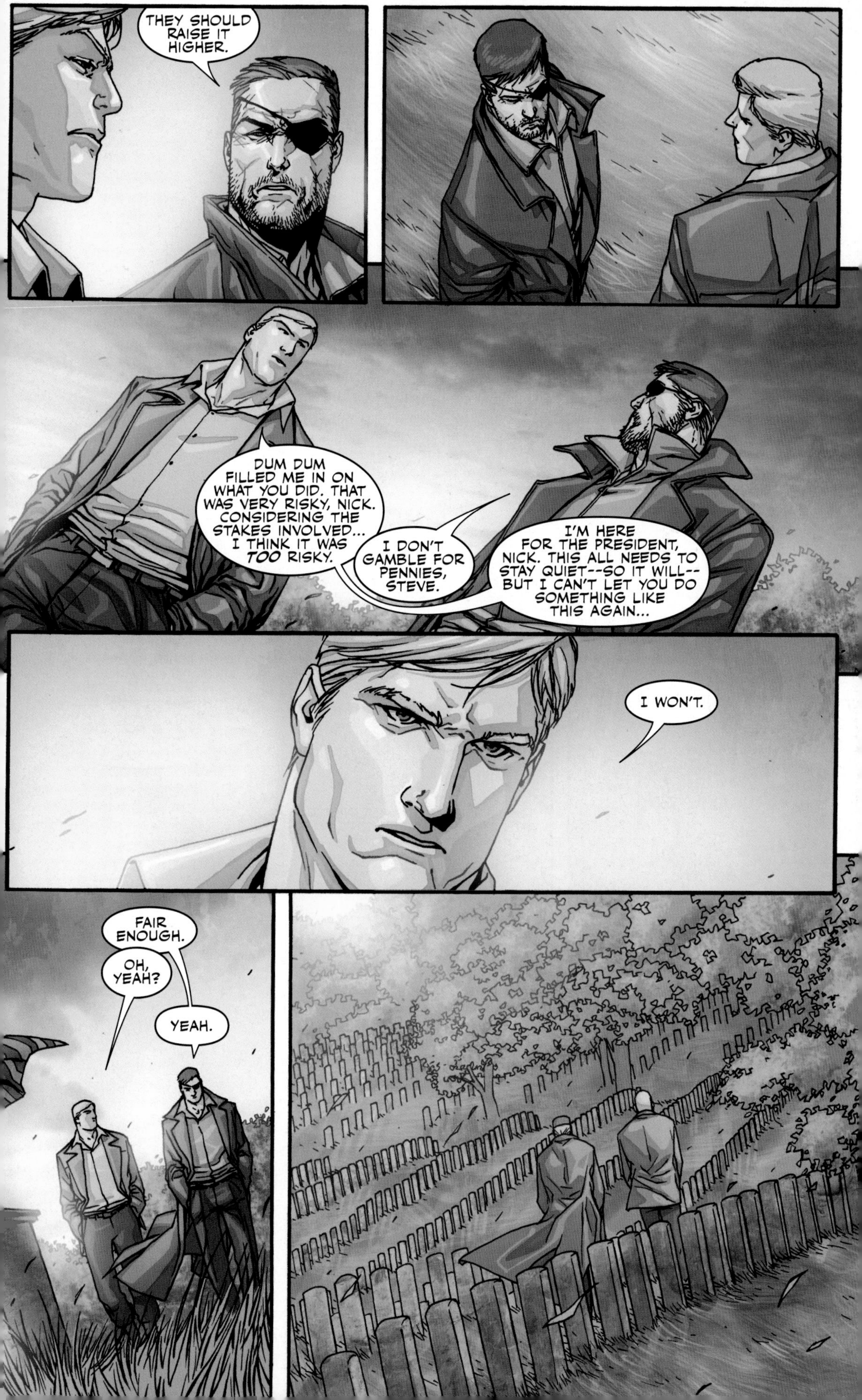
THEY SHOULD RAISE IT HIGHER.
DUM DUM FILLED ME IN ON WHAT YOU DID. THAT WAS VERY RISKY, NICK. CONSIDERING THE STAKES INVOLVED... I THINK IT WAS *TOO* RISKY.
I DON'T GAMBLE FOR PENNIES, STEVE.
I'M HERE FOR THE PRESIDENT, NICK. THIS ALL NEEDS TO STAY QUIET--SO IT WILL--BUT I CAN'T LET YOU DO SOMETHING LIKE THIS AGAIN...
I WON'T.
FAIR ENOUGH.
OH, YEAH?
YEAH.

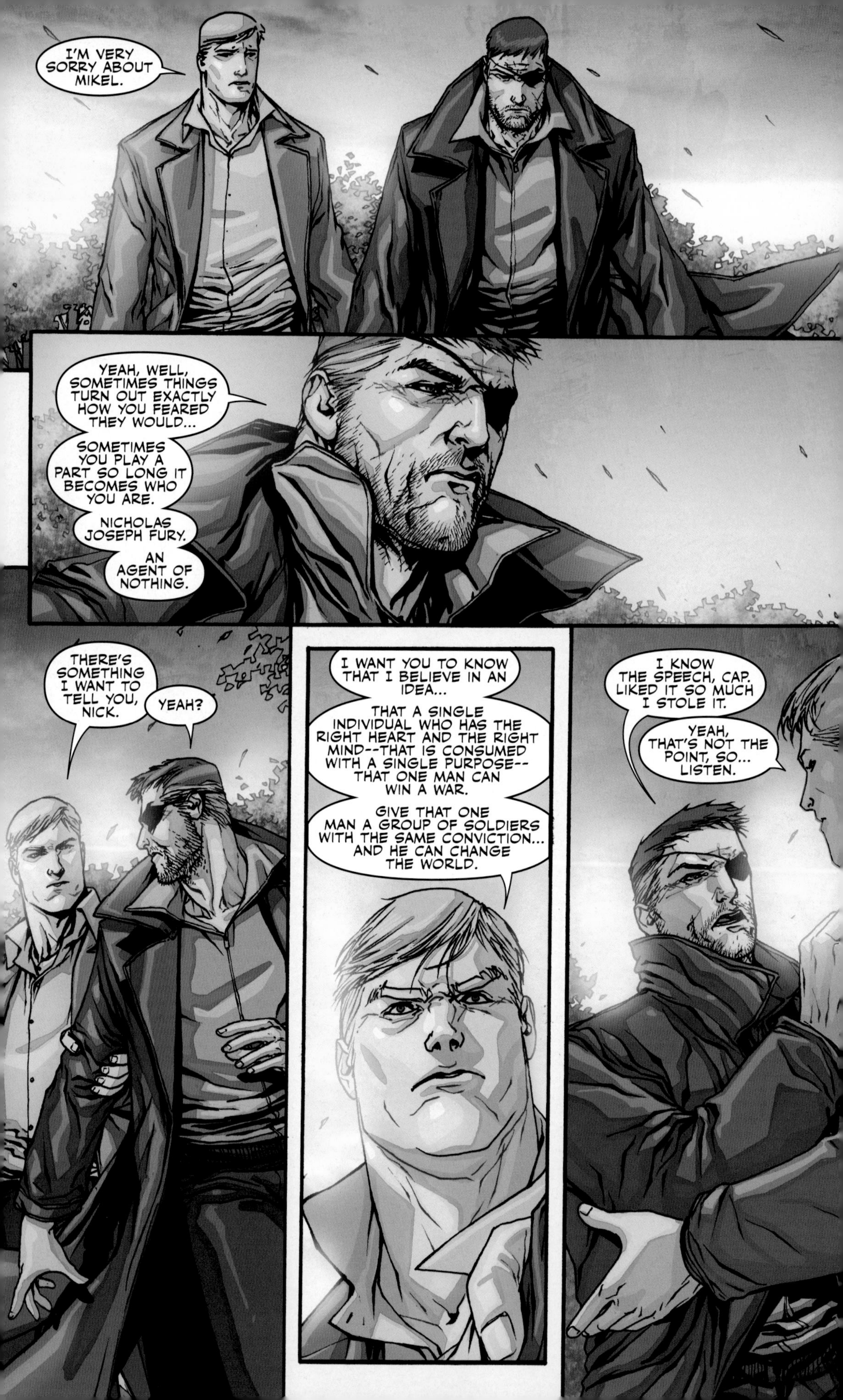
I'M VERY SORRY ABOUT MIKEL.
YEAH, WELL, SOMETIMES THINGS TURN OUT EXACTLY HOW YOU FEARED THEY WOULD...
SOMETIMES YOU PLAY A PART SO LONG IT BECOMES WHO YOU ARE.
NICHOLAS JOSEPH FURY.
AN AGENT OF NOTHING.
THERE'S SOMETHING I WANT TO TELL YOU, NICK.
YEAH?
I WANT YOU TO KNOW THAT I BELIEVE IN AN IDEA...
THAT A SINGLE INDIVIDUAL WHO HAS THE RIGHT HEART AND THE RIGHT MIND--THAT IS CONSUMED WITH A SINGLE PURPOSE--THAT ONE MAN CAN WIN A WAR.
GIVE THAT ONE MAN A GROUP OF SOLDIERS WITH THE SAME CONVICTION... AND HE CAN CHANGE THE WORLD.
I KNOW THE SPEECH, CAP. LIKED IT SO MUCH I STOLE IT.
YEAH, THAT'S NOT THE POINT, SO... LISTEN.

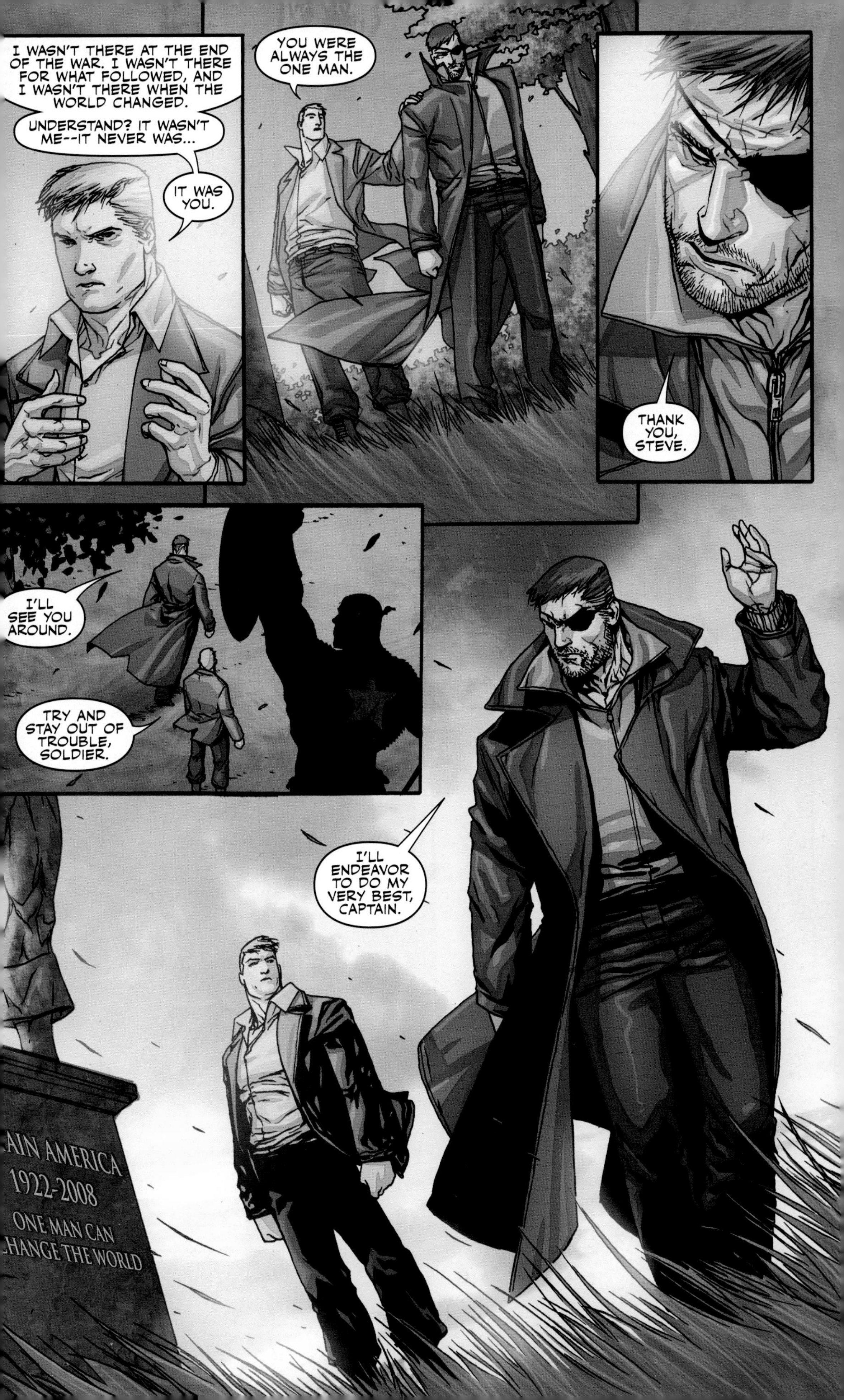
I WASN'T THERE AT THE END OF THE WAR. I WASN'T THERE FOR WHAT FOLLOWED, AND I WASN'T THERE WHEN THE WORLD CHANGED.
UNDERSTAND? IT WASN'T ME--IT NEVER WAS...
IT WAS YOU.
YOU WERE ALWAYS THE ONE MAN.
THANK YOU, STEVE.
I'LL SEE YOU AROUND.
TRY AND STAY OUT OF TROUBLE, SOLDIER.
I'LL ENDEAVOR TO DO MY VERY BEST, CAPTAIN.
AIN AMERICA
1922-2008
ONE MAN CAN
CHANGE THE WORLD

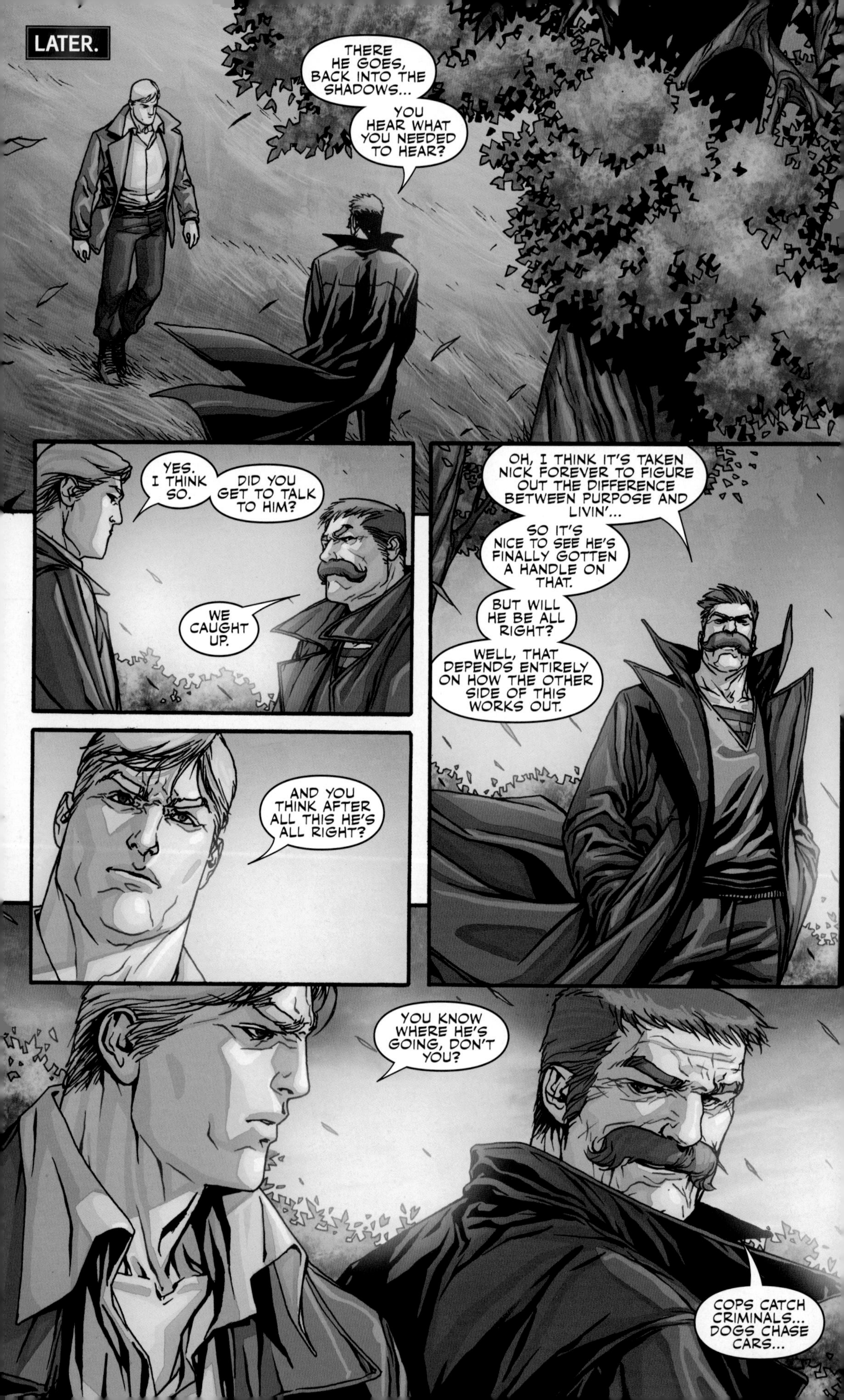
LATER.
THERE HE GOES, BACK INTO THE SHADOWS...
YOU HEAR WHAT YOU NEEDED TO HEAR?
YES. I THINK SO.
DID YOU GET TO TALK TO HIM?
WE CAUGHT UP.
AND YOU THINK AFTER ALL THIS HE'S ALL RIGHT?
OH, I THINK IT'S TAKEN NICK FOREVER TO FIGURE OUT THE DIFFERENCE BETWEEN PURPOSE AND LIVIN'...
SO IT'S NICE TO SEE HE'S FINALLY GOTTEN A HANDLE ON THAT.
BUT WILL HE BE ALL RIGHT?
WELL, THAT DEPENDS ENTIRELY ON HOW THE OTHER SIDE OF THIS WORKS OUT.
YOU KNOW WHERE HE'S GOING, DON'T YOU?
COPS CATCH CRIMINALS... DOGS CHASE CARS...

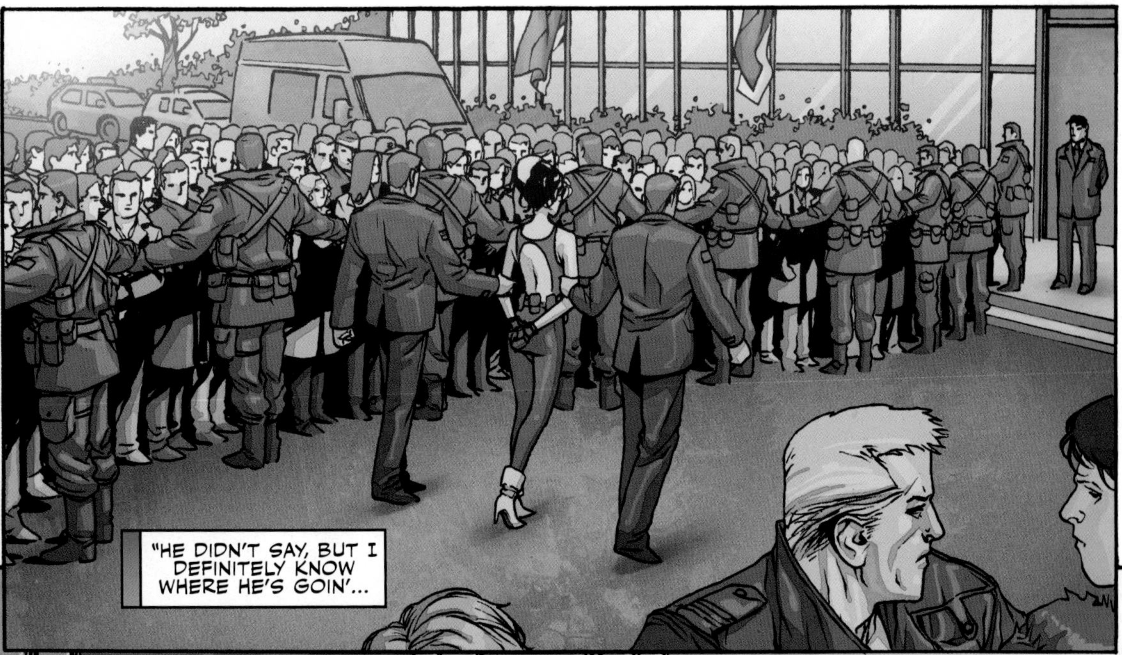
"HE DIDN'T SAY, BUT I DEFINITELY KNOW WHERE HE'S GOIN'...

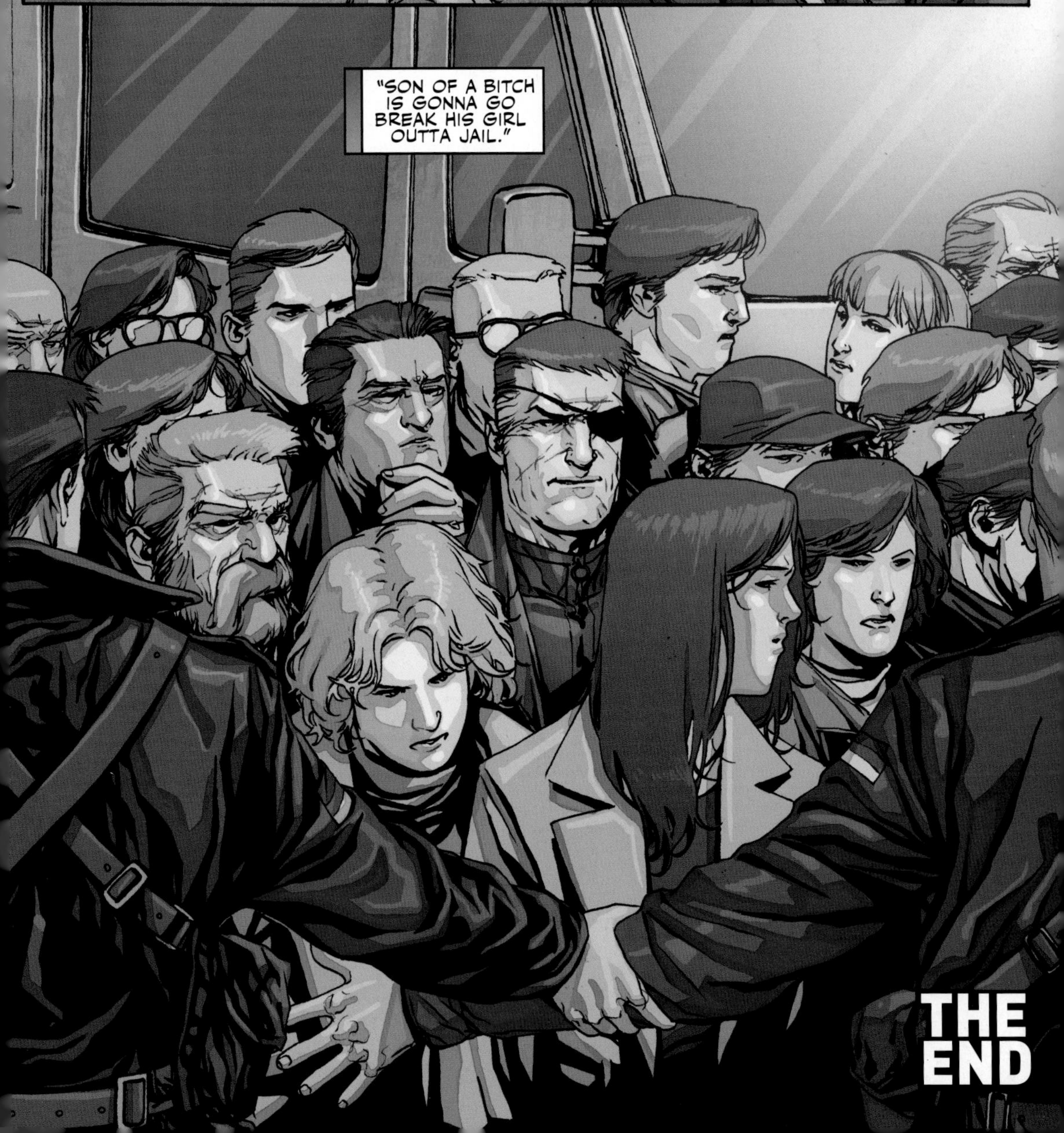
"SON OF A BITCH IS GONNA GO BREAK HIS GIRL OUTTA JAIL."
THE END

THE ONE MAN

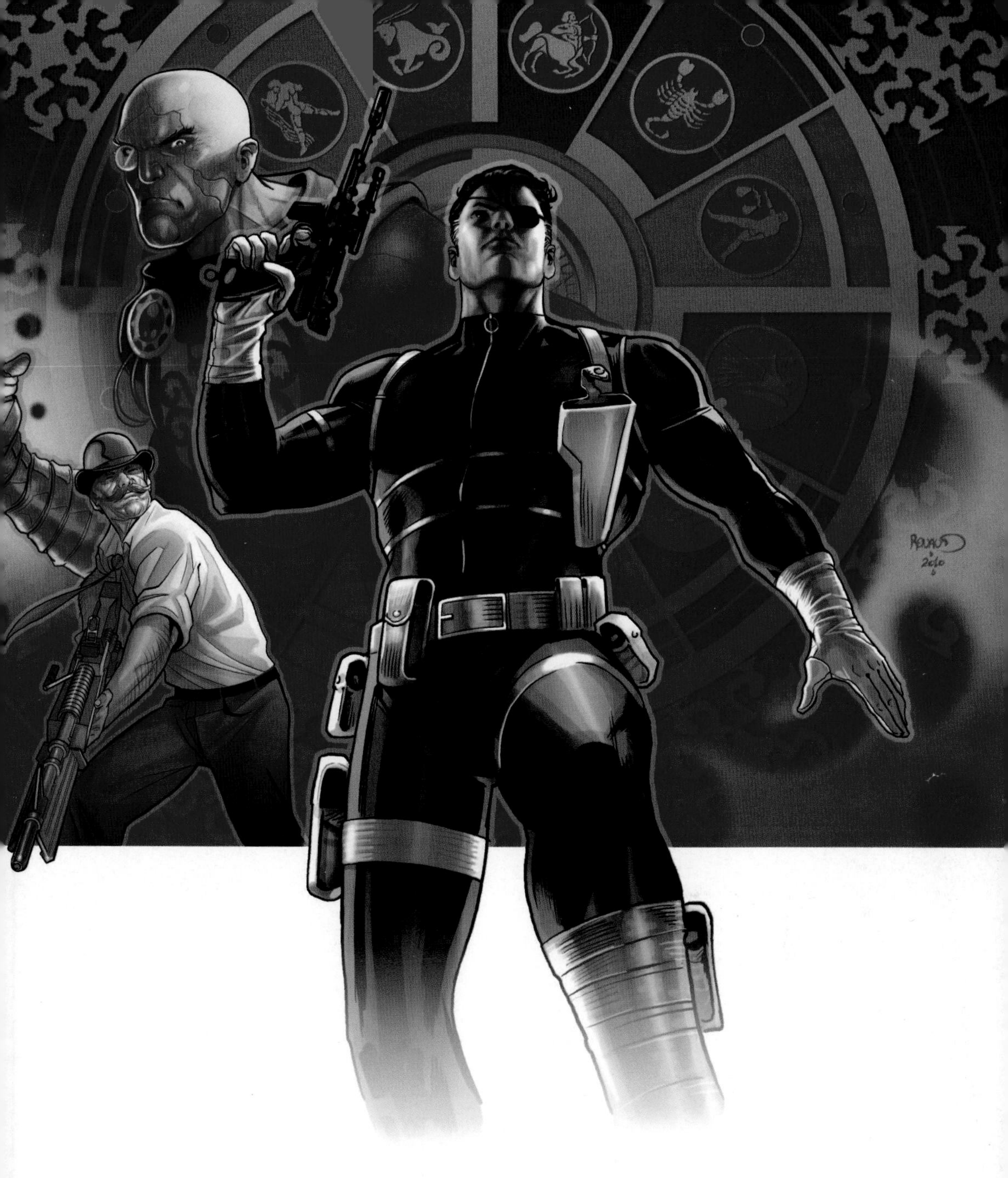

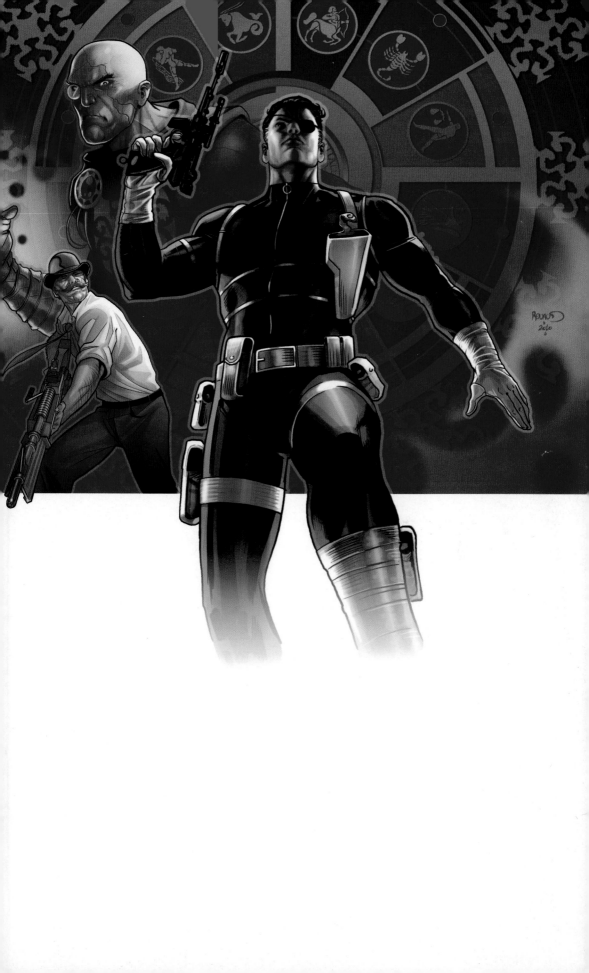

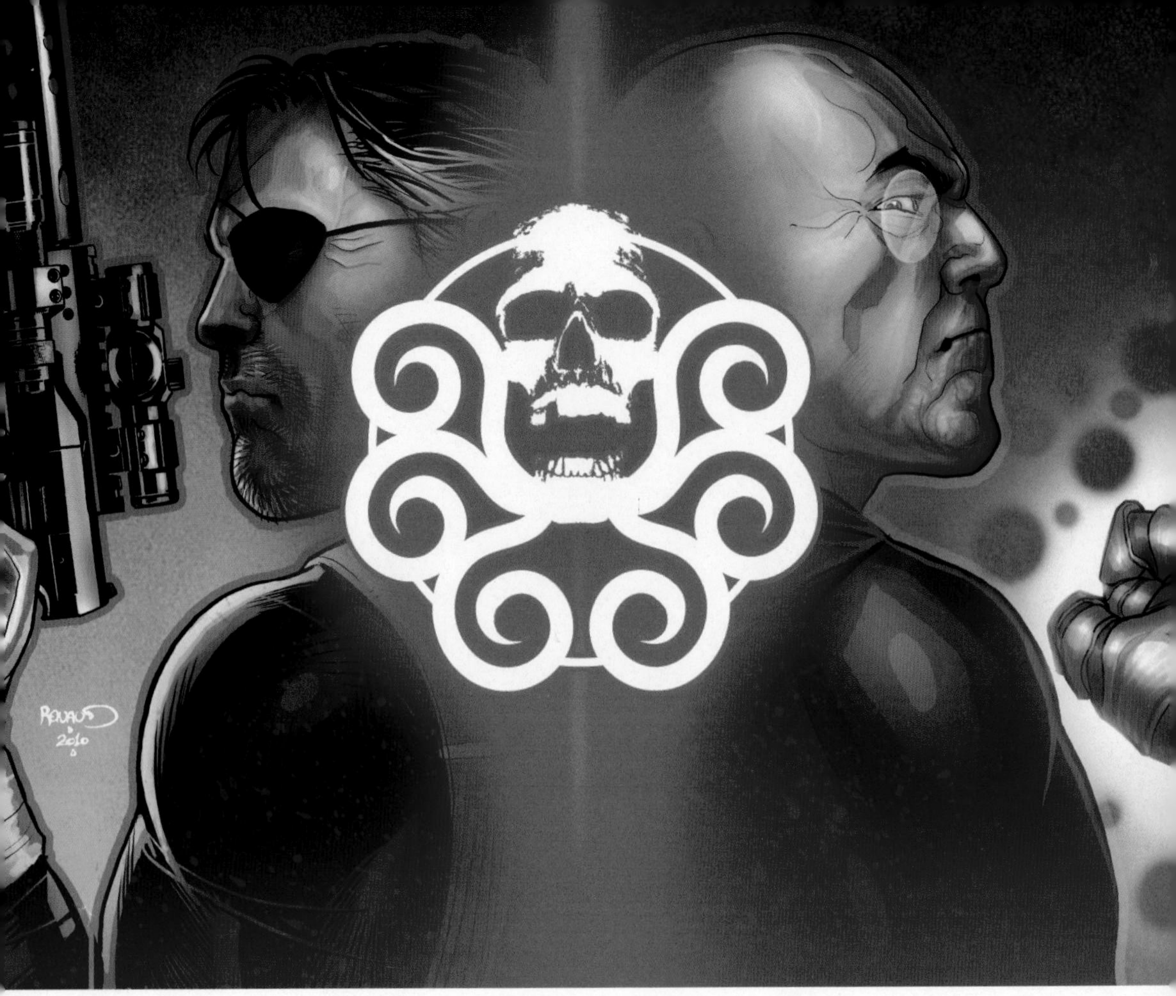

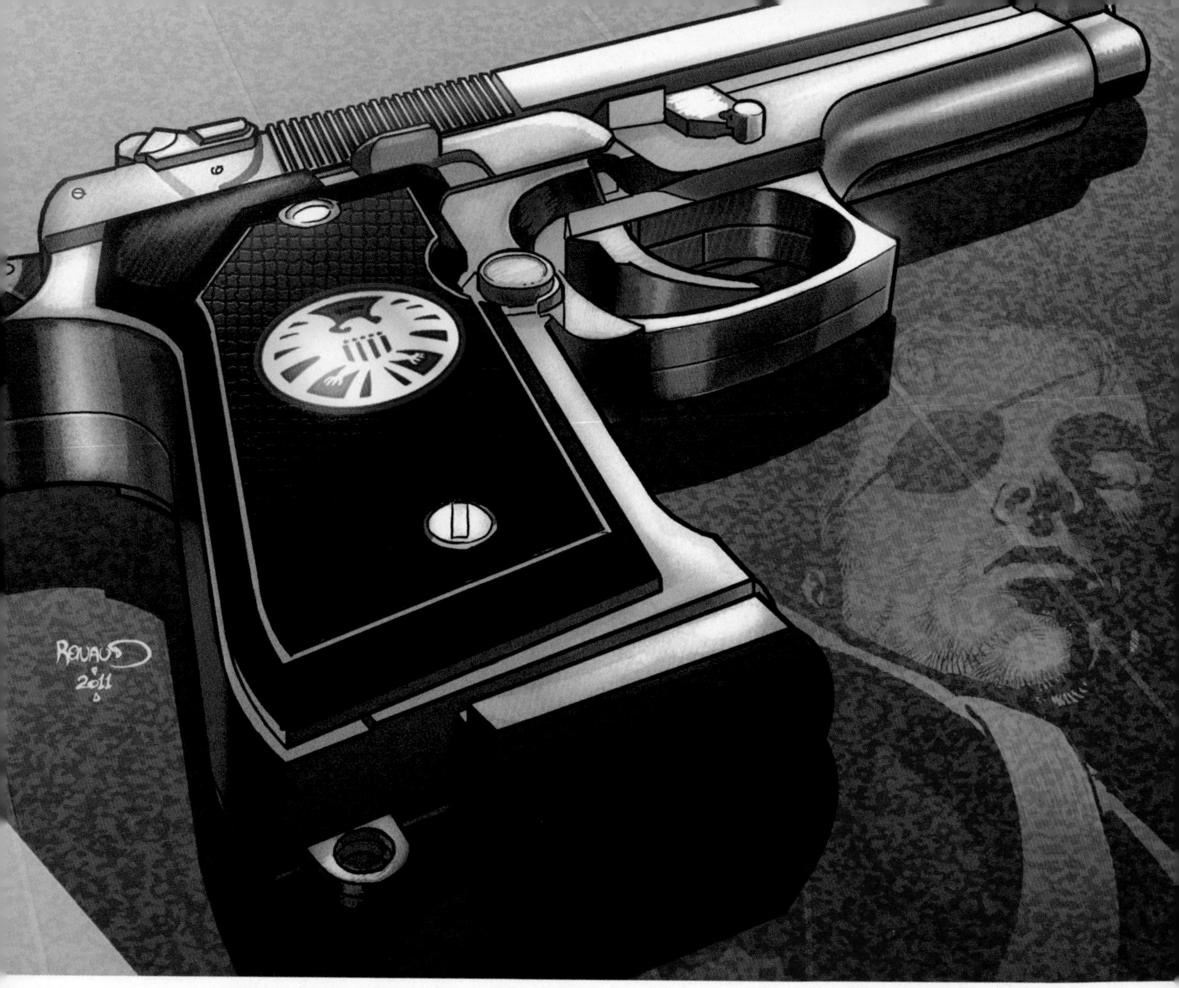
RENAUD
2011

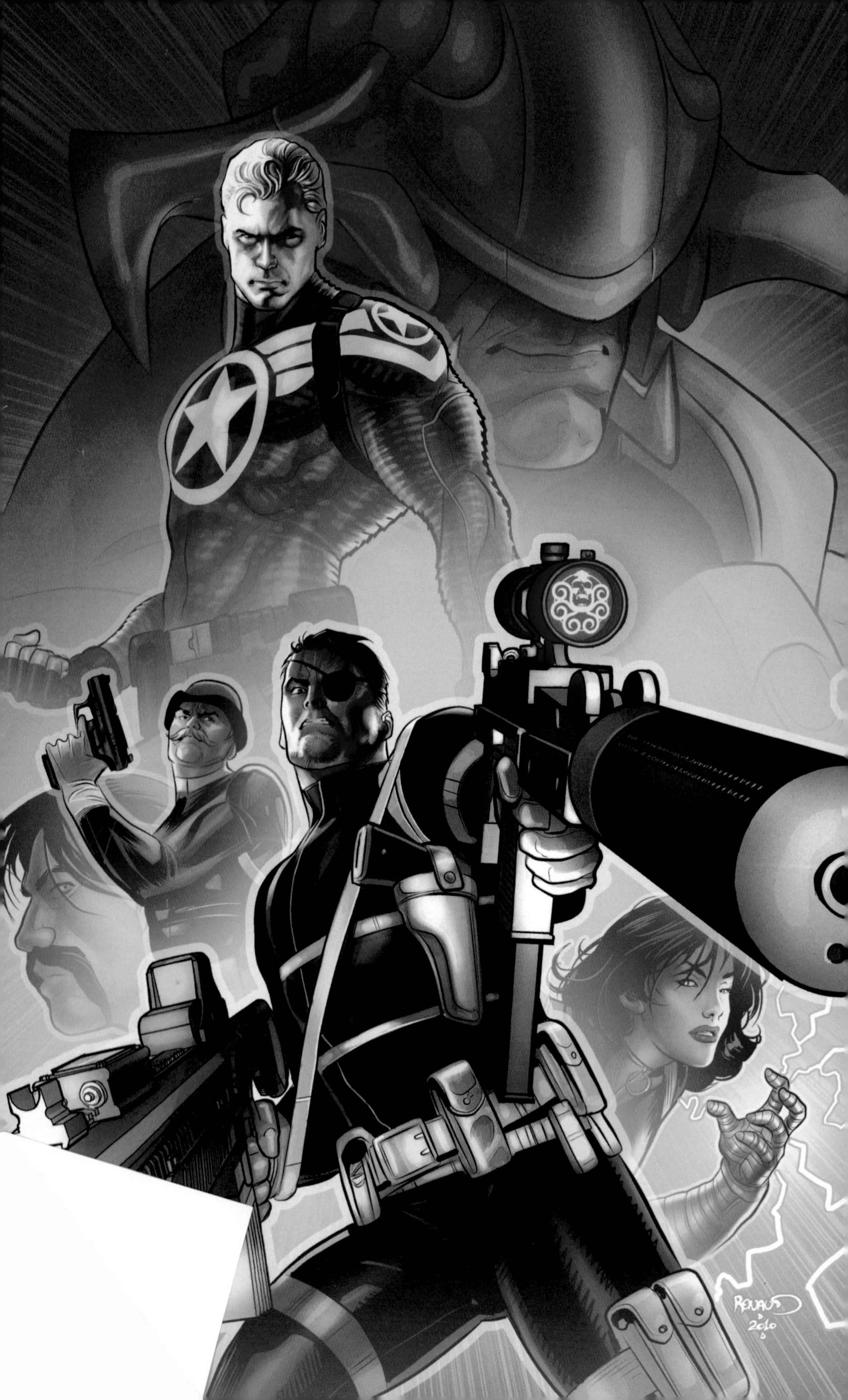